C.L.R. JAMES AND CREOLIZATION

C.L.R. JAMES

AND CREOLIZATION
Circles of Influence

NICOLE KING

University Press of Mississippi
Jackson

www.upress.state.ms.us
Copyright © 2001 by University Press of Mississippi
All rights reserved
Manufactured in the United States of America
Print-On-Demand Edition
∞
Library of Congress Cataloging-in-Publication Data

King, Nicole.
    C. L. R. James and creolization : circles of influence / Nicole King.
      p. cm.
    Includes bibliographical references and index.
    ISBN 1-57806-364-7 (cloth : alk. paper)
    1. James, C. L. R. (Cyril Lionel Robert), 1901—Criticism and interpretation.
2. Pluralism (Social sciences) in literature.   3. Intercultural communication in literature.
4. Influence (Literary, artistic, etc.)   5. Cultural relations in literature.   6. Caribbean
Area—In literature.   7. Trinidad—In literature.   8. Blacks in literature.   I. Title: Cyril
Lionel Robert James and creolization.   II. Title.
PR9272.9.J35 Z75   2001
813'.52—dc21   00-053404

British Library Cataloging-in-Publication Data available

For my mother and father

CONTENTS

Acknowledgments ix
Preface xiii
Abbreviations xix

Mapping Creolization 3

Double or Nothing
The Two *Black Jacobins* 30

Framing Community
Minty Alley, *La Rue Cases Negres*,
and Class Consciousness 52

Factions and Fictions
Considerations of the "Negro Question" 78

Family Matters
Nation, Federation, Integration 102

Metaphors of Nationalism
Music, Sport, and Racial Representation 118

Coda 143
Notes 145
Works Cited 153
Index 165

ACKNOWLEDGMENTS

This project began unexpectedly one evening when, at a gathering, Basil Paquet suggested I read a slim text called *Mariners, Renegades, and Castaways* to help with my study of *Moby Dick* as I prepared for my oral examinations for a master's degree. While the texts proved quite useful to read together, the smaller one seized my curiosity and launched my investigations into C. L. R. James. Since then, a series of such serendipitous and generous suggestions from friends and colleagues shaped my dissertation and then this book. I know, therefore, that while all its errors are my own, whatever achievements this book may lay claim to are wholly derived from such contributions and from a variety of collaborations I have been fortunate enough to take part in.

Several organizations provided funding and venues for me to complete and share my work. I especially thank the Mellon Fellowship Program, which funded the dissertation project, the Ford Foundation Post Doctoral Fellowship Program, and the University of Maryland for funding a semester away from teaching. For access to their archives and inclusion in their fellows program, I thank the Schomburg Center for Research in Black Culture. I carried out additional research at the Institute for Commonwealth Studies, University of London, the University of the West Indies, and the Trinidad Oil Workers Union Library, San Fernando, Trinidad.

Of the many people who graciously lived the composition of this book with me I would especially like to thank the following for their contributions of wise council, encouragement, extensive comments, and friendship: my advisors on my original dissertation project, Sandra Pouchet Paquet, Betsy Erkkila, and the late Lynda Hart; my mentors Valerie Smith and Emory Elliott; the friends whom I happened upon so unexpectedly in 1988, Elizabeth Alexander, Lindon Barrett, Jennifer Devere Brody, Anne Cubilié, Lisa Freeman, and Amy Robinson; new friends and colleagues well met after 1993, especially Mary Helen Washington, who helped to generate many key ideas of this text, not least of which was to get James "into quotation," and also Theresa Coletti, Merle Collins, Jane Donaworth, Bob Levine, Carla Peterson, Sangeeta Ray, Marilee Lindemann, Martha Nell Smith, Bill Sherman, Bill Cohen, and Kandice Chuh, who helped in more ways than she can know. I thank as well my students in various courses and seminars at the University of Maryland; Phyllis Marie Jeffers deserves special mention for her editorial and research assistance. Kevin Meehan's careful and enthusiastic reading of my work made manifest its shift from a dissertation to a book.

This project took a pivotal turn in a better direction when I began my affiliation with the C. L. R. James Institute in 1997. I would like to thank institute director Jim Murray for his unflagging support, for tirelessly culling materials from the archive for me, for creating a welcoming work space, and, not least, for being a great friend. I have relied heavily on the work of others concerning James, and would especially like to thank Brian Alleyne, Anna Grimshaw, and Aldon Lynn Nielsen for their encouragement and kindness. I also wish to thank the expert staff at the University Press of Mississippi and particularly the director Seetha Srinivasan, who saw this project's potential well before I did and waited patiently for its completion. For stewardship of this project I owe a great debt to the anonymous reader whose criticisms kept pushing my ideas to their limits.

Many other people helped me to do this work by virtue of their caring and understanding over the years; a profound thanks goes out to each of my "big sisters," to Addette Williams, to my Aunt Ivy and other extended family in New York, and to my friends and family in London.

I thank my parents, Ina Hope King and the late Robert F. King, for their relentless faith in my abilities. They were my first teachers and most enduring ones, and I continue to learn from them both.

My sister, Sabrina Hope King, has helped in innumerable ways. Her own example and her infectious enthusiasm for hard work advanced me through some of the more arduous periods of writing, for which I cannot thank her enough. For shared moments of reckless hilarity and sweet affections, of which I greedily indulged myself at every opportunity, I am grateful to my buddy, Ayanna-Grace.

Finally, Brett St Louis has shared so much of his intellect and insight that the task of writing this book was often made easier and more difficult at the same time, for he continually raises the bar against which studies of James must be measured. I cannot thank him enough for that, as a scholar and as a friend. At great distances and with uncommon tenderness, his love has given me the strength to do the work and has underscored the satisfaction of getting it done.

PREFACE

When I began reading and writing about C. L. R. James ten years ago, I found him a compelling subject because his lived experience and published works suggested concrete links between literature and political struggle against imperialism, capitalism, and colonialism. His friendships, associations, and collaborations shed light on the convergences and divergences of intellectual and grassroots activities practiced within the black diaspora. Although my training has been explicitly in the analysis and interpretation of literature, these pursuits have only held meaning and relevance for me insofar as I could use such analyses and interpretation to expose and discuss issues of political importance. In C. L. R. James, therefore, I found a fascinating, if not a perfect, model.

In my early research on James, I was struck by how certain assessments of his work saw his forays into fiction as finite, and as antecedent and subordinate to his activities and writings as a socialist and political theorist (see, for example, Robert Hill's essay "In England 1932–1938"). For my part, I recognized James's affinity for fiction and narrative in nearly everything he wrote but especially in his speeches and in the book-length works *Beyond a Boundary*, *The Black Jacobins*, and *Mariners, Renegades, and Castaways: Herman Melville and the World We Live In*; in these texts, he seemed to like nothing better than to tell a story. In the years since C. L. R. James's death in 1989, there has developed a significant body of scholarship that has sought to introduce his ideas to new publics and to bring to light his large body of unpublished works. *C. L. R. James and Creolization* also seeks new interpretive communities for James. By asking questions of James through the use of literary, historical, and biographical paradigms, I hope to avoid scholarly fragmentation of him and, in a creolist gesture, observe the changing whole, James's oeuvre, in its diversity rather than as isolated within discrete formations of history, literature, politics, or cultural studies.

This book recognizes within the diversity and the contradictions of James's career a useful metaphor and starting point for considerations of "international blackness," for contributing to discussions of black identities that eschew singularity and monolithic formations. Specifically, in its investigations of certain key James texts, this book seeks to understand how gender, class, ideals of nationalism, and aesthetics place pressure on James's attempts, and therefore on our understanding of James's work, to codify and represent Caribbean identities, black radical political formations, and resistant nationalisms. My investigation unfolds against a shifting backdrop of James's migrations from Trinidad to England and from England to the United States, and within the theoretical frameworks of creolization and hybridity.

Throughout his career, whether writing a short story or a political history, James articulated his attempt to produce revolutionary and/or radical discourses with a consistent methodology that I call an *aesthetics of creolization*. Whereas the term "creolization" generally refers to the amalgamation of cultures that occurred in the Caribbean around the colonial encounter and created new cultures altogether, I also use it to refer to James's amalgamation of scholarly disciplines and his methodological approach to cultural and political criticism.

In this work, I explore his consistent intellectual contention that revolutionary and/or radical narratives could be fashioned from within white European bourgeois forms. James articulates this contention from political, authorial, and personal perspectives. And while some perceive James's self-description as a "Victorian intellectual" (in *Beyond a Boundary*) as evidence of detrimental conservatisms, following Belinda Edmondson, I treat that description and the larger phenomenon of his working within white European bourgeois forms as evidence of a writer made more compelling and more human because of his complicated allegiances. My book engages the dialectics of those allegiances that both ignore and interpret racial categories, and that both dismantle and reconstruct class as a means of stratifying populations.

James rarely wrote from within the confines of a single discipline; unrestricted by the conventional boundaries of history, literature, and philosophy, he layered and converged one upon the other creatively and sometimes radically to make his point. No matter which writerly medium he used, he was preoccupied with how to represent the individual personality and at the same time represent the community.

C. L. R. James and Creolization, therefore, is definitely the work of a "literature person," but now I am far less interested in claiming James for literary studies or for canonization in West Indian literature; that work has been done. The continued relevance of James to our world is exactly the difficulty we meet when we try to squeeze him into a specific category or discipline. My engagement of a cross section of James's works, drawn from different periods of his life and generated out of his own shifting political concerns is organized as close readings. These readings are offered as a way of understanding and historicizing contemporary debates having to do with transnationalism, race, modernity, cultural studies, and postcolonialism. At the same time, I offer up as the twin pursuit of this book my desire to theorize and historicize intra-Caribbean and black U.S./Caribbean dialogues that contemplate the intersections of art, resistance, and identity.

In chapter 1, I outline the book's theoretical architecture and present an extended discussion and overview of theories of creolization and hybridity, drawing heavily on the works of Edouard Glissant (*Caribbean Discourse*) and Edward Kamau Brathwaite (*Contradictory Omens* and *The Development of Creole Society in Jamaica, 1770–1820*). My principal contention is that creolization and hybridity are organic to James's diverse ideas and themes; therefore, this chapter establishes how creolization and hybridity specifically manifest within James's oeuvre. Drawing upon James's discussions of creolization and hybridity in *Beyond a Boundary*, his ideas about blackness, anticolonial politics, and West Indian cultural formations are illuminated and serve to undergird the discussions of the following chapters.

In 1936 and 1938, James completed two narratives of the San Domingo Revolution. Asserting that cross-reading the play and the history help to decode crucial components of each narrative and often mutually close gaps within the other, chapter 2, "Double or Nothing: The Two *Black Jacobins*," offers their first comparative reading. In these two texts, James grapples with usages of the written and the spoken word in his effort to analyze the political and strategic centrality of Vodun to the seventeenth- and eighteenth-century Haitian revolutionary effort. Additionally, the play and the history both serve as early opportunities for James to voice his political beliefs as a socialist and as a Pan-Africanist. A central aim of this chapter is to destabilize the idea that James's career in socialist politics and revolutionary activism can be represented as either chronologically or textually distinct from his career as a fiction writer and his concerns with literary representations. This idea is developed further in chapter 3.

In chapter 3, I argue that James's brief career as a fiction writer has relevance and importance that stretches beyond the *Beacon* era of Caribbean letters. As part of this argument I place James's novel *Minty Alley* (1936) in conversation with the film *La Rue Cases Negres* (*Black Shack Alley*) (1985), directed by feminist filmmaker Euzhan Palcy. Whereas the relationship of the individual to the community characterizes many twentieth-century Caribbean novels and is constituent to the *bildungsroman* form, it is also a theme central to James's career as a nonfiction writer. The film shares both thematic and formal attributes with *Minty Alley* and provides the opportunity to critique productively the aspirations of *Minty Alley* as a radical text. Further, my comparison of the film and the novel unearths an inherent aesthetics of creolization. Both texts' creolizations of the bildungsroman are realized through discourses of "folk" culture located within the community as well as through each protagonist's meticulously marked achievement of class consciousness.

Turning to James's first American period (1938–53) I use the fourth chapter, "Factions and Fictions: Considerations of the 'Negro Question'" to compare James's responses to the "Negro Question" with those of Richard Wright. Despite their friendship and similar journeys towards politicization through self-teaching and leftist organizations, Wright and James held very different opinions about the revolutionary potential of America and black Americans in particular. My analysis highlights where certain convergences appear and posits explanations for where they don't. As a major influence on James, Wright helped to shape and direct many of James's ideas about the intersections of race and class. A particular congruence is the power both men attributed to fiction, especially the novel, as an insurgent political mechanism. The migrations of James and Wright to and within America can be understood as a technology of creolization that directly informs their differing suppositions about race and revolution. This chapter is the first of two that seek to compare James's perspective on U.S. racial politics and black identity with that of one of his contemporaries. As such, it aims to contribute to the body of scholarship that accentuates the porousness of national borders in investigations of black identities and black epistemologies. The premise of this chapter hinges on the question of why, given their similar political perspectives on the United States, James was so anxious to stay and Wright was so anxious to go? The answer involves an analysis of Wright's essays "Blueprint for

Negro Writing" (1937) and "I Tried to Be a Communist" (1944) and James's essays "The Revolutionary Answer to the Negro Problem in the United States" (1948) and "With the Sharecroppers" (1941).

In chapter 5, I continue my focus on James's first American period with a comparative analysis of *Mariners, Renegades, and Castaways* (1953) and *American Civilization* (1992). I situate both texts as examples of "resistance literature" and describe their resistance as manifest in form, content, and context. James employs a creolized methodology in writing these texts—their unfinished, or unpublished status, their hybrid categorization, and their multiple imperatives of composition are all aspects of this methodology. My argument in this chapter juxtaposes James's personal quest for belonging and family with his critique of the American government as exclusionary and hostile. James's maintenance of his admiration for the American people and their revolutionary potential makes his expulsion in 1953 significantly more difficult.

The last chapter, "Metaphors of Nationalism: Music, Sport and Racial Representation," returns the discussion to *Beyond a Boundary* (1963) and the question of black identities in the United States and the West Indies. When Ralph Ellison talks about jazz in *Shadow and Act* (1964) and when James discusses cricket in *Boundary*, they are interested in delineating fine art, politics, and racialized, nationalized identities. Thus, this chapter offers a final contemplation of creolization's migratory possibilities. Pairing James's articulations of creolization through cricket and Ellison's discussions of Americanness through jazz, I ask whether as a theory creolization can be moved out of its specificity and used to compare constructions of black identities transnationally. Each author's concern with aesthetic value in evaluating the art forms of jazz and cricket precipitate similar contradictions in their individual theorizations. The organic colloquy presented by these two texts and their authors provides an opportunity to specify how ideologies of creolization can contribute to a discussion of comparative black subjectivities. Turning now to these multiple dialogues as led and shaped by James himself, I hope to display what Silvio Torres-Saillant calls "the transgression of disciplines and fusion of genres that we witness in the most central Caribbean authors" (18).

ABBREVIATIONS

CP	Communist Party (USA)
INS	Immigration and Naturalization Service (USA)
JFT	Johnson-Forest Tendency
PNM	People's National Movement (Trinidad)
PNP	People's National Party
QRC	Queen's Royal College
SWP	Socialist Workers Party (USA)
UNIA	Universal Negro Improvement Association
WIFLP	West Indian Federal Labour Party
WP	Workers Party (USA)

C.L.R. JAMES AND CREOLIZATION

MAPPING**CREOLIZATION**

There are, I am sure, many approaches to the ideas, themes, and concepts embodied in what is called "creoleness." My main interest in writing this essay is to seek to trace how creoleness may apply to fiction, indeed to the genesis of the imagination of the living soil of South America and the Caribbean. May I say at the outset that such genesis for me is ceaselessly unfinished and that this sensation of *unfinished genesis*—in worlds of space and nature and psyche—has its roots as much in Old Worlds as in New, in the crossroads of a civilization upon which we may have arrived in subtle and complex and involuntary ways that are altering conventional linearity and conventional frameworks.

Wilson Harris, "Creoleness: The Crossroads of a Civilization?"

In 1975, C. L. R. James wrote a five-hundred-word piece titled "Cricket and Race." Most of the short piece is taken up by the theme of "racial ideas" and sport, a subject James says he would have liked to have discussed with his recently deceased friend of six decades, Sir Learie Constantine. James asserts, "I believe the Constantine I knew would have been an ally against these racial ideas, benign as they may appear." James's extreme distaste for the tendency of the press to construct racial essentialisms around black sportsmen and his own globalized stance on the nexus of race, sport, and nationalism are the ideas to which he refers. These are themes that James elaborated upon at much greater length elsewhere and presumably did have a chance to discuss with Constantine; the succinctness of their presentation in "Cricket and Race" serves as an appropriate entry into this book. Reacting to a statement about baseball player Willie Mays, James expresses how he understands racial essentialisms as delimiting an appreciation of the artistry of an individual or culture. James first quotes a *Washington Post* article on Mays and then proceeds to articulate what I consider a characteristically Jamesian position on the meeting point of the production of beauty by overtly racialized subjects within a particular historical context: "On July 4 the *Washington Post* published an article on Willie Mays, the greatest baseball hero since Babe Ruth: 'Mays . . . was a black athlete. He ran black, swung black, and caught black.' Baseball had deteriorated into boredom. But Mays expressed on the field what James Baldwin (the famous black novelist) and others would later try to say in words: 'You need to learn something again about joy and suffering, about risk and those possibilities of uninhibited expression without which neither life nor art can survive.'" Aligning himself with Baldwin's words, James goes on to blast the idea of race as capable of representing essential characteristics in a group or individual:

> I have expressed similar ideas about cricket but from this "blackness" I recoil: it is not new, it is not Black. . . . When Frank Worrell and his team tried to restore to cricket what it had lost, they were not expressing a blackness.
> I believed and still believe that the generations of Grace, Trumper and Ranjitsinhji, of Worrell and his men, all were expressing powers inherent in a section of society but hitherto dormant.

Finally, James links beauty and elegance to effectiveness and power, not to read sports *as* politics, but rather to read the participation in sport by the groups under discussion as woven into the tapestry of world historical events:

> On 16 July I went to Detroit to see Mays. . . . Within his elegance and dignity, there is the ferocious effectiveness of Frank Worrell and I cannot see that Barbadian as an exemplar of blackness.
> Does Sobers bat, bowl and field black? He plays the game of powers emancipating themselves in a field that needs emancipation. (*Cricket* 279)

James's invocation of a diverse group of cricketers here, Afro-Caribbean, Indian, Australian, and British, whose play spanned the 1860s to the 1960s elevates certain political and social struggles above race because, as James would put it, "commentators and analysts do not pay sufficient attention to a very important aspect of the game, the way in which at any particular period it reflects tendencies in the national life" (*Boundary* 214). To use Sir Frank Worrell as an example, although he was the West Indian cricket team's first black captain,

James recognizes the fact of his blackness as secondary to the circumstances that made his captaincy a reality. The moment of his captaincy, the early 1960s, is the moment of independent nationhood for Trinidad and Tobago, and for many of the other British colonies. That moment, however, is not fleeting; the long struggle for independence and the indeterminate transition into a so-called postcolonial existence is the process that, according to James, so crucially characterizes and influences the West Indian players on the cricket pitch. James felt that it was from the bounty of independence, what he calls in *The Black Jacobins* the West Indies' "entrance into the comity of nations," that Worrell and "his men" drew their great cricket, not from the fact of (some of) their team's unsituated or raw "blackness." While these ideas may beckon in the direction of the sociological implications of black bodies and sports culture in the contexts of capitalism and postcolonialism, I wish simply to establish the cues and signals inherent in James's work that cast light upon the project and imperative of placing the subject of blackness as well as black subjects from the Caribbean and the United States into conversation with one another.

Born on January 4, 1901, James's long life and exploration into ideas of race, independent nationalism, Marxism, literature, colonialism, and sport began in a small village in Trinidad.[1] James died eighty-eight years later in Brixton, England. The son of a schoolteacher father and highly literate mother, James grew up in a family that commanded status and respect from the surrounding community but that was nevertheless quite poor. James's scholastic aptitude was recognized early, and, according to him, he was therefore expected to secure middle-class financial status by entering the civil service after graduating from school. Rejecting that dictate, his love of literature and cricket led him down a slightly more bohemian path: he supported himself as a teacher at his old school, the Queen's Royal College (QRC) in Port-of-Spain (a secondary school cast in the Oxbridge mold), and began writing short stories and his first novel as part of the now famous *Beacon* group.[2] In pursuance of his literary career James emigrated to England in 1932, where he published his novel, *Minty Alley*, became a cricket journalist for the *Manchester Guardian*, and entered the world of socialist organizations as well as Pan-Africanism. In 1938, after publishing several nonfiction works, including a history of the Haitian Revolution, *The Black Jacobins*, and *A History of Negro Revolt*, James traveled to America under the auspices of the Socialist Workers Party (SWP) for a year's lecture tour. Overstaying his visitor's visa, he remained for fifteen years and left then only under protest, a victim of American Cold War politics and its attendant paranoia about Communism. Originally a follower of Trotsky, while in America, James would formulate a critique of Trotsky's philosophical and political method and, together with Raya Dunayevskaya (Trotsky's former secretary) and Grace Lee (a Chinese American philosopher and activist), form a tiny splinter organization, the Johnson-Forest Tendency. The name of this group was taken from Dunayevskaya's pseudonym, Freddie Forest, and the pseudonym James used most frequently: J. R. Johnson. Although James's life in America was complicated by ill health and by his leftist politics, which forced him underground to escape pursuit by immigration authorities, this period was nevertheless one of his most prolific as a political theorist and writer. His deportation in 1953 occasioned a return to England and then to Trinidad and Tobago in 1958 where Eric Williams, James's former student, was preparing to lead the almost independent island nation as its first prime minister. Working as an editor for the *Nation*, the newspaper of Williams's People's National Party (PNP) and as a delegate to the West Indies Federal Labour Party (WIFLP) (the political arm of the short-lived West Indies Federation), James ultimately failed to influence the moderate Williams to adopt more radical platforms and was unable to create a political base of his own. A near-fatal car accident in 1961 compounded James's ill health and greatly reduced his capacity to write and exert himself; this did not, however, reduce his productivity or significantly curtail his global travels. His post-American period also saw James return in force to Pan-Africanism. The revolutions in Hungary and the Gold Coast (Ghana) and decolonization in general were of great significance to James and bore out many of his theories of how the modern world was going to be shaped by ordinary people. His four-year return to Trinidad was followed by work with Kwame Nkrumah in Ghana, a variety of teaching posts in the United States (he was allowed back in by the late 1960s), visits to the Caribbean, and finally, a sort of settlement in Brixton, where he lived at the *Race Today* collective from 1981 until his death in 1989. The last twenty years of James's life afforded him a measure of fame, and, in the late 1970s and during the 1980s, his books and essays began to be republished and made available to new generations of readers, activists, and academics in England, the West Indies, and the United States.[3]

As one such U.S.-based academic, I find the connections that James makes in "Cricket and Race" emblematic of his challenge to both himself and his reader to think outside the proverbial boxes of nation, chronology, genre, and discipline. The subtle parallel James draws between Worrell and the West Indian cricket team and Mays as a peculiar representative of American baseball then provides a conduit for the sorts of parallels I will make throughout this book. Apprehending the representational juggernauts contained within the signification of black West Indian and black American sports figures, James encourages the reader to recognize their different yet overlapping contexts of racial ontologies and, further, their relationship to anticolonialism and art as resistant epistemologies. In other words, the deceptive ease of placing Mays, Worrell, and Baldwin in the same essay does not effect a collapse of the national, generic, subjective, or political circumstances that distinguish them from one another. James's juxtaposition seems to encourage us to find the bridges that preserve yet connect across such differences. First, the Mays/Worrell example shows how James understood Caribbeanness and black U.S. identities mattering to one another as they articulate overlapping and often parallel struggles for multiple emancipations. Second, James states how Willie Mays's play expresses a humanistic "joy and suffering," not a generic blackness that automatically connects all black people or separates them from all nonwhite peoples; James generally tried to steer away from such monolithic racial formations. Certainly, the argument can and should be made that Mays's expressive abilities *grow out of* his experiences as a Negro American, but the artistry of his play is not so easily or quickly locatable. For James, an aspect of artistic value resides in the ability of an individual artist to convey "joy and suffering" to any spectator. Third, the work of representing and comprehending artistic value, and the political, social, and economic circumstances that help it to thrive or perish, cuts across what James calls "arbitrary" disciplines of literary, political, or "popular" lines of inquiry; thus he enlists Baldwin to help make his point about sport.

However, even as James eschews racial and racist essentialisms, he is unavoidably formed and influenced by them. Although James may "recoil" from "this blackness," he inadvertently qualifies Baldwin as a "famous *black* novelist." A tireless advocate for the struggles of ordinary black people in different geographical locations and at various historical moments, James nevertheless consistently attempted to read race and to read blackness as important only in relation to other equally important phenomena, such as class position and historical circumstance. The cross section of James's works and the authors with whom I place him in conversation all traverse these slippery trails of race, artistry, and emancipatory struggle that at different coordinates accommodate or reject a racialized poetics.

As the referents within the quoted passage from "Cricket and Race" suggest, James presumed an audience familiar with the game of cricket, its history, and its outstanding players; obviously, he was not writing for American readers. And yet, to make his point, he utilizes two black Americans not necessarily familiar to his intended audience. Nevertheless, James impresses upon the reader the importance of knowing and being aware of Baldwin and Mays, not just because of their fame and accomplishments within the realms of literature and sport but because of how their work is connected *and* how their work informs and illuminates the work of cricketers in the "Old" and "New" Worlds. The ease with which James constructed such comparative frameworks is the inspiration for this book.

James's facility with comparative frameworks does not prevent me from cautiously avoiding the universalization of diaspora black experiences or positing the "New" World as a coherent entity or uncontested space. I do hope, however, that my own comparative devices make James available to more diverse audiences. Each chapter turns on a point of comparison that involves James's interest in different genres of writing, his shifting political affiliations, or the ways his work can be understood in conversation with other artists, some of whom he counted as friends. I proceed from an idea of black cultures that understands them as often connected to one another and as similarly (although not identically) connected to other cultural formations as mediated by race, ethnicity, relations of political power, gender, and class. James's reading of Mays, Baldwin, and Worrell through and against one another does not collapse them into representatives of some universal blackness; rather, in the pursuit of more complex understandings of art and artistry, James characteristically makes plain the diversity of experience and expression housed within the black diaspora. My efforts to theorize and understand as fully as possible James's shifting positions on art, blackness, and politics have been greatly assisted through my application of creolization and hybridity theories; I use the rest of this introductory chapter to elaborate my usage of these theories as interpretative mechanisms for the work of C. L. R. James. Happily, neither James nor blackness can lay claim to particular purities or orthodoxies. As Stuart Hall has most aptly put it, specifically referencing black popular culture, purity as such does not adhere to blackness or its cultures. Rather, "always these forms are the product of partial synchronization, of engagement across cultural boundaries, of the confluence of more than one cultural tradition, of the negotiations of dominant and subordinate positions, of the subterranean strategies of recoding and transcoding, of critical signification, of signifying" ("What Is This 'Black' in Black Popular Culture?" 28).

The same sort of recognition of the instability of cultural, racial, and transnational identities is discernible at various points in James's thinking.

To place James in conversation with one Martinican filmmaker and two black U.S. writers privileges the U.S./Caribbean relationship above other national and international relations that informed James's life and work. My choices, however, seek to engage certain specific manifestations of creolization in order to interrogate both the specifics of U.S./Caribbean intellectual and historical relationships as well as the viability of creolization as an epistemology suited for making sense of black diasporas in the Atlantic world. At the same time, the Caribbean of Toussaint L'Ouverture and Fidel Castro as well as the America of Herman Melville and Richard Wright are important to James as histories and spaces of (differentiated and diverse) social change. He had similar ideas about Hungary and Ghana in the twentieth century, to be sure, but I have found there to be a particular urgency in my pairings. This urgency is generated from a desire to address the "dialogic discourses" at play within creolization and at work when James discusses America and the Caribbean.

Creolization: Revisioning the Enlightenment

As the modalities that usher the Caribbean into discussions of the modern, modernity, modernism, and postmodernism, creolization and hybridity must be defined in order for us to understand how they are to be differentiated from one another. Creolization and hybridity are tools that aid the apprehension of what Torres-Saillant calls the "differentiated entity" of Caribbean literature *and* that facilitate a cross-cultural comparison of Caribbean literatures with certain specific examples of black U.S. writing; James has contributed to both bodies of writing. I assert that creolization and hybridity are ways in which we can interpret Caribbean writing and "its cultural and intellectual interrelations with the West," without viewing it as "a passive receptacle of metropolitan influences" (23) and while simultaneously situating it within postcolonial discourses. Creolization seeks to be understood as an organic phenomenon of the Caribbean, but, at the same time, it is a mechanism through which the Caribbean positions itself in relation to and interacts with the rest of the world. I intend to draw on a diverse set of interpretations of creolization and hybridity theories so that the key differences and convergences between them can emerge. I then show how creolization and hybridity resonate specifically in the key themes that inform C. L. R. James's work and ideas.

Functionally, creolization is the term that attempts in one word to capture as much of the Caribbean region's articulations of diversity, mixture, and cross-cultural influences as is possible. By definition, it can be shown to challenge Western European colonial systems of categorization and their emphasis on order, absoluteness, singular national narratives, and fixed identity. Creolization is a term and a theory that consciously avoids political and historical stasis and can be pressed into service as a way of understanding the cultural, social, and political development of the "modern" Caribbean. (In this instance "modern" denotes the construction of the Caribbean and the wider circum-Atlantic world by diverse peoples after Columbus initiated its exploration and exploitation by Europeans in the fifteenth century.) Creolization is also connected to the cultures of the Caribbean "in play" before the arrival of the Europeans. Antonío Benitez-Rojo describes creolization as "a term with which we attempt to explain the unstable states that a Caribbean cultural object presents over time. In other words, creolization is not merely a process (a word which implies forward movement) but a discontinuous series of recurrences, of happenings, whose sole law is change" ("Three Words" 54). Creolization is more complicated, however, than just mixture and cross-cultural influence, as such phenomena can be identified all over the world at all stages of history. An important component of the creolist culture is that it is a culture formed out of an eclectic borrowing that it acknowledges, values, and privileges.[4] When creolization is understood as such, one can begin to discern the difference between it (creolization) or a creolist culture and a culture, like that of the United States, which often likes to imagine itself and regard itself as "a melting-pot culture," where the proposed end-product is unitary rather than multiple, homogenous rather than heterogenous. Joseph Roach calls this the "hypothetical monoculture of Anglo North America" (10) and more generally describes "the relentless search for the purity of origins" as a "voyage not of discovery but of erasure" (6). This distinction will be of particular importance when my discussion turns to James, Wright, and Ellison and their respective views on America. Creolization's advocates and practitioners emphasize how it challenges colonialism and, more inclusively, Western systems of value that presuppose stability through singular national histories and absolute identities. Such presuppositions have notoriously confined black people in many nations to static, subordinate positions in history.

Edward Kamau Brathwaite and Edouard Glissant are two authors who have greatly influenced the theorization of creolization, in both popular and scholarly circles. Brathwaite, in 1971, described creolization as "the acculturation and interculturation" that occurred between the European, African, Asian, and Amerindian populations of the Caribbean region over time. Despite the changes within creolization theory since Brathwaite inserted it as a principal term in the lexicon of Caribbean studies, his definitions are still considered to be foundational to creolization theories that have proliferated in more recent years. In recognition of its multiple definitions, Brathwaite specifies "creole's" usage "in Jamaica and the old settled English colonies" as referring to those "born in, native to, committed to the area of living," and denoting "both white and black, free and slave" (*Contradictory Omens* 10).[5] According to Brathwaite, West Indian creolization "started as a result of slavery and therefore in the first instance involving black and white, European and African, in a fixed superiority/inferiority relationship." With emancipation (1834 in British West Indian colonies), Brathwaite suggests how the process of creolization was "slowed/halted/altered" because of "the changed relationship of white and black, a new emphasis on culturation into English models, the arrival of East Indian and other immigrants occasioned by the changed black/white situation and the development, out of this, of a plural society" (11). Brathwaite's definitions resonate with James's personal recollections of the way his early life was a mass of different, sometimes conflicting influences. (*The Black Jacobins* also utilizes a creolized historiographic approach as James elaborates the multiple political and cultural influences on the Haitian rebels.) Jamesian ideals can likewise be discerned within Glissant's theorizations on creolization (written in the late 1960s and the 1970s and using Martinique as the focal point).

Glissant, moving away from his Francophone predecessors' articulations of *Negritude* and *Indiginisme*, forever connected creolization to the postmodern by emphasizing its infinite movement. Like Brathwaite, Glissant asserts that creolization is process, but whereas Brathwaite can and does locate an evolving end-product, creole society (which is different and new in relation to any of its originary components), Glissant insists on this process as incessant. In creolization, he determines, "we can see that the mingling of experiences is at work, there for us to know and producing the process of being. We abandon the idea of fixed being" (14). Expanding his opposition to the notion of fixed being as an impossible but pernicious construct of Western European ideology, Glissant locates creolization within a complex philosophy of being/becoming in the Caribbean that is always attended by specific politicized contexts and acts of resistance. Fixed Being or "Sameness" "began with expansionist plunder in the West," and "Diversity came to light through the political and armed resistance of peoples." Both hybridity and creolization urgently seek to subvert, invert, and where possible, replace (as a palimpsest replaces) Enlightenment and colonial ideologies of race, identity, and aesthetics. One of my main assertions in this book is that James uses theories of creolization and hybridity in most aspects of his writing. Through a series of readings, I show that James's aesthetic sensibility is uniquely and at times paradoxically stitched from the cloth of creolization and hybridity.

But what does it mean to link aesthetics and creolization and hybridity? Aesthetics carries with it the heavy baggage of universalism and connotes perceptions of beauty as connected to philosophies of taste. Does this not sit awkwardly besides creolization and its insistence on impurity, mixture, and instability? I argue in the following pages and throughout this book that within that awkwardness, within the very uneasiness of these terms placed side by side, is the portal to understanding the project of identity formation and cross-cultural comparison under the auspices of racialized and class-based discourses that are so crucial to much of what James has written and so distinctively articulated in wide Caribbean and black U.S. arenas. An appropriate next step then is to survey the definitions and interplay between Enlightenment aesthetics, creolization, and hybridity.

The European Enlightenment sense of aesthetics seeks to understand a work of art as being able to definitively signify a universal experience. In contrast, creolization understands art, culture, and language in a radically different manner. Unlike Enlightenment philosophy, which concerned itself with the creation of totalizing grand narratives—and interpreted the world as built on absolutes, on binary oppositions (especially of self and other), the postmodern perspective of creolization understands, without an inherent compulsion to classify, the cultures and politics of the Caribbean as complex and layered. As a philosophy nurtured in the colonial and postcolonial region of the Caribbean, and therefore under a comprehensive, although not exclusive, influence of Enlightenment philosophies, creolization acknowledges and celebrates this European antecedent as one amongst many. Inasmuch as it is an ideology that functions as a response to the diversified assault of colonialism, creolization is a postcolonial discourse. Hybridity, in the context of postcolonial discourse, responds to this generalized notion of Enlightenment aesthetics by proving the productivity of the hybridized subject. By asserting productivity in all senses of the phrase, hybridity as theory inverts its simple definition and hegemonic signification. Thus, one can begin to see the usefulness of both hybridity and creolization as ways to "read" the Caribbean and Caribbean literature and as ways to effect transnational and cross-cultural conversations within the black diaspora.[6]

The publication of *Caribbean Creolization* marks a concerted attempt to theorize creolization by considering the Caribbean's cultural and linguistic diversity. Whereas Brathwaite and Glissant's ideas about creolization are extrapolated from localized viewpoints (Jamaica and Martinique, respectively), and while I often focus on the Anglophone Caribbean, in their introduction to *Caribbean Creolization*, Kathleen Balutansky and Marie-Agnès Sourieau provide a needed regional overview of the term. Again, defining creolization in opposition to the European Enlightenment "ideology of order prevailing in all domains over chaos," Balutansky and Sourieau state, "In the New World, brute exploitation gave the lie to Western ethics, philosophy, aesthetics, and politics . . . Creolization is thus defined as a syncretic process of transverse dynamics that endlessly reworks and transforms the cultural patterns of varied social and historical experiences and identities. The cultural patterns that result from this 'crossbreeding' (or cross-weaving) undermine any academic or political aspiration for unitary origins or authenticity" (2–3). Importantly, their definition of the Caribbean frustrates an impulse to romanticize the phenomenon of creolization, and points to its paradoxes:

This not to say that the region's complex human mixtures, as well as its labyrinthine racial and cultural combinations, are not the result of, or do not result in, a painful pattern of confrontations and ruptures among racial groups and of considerable mutations of personal and cultural identity. Indeed, those who inhabit this region still dwell in a socially, racially, and spiritually fragmented world—one that yearns to imagine itself as a whole. From the early days of slavery to the present, this need has underscored the struggles, conflicts, and upheavals within communities as well as individuals. (3)

By emphasizing creolization as *process*, one which is often marked by violence and rupture, Balutansky and Sourieau's ideas about creolization are quite similar to Glissant's, and yet build upon theorizations that predate Glissant and include Brathwaite. The latter's etymology of creole specifies, as other theorists would continue to do, the Caribbean colonial encounter and landscape as essential to creolization's definition. He states, "The word itself appears to have originated from a combination of two Spanish words *criar* (to create, to imagine, to establish, to found, to settle) and *colon* (a colonist, a founder, a settler) into *criollo*: a committed settler, one identified with the area of settlement, one native to the settlement though not ancestrally indigenous to it" (*Contradictory Omens* 10). Brathwaite and his adherents wish to anchor creolization securely as a term and a phenomenon of the "New World," and specifically the Caribbean despite the fact that colonial encounters (such as that of Spain in the above example), cultural interventions, and ethnic mixing are common throughout history and can be recognized in many different areas of the globe. Equally important to Brathwaite's concept of creolization is his investment in Caribbean Creole languages, whether written or spoken, as liberatory mechanisms ("nation language") against colonialism. In an essay where he discusses creolization as "An Exploded Discourse," Glissant is more circumspect than Brathwaite in asserting creole languages as liberatory—"the language of the people, Creole, is not the language of the nation" (166)—in part because of their dependency on that which they wish to be liberated from (in Glissant's Martinique that would be both French and *the* French). Arguing that Creole (as a language) has not had enough time or latitude for the type of self-reflection that would aid its development into the language of a Caribbean poetics (self-expression), Glissant instead emphasizes the complex processes that motor both linguistic and cultural creolization when he asserts:

If the Martinican intuitively grasps the ambiguity of both his relationship with French and his relationship with Creole—the imposed language and the deposed language respectively—it is perhaps because he has the unconscious sense that a basic dimension is missing in his relation to time and space, and that is the Caribbean dimension. As opposed to the unilateral relationship with the Metropolis, the multidimensional nature of the diverse Caribbean. As opposed to the constraints of one language, the creation of self-expression. (*Caribbean Discourse* 165)

I find Glissant's formulation useful in its determination to understand the language, geography, and ruptured histories of the Caribbean as relational (to Europe and elsewhere) and continually developing. Taken together, Balutansky, Sourieau, Brathwaite, and Glissant offer a comprehensive portrait of some of the more prevalent creolization theories.

While Michael Dash critiques Brathwaite's definitions of creolization as premised on a closed and restrictive model, his critique usefully summarizes the evolution of creolization as a theory of identity and the Caribbean region, underscoring the fact that creolization's openness and valorization of indeterminacy is only its most contemporary self-description (*This Other America* 72). Yet, despite what I find to be a theoretically apt criticism, Dash forgets that creolization harbors within itself essentializing tendencies. Furthermore, whereas it is a current practice to speak of the Caribbean regionally, that has not always been the case. European colonialism in the region left a legacy of dividedness that is perhaps most obvious in the linguistic diversity of the Caribbean where there are at least five different official—"legitimate"—languages and many more unofficial languages spoken throughout its nations and territories. (Even at the beginning of the twenty-first century, the Spanish-speaking Caribbean is more often linked in public discourse to Latin America before or in place of it being understood as part of the Caribbean.) Paradoxically, Brathwaite's (and others) interest in conceptualizing the Caribbean as a whole was a necessary step toward theorizing the impossibility of it imagining itself whole. Brathwaite's famous image of a Caribbean "submarine unity" (*Contradictory Omens* 64), which replaces the image of disparate islands with one of a connected undersea mountain range, is an important articulation of resistance against the crippling notions of intra-Caribbean difference. Thus, I agree that Brathwaite's desire for a "therapeutic wholeness" is antithetical to a contemporary creolist model, but I see it nevertheless as a desire that helps to produce that model. As Balutansky and Sourieau state above, the entire region harbors a yearning "to imagine itself whole." The impossibility of realizing such a desire undergirds the power of a creolist paradigm. It provides the peculiar tension that creolization strengthens itself with through resistance. Later in his text, Dash recognizes this, although not in direct reference to Brathwaite, when he remarks, "one of the basic impulses in Caribbean thought is undeniably the need to reconceptualize power" (*This Other America* 105). In its desire to reconceptualize power and establish a new authority, creolization can be linked to discourses of hybridity that, of course, resonate and articulate well beyond the boundaries of the Caribbean and the Caribbean diaspora, and offer a set of similar yet differentiated interventions into colonial ideologies and social and political hegemonies across the globe. James's own efforts to show how "the general power of ordinary men and women could intervene critically in historical events" and his desire to "make the Caribbean people aware that they were indeed at the forefront of the struggle to found the new society" (Grimshaw, *Reader* 18) are at once evidence of his creolized consciousness and his desire to "reconceptualize power."

Creolization and Hybridity

Creolization and hybridity are similar; they are not synonymous. Perhaps their greatest distinction is hybridity's geographical nonspecificity and creolization's desired rootedness in a specific Caribbean space/experience.[7] "Hybrid" is defined in concise dictionaries as the offspring resulting from the union of different animal or plant species (as quoted in Ashcroft, Griffiths, and Tifflin, *Key Concepts in Post-Colonial Studies*, 118). Notably, within postcolonial discourse Homi Bhabha has broadened its meaning to connote a generalized postcolonial condition that is in fact reliant upon hybridity's geographical nonspecificity and emphasizes the "mutual constructions of colonizer/colonized subjectivities" (118).

Creolization, in contrast, positions itself at the "sociocultural" nexus of what Brathwaite identifies as "the four main cultural carriers of the Caribbean region—Amerindian, European, African and East Indian." Significantly, Brathwaite suggests that the interaction of these four cultural carriers is equally important for their collective interaction with the "*environment* to create the new societies of the New World" (emphasis added). Further, Brathwaite locates his definition of creolization in the context of creole societies in his work *The Development of Creole Society in Jamaica, 1770–1820*, where he states that the culture and society settled and formed by people from Britain and West Africa "developed . . . its own distinctive character or culture," which could not be described "as 'purely' British or West African and is termed 'creole'" (xiii). Brathwaite bases his study on Jamaica specifically; I feel, however, that his definition is applicable to the entire Caribbean region. Creolization, as invoked by Brathwaite and Glissant, cannot be separated from its place of origin; by definition it is a term that invokes the experience of people who settled in the New World after Columbus's voyages; hybridity's scope is much broader and has resonated with much greater controversy within postcolonial studies because of its usage in nineteenth-century racialist discourse of imperial powers. Brathwaite's definition is both dated and transcendent of the date of his research—by which I mean in the twentieth century, the main cultural carriers of the Caribbean region are significantly different from their configuration in *Development of Creole Society*, and now include, for instance, the United States. Nevertheless, his identification of cultural formation as the product of mixing and interchange remains both relevant and useful in destabilizing the persistent formulation of the cultural impact of colonization as unidirectional and emanating from the West. In contrast, Glissant's discussions of creolization emanate from the Caribbean, yet he cites examples of creolization from all over the world.

James's formal education as a British subject in early twentieth-century colonial Trinidad comprehensively presented Victorian England as a particularly rich culture and society to emulate and imitate. Inevitably, James came to identify with certain aspects of Englishness and famously describes himself in *Beyond a Boundary* as a "Victorian with the rebel seed." Thus, in my connection of James to creolization and hybridity, it is important to consider the ways in which hybridity was conceptualized and disseminated from a British Victorian viewpoint. By locating hybridity in the specific historical and geopolitical context of Victorian England, Jennifer Devere Brody constructs a useful bridge between hybridity's participation in ideologies of colonialism and imbalanced relationships of power imposed upon the Caribbean, and creolization as a discourse or modality of ideological resistance developing from within the Caribbean. In *Impossible Purities: Blackness, Femininity, and Victorian Culture*, Brody details anxiety-ridden discourses of cultural purity implicit in Victorian England's attention to hybridity. Drawing our attention to the hybridities of the colonizer class itself (represented by the English), Brody shows how in its wish to deny its own "taintedness," England projects a false (im)purity onto the colonial other. Hybridity in Victorian English discourse is most fundamentally concerned with purity and categorization in the face of multiple impurities and permeable boundaries in all aspects of its culture(s). Brody identifies this concern as one that troubles the constructed pure "history" of Englishness. That "history" functions as a narrative of nation that England both consumes, exports, and projects onto its colonies (134). Looping back to James, the negative connotation of hybridity makes it difficult for the Caribbean to sense how it can understand creolization, hybridization, and "mongrelization," in positive terms or how such an epistemological self-positioning might be understood as "legitimate." For James, however, it was a positive: it was the black Jacobins of Haiti bringing themselves and bringing something new to the world stage. It is also, in another iteration, Derek Walcott's "quarrel with history."

Creolization shares with hybridity the desire to deny the Englishman or generic colonizer what Brody calls "the illusion of order, as well as the fixity of the other" (138). But, whereas creolization refuses to engage, even as a means to subvert, the prevailing Victorian ideology that "named hybrids horrific" (139), at times hybridity reclaims and revises the hybrid's negative connotations. Creolization asserts the necessity of examining Caribbean cultures from within the Caribbean while hybridity casts its net further to corral an examination of both the point of encounter and the multiple points of origins that lead to these encounters. In some senses then, creolization is positively attached to the forming "nations" of the Caribbean in terms of the politics of past and present anticolonial and national independence movements. Many of these political and related cultural movements (Negritude, Creolité, Indiginisme, the Caribbean Artists Movement, and Black Power) are heavily invested in asserting an identity independent from the colonial metropolitan power; however, they are not necessarily also invested in denying the types of transculturations occasioned by the (ongoing) colonial/postcolonial encounter. For James, the prismatic relationship of anticolonialism and the politics and cultures that attach to independence movements is captured in 1963 when, in his appendix to *The Black Jacobins*, he situates the creative writers of the Caribbean as most likely and best equipped to carry on the "political work" of both developing, inhabiting, and expressing a nascent, still resistant West Indian nationalism (416–17). James also describes the creole development of West Indian society as a struggle between the "modern population" of laborers bound to the colonial system, which James calls "the oldest Western relic of the seventeenth century still alive in the world today" (*Jacobins* 405). Significantly, James outlines the borrowing and acknowledgment of creolization discussed earlier and calls attention to its lack of duality: "The West Indies has never been a traditional colonial territory with clearly distinguished economic and political relations between two different cultures" (405). Noting the decimation of aboriginal Amerindian civilizations, James asserts that this decimation was partly responsible for one aspect of creolization, inasmuch as "every succeeding year . . . saw the labouring population, slave or free, incorporating into itself more and more of the language, customs, aims and outlook of its masters. It steadily grew in numbers until it became a terrifying majority of the total population" (405). That terror, James's interpretation of the "masters'" reaction, signals the recognition of a dialectical position in which the masters, in producing this slave population, are also producing their own downfall: "the ruling minority therefore was in the position of the father who produced children and had to guard against being supplanted by them" (*Jacobins* 405). This oblique discussion of creolization in *Jacobins*, then, should also be understood as related to some of the influential conclusions that Homi Bhabha has reached regarding hybridity and the postcolonial condition.

In "Signs Taken For Wonders," Homi Bhabha draws upon psychoanalytic theory to make the argument that hybridity is claimable as a theory of postcoloniality because it is a sign that negates through repetition, "it unsettles the mimetic or narcissistic demands of colonial power but reimplicates its identifications in strategies of subversion that turn the gaze of the discriminated back upon the eye of power" (173). This "strategic reversal of the process of domination through disavowal" disrupts the binary opposition of self and other that functioned as the brick and mortar of colonialism. Bhabha's "revaluation of discriminatory identity effects" suggests the inherent inequality and subjugation on which colonial Caribbean societies were based *and* the negative association of hybrid identity that Brody points out. (In *Boundary* James uses hybridity most often to describe his own experience and personality while he generally invokes a notion of creolization when discussing aspects of the Caribbean society in which he grew up. For instance, the creolization of cricket is discussed by James, without using the term, both in reference to race and to the culture that sprung up around West Indian cricket.) Perhaps, most significantly, Bhabha raises the issue of mimicry in relation to postcolonial subjectivities.[8] Postcolonial discourse consistently struggles with the negative significations attached to the word *hybrid* and seeks to reclaim hybridity as a productive, positive signification; it has not for the most part, however, been able to connect the ideology of hybridity to specific political struggles even as it proffers itself as a mode of agency for postcolonial subjects.[9] Nevertheless, Bhabha's formulations of hybridity as a means for colonial subjects to both perform and embody resistance to the various colonial hegemonies of power speak directly to the nineteenth century usages of hybridity outlined by Brody and to late twentieth century anticolonialist projects.[10]

James is both unapologetic and proud of his own hybrid identity as a "Victorian with the rebel seed" and can thereby be understood as considering hybridity as a compelling ontological position to occupy. Nevertheless, the lived reality of his peculiar experience of hybridity situated him as an outsider to various communities for most of his life. As such, it is perhaps more useful to consider the different/shifting connotations of hybridity without employing a binary apparatus of positive and negative valuation. Instead, it will be important to recall and recognize hybridity's shifting connotations in both its abstract formulations and also when it is understood as delineating the lived experience of individuals. In *C. L. R. James's Social Theory: A Critique of Race and Modernity*, Brett St Louis includes James in a long line of twentieth-century black intellectuals whose "hybrid" existence is at various times articulated through W. E. B. Du Bois's notion of double consciousness and Richard Wright's "outsiderism" (21). St Louis's insight is part of his larger thesis, which recognizes the "precarious positioning of the black diaspora as simultaneously included and excluded from the West," (iii). Crucially, St Louis notes significant experiential differences between black American and black West Indian positioning within racialized landscapes (20).

Without attention to historical specificity or individual experience the multiple theorizations of both hybridity and creolization sometimes obscure their materialist realities. However, in considering both a contemporary as well as geographically specific politics of hybridity from an Asian American perspective, Lisa Lowe can be understood as responding to the more abstract formulations of hybridity. Emphasizing the material realities of hybridity in the colonial encounter of immigrant Asian communities and the United States, Lowe asserts that hybridity "does not suggest the assimilation of Asian or immigrant practices to dominant forms but instead marks the history of survival within relationships of unequal power and domination" (66). For James, his sense of developing into a hybrid was created out of the specific social and political colonialism of the British, which taught him a specific curriculum and oriented him towards its metropolitan center, London. Lowe's ideas are useful to our discussion not just because they insist we recognize the mantles of capitalism and violence worn by hybridity—and, I would add, creolization—as a phenomenon of colonial and postcolonial encounters, but because these are James's concerns as well (82). Lowe's work is also instructive inasmuch as she makes the Asian immigrant visible: these groups are given short shrift in James's, Glissant's, and Brathwaite's formulations of culture, creolization, and hybridity and in terms of how they theorized Asian immigration relating to the politics of resistance understood within concepts of creolization and hybridity.

Creolized Identities and the Need for Multiple Dialogues

There are numerous instances where James uses and embraces the notion of hybridity, both within the peculiarities of his West Indian identity and in his extra-Caribbean activities, migrations, and publishing. Significantly, James's acknowledgment and embodiment of hybridity does not suggest as it does with V.S. Naipaul, for instance, a crippling alienation from the Caribbean or a derogatory assessment of his West Indian years. Ultimately, both creolization and hybridity serve as tools with which to apprehend James and his relevance to contemporary, diverse communities. Even though relevant passages from *Beyond a Boundary* are frequently quoted to note James's double consciousness expressed as Victorian self-identification, James has not yet been engaged as either a subject or theorist of creolization and hybridity; such a sustained engagement is launched in this volume.

The need, indeed the point, of using creolization and hybridity to engage

James's works is quite simply that these theories allow for both a privileging and a questioning of racial categories, of the black diaspora, of how we go about the tricky business of representing history and assessing our (multi-) cultures. Contained within the ideologies of creolization and hybridity is the elasticity of all racial signifiers, none more so than blackness. As later chapters will bear out and as demonstrated by the piece this chapter opened with in its juxtaposition of Mays, Baldwin, and Worrell, where I bring other writers into my discussions of James the purpose is to broaden the contexts and especially the constructs available to interpret and critique James with. As such, creolization and hybridity have proven the most suitable theoretical frameworks since the different ways they each privilege race and class mark interesting parallels with James's own differing (over time) privileging of these categories as demonstrated by his participation in (and narration of) globally diverse class struggles, black struggles, and black class struggles.

To return to the issues with which I began this chapter, James consistently demonstrated that he understood and valued the specificities of "black" struggles, yet he also abhorred racialist thinking that asserted blackness as possibly superseding other distinguishing aspects of struggle such as gender, class, or ethnicity. In James's abhorrence of an essentialized, universalized "blackness," he recognizes how it can be an overdetermined category, one which, like the hybrid in the English Victorian sense, can function hegemonically to delimit what James, creolists, and postcolonial theorists alike recognize as complex "new," "old," "third," and "first" world subjectivities. Blackness in all of these instances can simplistically obscure the ways in which class, class antagonism, ethnicities, and gender work to negatively fragment a society. Conversely, these same elements can, when strategically aligned, manifest as viable modes of resistance to, for instance, colonialism. James's ability to formulate such conclusions without using the language of later creolization and hybridity theorists, some of whom I have referred to in this chapter, can be attributed to the multiple identities he inhabited and his ability to discern the multiple, creolizing influences that shape human existence, especially during the twentieth century.

The ideas of postcolonial theorists such as Glissant and Bhabha are embedded not only in the subjects James takes up but also in *how* he analyzes them.[11] *Beyond a Boundary*, for instance, reveals the ways in which hybridity is always already a component of the colonial enterprise; *Minty Alley* attests to the ways in which Victorian ideologies of race and class circulate and re-vision themselves in a fictional Trinidadian community; *Mariners, Renegades, and Cast-*

aways invites American literature as well as American politics to recognize how their sacred discourses of democracy are situated within discourses of totalitarianism.

James intermittently understood and exposed the problematics of "purity" in his discussion of various manifestations of cultural imperialism by the English in Trinidad. His repeated use of "purity" and "Puritan" in *Boundary* was one of the first reasons I began to connect him to theories of creolization and hybridity. On one hand, "Puritan" is part of *Boundary*'s cricket discussions and conveys the British notion of fair play, but "purity" has less exact connotations as it is applied more widely in the text. James recognizes that the colonial encounter itself destroys any notion of "purity" in either the sense of racial boundaries desired by the English or the moral standards they professed to have. James's prefatory remark in *Boundary*, when he quizzically declaims, "What do they know of cricket who only cricket know?" suggests that *Boundary* (in a creolist move) will offer a way of seeing or knowing, even as it calls into question the very possibility of stabilized knowledge. He adds, "if the ideas originated in the West Indies it was only in England and in English life and history that I was able to track them down and test them." This comment situates West Indianness as an ever-evolving identity that requires, at any given moment, both historical and cultural specificity. Those specificities, in turn, are impossible for James to disentangle from particular types of Englishness. Within the text, he describes Puritanism as a code of honor, gleaned from the British, and as learned through cricket while he attended primary and secondary school. It represents a discipline of character, especially moral discipline, that made him prefer to "cut off his fingers than do anything contrary to the ethics of the game." Retrospectively, James acknowledges the ways in which cricket was not pure and sometimes, in fact, promoted "racialism." These ironies of racial, national, and cultural identities are often discussed by James through the use of autobiographical anecdote. The hybridity contained within himself and the creolized society in which he came of age are recognizable in many of James's grander pronouncements about modernity. The emphasis that James places on puritanism can often be read as a synonym for the positive value he places on his Britishness, which made him an outsider in Trinidad.

There is much written about the chapter in *Boundary* called "The Light and the Dark," which typifies the conflicting instances, usages, and appearances of creolization and hybridity in James's work. James's anxiety as a young man in Trinidad over which amateur cricket club (team) to join and the extraordinary detail with which these clubs defined their membership (via profession, race, skin color, associates, family), and by extension, Trinidadian society, corresponds to the metropolitan English Victorian concern with classification as well as its obverse: an apprehension of misclassification, recognized negatively as miscegenation and hybridity. James, "a promising cricketer," narrows his choices down, from the all-white teams, Queens Park and Shamrock; and the all-black teams of Constabulary and Stingo. Constabulary was the team of the local police (captained by a white man and not a secondary education amongst them) and Stingo was comprised of "plebeians: the butcher, the tailor, the candlestick maker, the casual laborer, with a sprinkling of unemployed. Totally black and no social status whatever." James is left with only two true possibilities, Maple, the club of "the brown-skinned middle class," to whom color mattered more than class, and Shannon, the club of "the lower black middle class," whose membership included "the teacher, the law clerk, the worker in the printing office and here and there a clerk in a department store" (56). James uneasily chooses Maple. As he often comments, the full significance of his choice, made in the 1920s, did not arrest him until decades later. How his choice can be read as an articulation of both creolization and hybridity is suggested by a particular set of comments found elsewhere in *Boundary* that forecast the contested categories that James occupied and tried to negotiate.

He describes himself as "the strange fruit" of a "hot house flower," by which he means English society and culture as gleaned from the West Indian colonial system. James saw himself as a hybrid: "I would not deny that early influences I could know nothing about had cast me in a certain mould or even that I was born with certain characteristics" (50). He writes: "As far back as I can trace my consciousness the original found itself and came to maturity within a system that was the result of centuries of development in another land, was transplanted as a hot house flower is transplanted and bore some strange fruit" (50). James speaks of his personal "original consciousness" but immediately complicates the possibility of originality. "Original consciousness" implies subsequent types of consciousness that James acquired along with multiple systems of influences. Although the tone James uses here may be ambivalent, describing himself as a hothouse flower is no self-abnegation but rather a self-conscious truth that refers to the relentless indoctrination of the British educational system in a West Indian setting.

The experience of having to choose a team to play for is the point in the text where politics, race, literature, class, and cricket come into uncomfortable conflict for James and marks the point at which he says he begins to unconsciously engage "racialized class politics." It is not a smooth transition. James, the educated "British/West Indian" intellectual, finds himself incompatible with being a player on Shannon, "the people's" cricket team. Indeed, except for his burgeoning reputation as a man of letters, the self-identified "dark-skinned" James would logically "fit" Shannon, the best team around. Maple, on the other hand, with its crude colorism, housed many of James's friends and school chums. Several others have written compellingly about this defining moment in James's life.[12] James recalls that his younger self, yet a stranger to Marx and Trotsky, somehow knew it was a conservative move and even his "social and political instincts nursed on Dickens and Thackeray" (58) pushed him toward joining Shannon, the club that "played as if they knew they represented the great mass of black people on the island" (61). And yet he joined Maple. It was a conservative move by a person who would ultimately make his reputation as a radical.

By using himself in the discussion of Shannon and Maple to illuminate the complexities of race, class, and place in colonial Trinidad, James highlights the dialectic of personal and collective identity. That is, even as he describes himself as a "Westerner, particularly of British formation, a puritan in the West Indies," he shows the circumstances of his birth, lineage, as well as location, to be unresolvable. Even so, James reaches for an "impossible purity" over and over again in the text; the examples of puritanism that he cites paradoxically expose what is not pure. The "logic" of his choice is shown as an act riddled by hesitation and apprehension. The "purity" of the "code" fails to manifest itself in the coalition of race, class, and cricket. As much as James insists that "they were men who could behave as equals on the pitch," he concurrently shows how, in an Orwellian sense, some men were "more equal than others," and he, James, chose to be more equal.

The world that consumed James, "for cricket and English literature I fed an inexhaustible passion," was a world that James recognized, bitterly, for its severe impracticality: "There was no world for which I was *fitted*, least of all the one I was now to enter" (emphasis added, 43). He recognized himself as "an alien in his own environment," and as a "British intellectual long before he was ten." His distance from "his own people, even his own family," was great. When James recalls the particulars of the Shannon/Maple choice we begin to discern how the problem of choosing a place to fit himself into semi-professional island cricket is a new iteration of a recurring childhood dilemma: "My social and political instincts, nursed on Dickens and Thackeray, were beginning to clarify themselves. As powerful a pull as any was the brilliant cricket Shannon played. Pride also, perhaps, impelled me to join them. In social life I was not bothered by my dark skin and had friends everywhere. It was the principle on which the Maple club was founded which stuck in my throat" (52). Here, James is most overtly commenting on his racialized and class-based identities. However, he implicitly suggests, especially by his invocation of Thackeray, an understanding of how he is provisionally accustomed to transgressing and polluting boundaries of race and class; while others might suffer racial restrictions "in social life," he did not. Furthermore, Trinidad's creolized society, its Byzantine admixtures of human life, and its middle classes under the sway of Englishness, is as ineffectively disguised on James's idealized cricket pitch by the attempted rigid construction of the teams as it is by the symbolism of the sport's white uniforms. James himself is situated in an in-between space as he both questions *and* endorses these boundaries. He is both eager to chart new directions for his material and social existence and yet remains deeply reliant on the conventions of "how things are done." He recalls, "none of the lines were absolute" (50).

Thus, even as James was "negotiating directly between his middle-class background . . . and his nascent attempts to situate himself within the experience of working-class Trinidadians," as Grant Farred observes, indeed even as James reflects on this "social and moral crisis" of choice, one that profoundly affects his political development, the circumstances and criteria of this choice signal a rejection of that which creolization represents and an endorsement of "the performed hierarchies of colonial cultural and ideological control" ("Maple Man" 168). The methodology employed by James as he made his decision considered his hybrid existence as an intellectual and a sportsman, as an English intellectual and a Trinidadian native son, and as a member of the precariously situated middle class, which was nevertheless distinct from the "lower middle class." The anxiety induced by the rigid social stratification, the boundaries, and the apparent binary oppositions of his world, present a picture of a creolized Trinidadian society. As Farred points out, it is not so much that James makes a move to the political right by joining Maple but rather that "he remained in the place where he had always been, deeply rooted in his middle-class experiences" (168). Thus, it is a conservative and not a reactionary choice, a move that is made by James in the hope, the belief, that the rightful categories, the known and practiced stratification, would prove themselves comfortable and nurturing. Predictably, as James's own ambivalence over the decision suggests, no such comfort or promise of stability that that categorization tempts and teases him with actually exists.

We are confronted then by a set of questions about James, creolization, and hybridity. James repeatedly describes his childhood as one spent defying the rules and boundaries set before him by his parents and teachers; he impresses upon the reader a particularized embrace of hybridity, most eloquently perhaps in the hothouse flower passage, all of which leads to the query, why was so much anxiety expended over the Maple/Shannon choice if James already understood himself as distinctly uncontainable? Certainly, the magnitude of the choice is heavily weighted by hindsight, but I wonder if the choice, as it appears in *Boundary*, exposes the lie of James's famous self-description as a "Victorian with the *rebel* seed"; in fact, had he been drawing within the lines all along? Or rather, is it that the Maple/Shannon choice places on view the difficulty of consistently maintaining and negotiating a "rebellious" persona? Further, the circumstances of choosing a cricket team illuminate not only James's understanding of the types of hybridity he performed but also demonstrate how the layered, creolized nature of Trinidad's 1920s society was disordered by the sometimes competing ideologies of hybridity and creolization, not to mention colonialism and anticolonial activities.

James reveals himself to be caught up in the web of signification that preyed upon him because of the class and social position he occupied in Trinidadian society and his developing political allegiances. He understands exactly how cricket is a tool of colonization and how it is a mode of advancing *Englishness* as an idealized identity and epistemology that can forestall "grotesque hybrids" even as it attempted to civilize and humanize colonial subjects/savages. He both endorses and critiques this hegemonic enterprise. One could say that, in *Boundary*, James's repeated utterances and discussion of the concept of whether or not something "is cricket" can be understood both as a form of what "English" in the ideal stands for as well as a transmutation of James's attention throughout the text to his own "puritan" sensibilities. James shows how cricket exchanges its singular association with English culture for a role as a sign that simultaneously articulates nationalisms and internationalisms that are non-English, post-English, and in some senses a performance of Englishness. Recalling that *Boundary* was written in the late 1950s and early 1960s, its attendant themes of class struggle and self-government in a nascent nation state on the eve of colonial independence draw upon the decades James spent in England and America, immersing himself in Marxist theory and practice and Pan-Africanist struggle. Indeed, it is difficult fully to appreciate the significance of *Boundary*'s articulations about both creolization and politics through cricket without an awareness and incorporation of these antecedent events in James's life and his prior writings, which form the bulk of his life's work, as the ensuing chapters will attempt to delineate. As James functions as a metonym for understanding multiple identities, cricket's own multiple significations and materialist functions help to articulate the transnational creolized society that produced James. Even as it was simultaneously an authoritarian mechanism with which colonial Trinidadian subjects encountered the sometimes subtle hegemonies and at other times overt physical violences of colonial rule, James shows how cricket was also an integrative mechanism for the burgeoning republic of Trinidad. The simultaneous potential for destabilizing radicalisms and reified romanticizations that attend to "creolization" and "hybridity" in Caribbean studies can be discerned within the work of James and can be carefully extended to other black diasporic cultures such as that of the United States. My engagement of James is meant to guide the reader into a meditation on the ways in which he forces us to think in new terms about the Americas and black people in the Americas and allows us to understand black "American" identity dialectically: as that which is articulated transnationally and transracially, through the personal, the political, often from multiple class positions, and as always mediated through gender.

An Aesthetics of Creolization

By placing James in conversation with artists like Euzhan Palcy, Richard Wright, and Ralph Ellison, the multi-dimensionality of his ideas becomes visible and gains significance across cultures and time periods. For my purposes, the differing resonances of race and blacknesses to be found within hybridity and creolization theories surface the contradictions, ironies, and insights that James and numerous artists, but especially the ones discussed in the following chapters, provide in their investigations of mostly black, mostly male, and mostly artistic Caribbean and black U.S. subjects.

In James, Ralph Ellison, and most of the texts and authors included in the present study, there is a shared ambivalence about wanting to or being able to define a racialized culture. Their definitions are inflected with what we would now call, positively, postmodernist doubts as to any sort of absolutes, but understood in their specific historical contexts these definitions can also be understood as a "revolutionary humanism" energized by the resistance and independence movements most audibly articulated in the 1960s perhaps but that pepper the entire black diasporic experience of the twentieth century.

James's aesthetics of creolization can be understood as an organically developed mechanism used to mediate the productively conflicting influences on his life, including his colonial education, his middle-class upbringing, and, eventually, his radical politics. Sometimes he interprets revolutionary or radical discourse as that which is expressed by the community as opposed to that which is expressed by the individual; we see this in Minty Alley, both Black Jacobins, Mariners, as well as in Boundary. At other times, however, and in many of James's letters, we also witness him contradict this interpretation, especially when he speaks autobiographically; often James allows the individual male or other elite voice priority over women's voices or other collective utterances. There is a conversation, then, that goes on in James's work. St Louis and others have identified James's valorization of charismatic individual male "leaders." The portrayal of Haynes in Minty Alley, Toussaint in The Black Jacobins, Ahab in Mariners, Renegades, and Castaways, Nkrumah in Nkrumah and the Ghana Revolution, numerous outstanding cricketers in Boundary, and James himself as seen in his letters and personal writings are all relevant examples. These individual personalities contend and converse with James's narrations and historicizations of ordinary communities and their struggles to be heard, both locally and globally. Therefore, of equal importance to Haynes are his working-class neighbors; the hubris of Toussaint is his failure to communicate "his" plans to the people whom he was attempting to lead; scattered throughout Boundary's pages of homage to the likes of Constantine, Headley, and Grace are numerous anonymous or near anonymous cricketers whose brilliant strokes or distinctive body lines imprinted themselves on James's memory. Stylistically, James's works speak to each other, and he himself can be seen to struggle over which voices, the outstanding individuals or the outstanding community, might dominate his narratives.

Rubrics of leadership are another way of establishing the significance of creolization and hybridity to James's corpus and thinking. In Minty Alley and the history version of The Black Jacobins, for instance, those who would lead and are chosen to lead, Haynes and Toussaint L'Ouverture respectively, are ultimately ineffective and fail because of a combination of factors that James consistently calls our attention to. These factors include the inability to subsume one's own leadership to the leadership initiatives cultivated by the masses themselves (this is also a major component of James's critique of the Socialist Workers Party's approach to the "Negro Question"). Also significant, however, is the partial accommodation on the part of would-be leaders toward a creolized sensibility. In this light, Toussaint's failure can be seen as his inability to unlock his unidirectional gaze toward France as purveyor of the best model for emancipation and national identity. Haynes, in an admittedly nonanalogous leadership situation as a middle-class outsider in a working-class community, not so much fails but exerts only a tenuous and impermanent influence over that community. Leadership and obstacles to sustained and successful leadership preoccupied James and offer productive insights into the overlap and mediation between his work as a writer and theorist and his work as a (sometimes) leader of political organizations, especially in the period spanning the 1940s to the 1960s.

This tension presented itself most clearly to me when I read James's lesser-known dramatic version of *The Black Jacobins* alongside the history. After analyzing in full the dialogue presented by the *Jacobins* texts, the following four chapters introduce new voices into this Jamesian tête-à-tête, both to amplify and extend the conversations within his texts. I explore how his ideas are taken up and are complicated by future generations and how they are offered with slightly different, and therefore illuminating, calibrations by some of his contemporaries.

DOUBLE OR NOTHING

THE TWO *BLACK JACOBINS*

History and Literature form part of the same problematic: the account, or the frame of reference, of the collective relationships of men with their environment, in a space that keeps changing and in a time that is constantly being altered.

Edouard Glissant, *Caribbean Discourse*

DESSALINES: Well, that suits them in France. In France they write plays. But listen, listen. That is San Domingo. We can't write plays about voodoo!

C. L. R. James, *The Black Jacobins*

"There is no drama like the drama of history" wrote James in his historical study of the Haitian Revolution, *The Black Jacobins: Toussaint L'Ouverture and the San Domingo Revolution* (1938). Indeed, between 1792 and 1804, the French Caribbean colony of San Domingo accomplished what was to be the only successful slave rebellion in the history of the New World by defeating Napoleon, the British, and the Spanish. (Upon their victory the people of San Domingo reclaimed the Amerindian name of their country, Haiti. I use the two names interchangeably.) In 1936, drawing from his manuscript notes and research for the history, James also wrote a dramatic version of the Haitian Revolution, *Toussaint L'Ouverture,* and saw it produced that March by the Stage Society in London. Despite casting Paul Robeson in the leading role, James was unable to make the drama either dramatic or compelling: it received poor reviews, had a short run, and, but for Anna Grimshaw's republication of it in *The C. L. R. James Reader*, would have remained in near total obscurity.[1] In the 1960s, James would revisit each work, make additions and revisions to both, and rename the play *The Black Jacobins* (forthwith I will refer to the history as *JacobinsH* and the play as *JacobinsP*). The history, one of the first to juxtapose the San Domingo Revolution and the French Revolution as wars that informed and influenced each other, has enjoyed far greater success with three English-language editions and translations into French, Italian, and German (*Reader* 430).

In this chapter, I argue that the historical and theatrical versions are key components of a larger Jamesian narrative; they are twinned parts of an elusive whole and should be read together. James's aesthetics of creolization can be discerned at three levels when the two *Jacobins* are read in partnership: each text helps us to decode crucial components of the other and often fills in the other's gaps; jointly, the narratives articulate James's developing Pan-Africanism and general interest in making historical and revolutionary connections amongst movements and people of the African diaspora; lastly, James's applied Marxist analysis of what he calls the Haitian proletarian movement, marks his expertise at creating and using multiple frames of investigation to achieve a prismatic view of history, culture, and politics. The act of using and extending a "Western" discourse to fit the needs of Caribbean/"New" World discourses can also be understood as a form of creolization. Disregarding the play's "failure" and the history's "success," their co-creation speaks quite forcefully to James's penchant for crossing and recrossing boundaries of genre in an effort to write the grand narratives of black people into otherwise monochromatic historical and cultural records.

In the preface to the 1980 edition of *JacobinsH*, James reminds the reader of the larger narrative to which it belongs and explains the ideas that propelled the initial project: "I was tired of reading and hearing about Africans being persecuted and oppressed in Africa, in the Middle Passage, in the USA and all over the Caribbean. I made up my mind that I would write a book in which Africans or people of African descent instead of constantly being the object of other peoples' exploitation and ferocity would themselves be taking action on a grand scale and shaping other people to their own needs" (v). While Kara M. Rabbitt has suggested that in *JacobinsH* James "is engaged in a tenuous, genre-bending enterprise," I read his endeavor more positively (120). The two *Jacobins* attest to the way James saw generic divisions as inherently false, if generally useful. James's production of distinct narratives of the San Domingo Revolution further reveals his struggles with how best to represent the Caribbean, how best to incorporate the voices of the masses, and how best to convey stylistically what he considered to be a spectacularly complex period of revolutionary action at the close of the eighteenth century. The act of creating two versions in different genres, the very need to do so, demonstrate James's intense intellectual struggles, which he came closest to resolving decades later in his autobiographical history of cricket, *Beyond a Boundary*. These struggles have to do with history and fiction, the popular and the elite, which voices and which forms to use and when, in order to reach and influence the largest number of ordinary people and to facilitate revolution. Together the two *Jacobins* surface the paradoxical issues affecting and effecting James's black intellectual voice in the 1930s. They offer an early glimpse of the balancing act James attempted his entire intellectual life: the negotiation between the intellectual elite and the revolutionary masses. When examined side by side the two texts diagram the methods and tools James creates to bridge the gap between his various audiences—these are methods and tools he will utilize again and again as a writer and as an activist.

When we examine both *Jacobins*, we are doubly rewarded by the different ways each text tells the same story. Within each narrative James examines the consequence of European, African, and New World influences on the revolutionary development and triumph of the San Domingo masses. Vodun, one of the key cultural signifiers I will discuss, is represented in both the play and the history as generating the collective uprising by the Haitian slaves. In the history, however, James shifts his focus away from the collective revolutionary enterprise after the opening chapters and begins to emphasize the leadership of Toussaint L'Ouverture. By looking at both *Jacobins* we see how James grapples with the written and the spoken word in his effort to analyze the political and strategic centrality of Vodun for his non-Haitian audiences. Why James provides us with two narratives with different emphases, which speak to distinct audiences and stress the creolized (not just double) consciousness of Caribbean revolutionaries, is a tale the two *Jacobins* tell together, reflecting James's concern with audience and the contemporary relevance of history to everyday people. Both *Jacobins*, therefore, draw upon twentieth-century ideas of anticolonial movements of which James himself was a principal architect. Specifically, Italy's 1935 invasion of Abyssinia (now known as Ethiopia), the only independent African nation, was a crisis both *Jacobins* were partially written in response to.

As Haiti asserted its own sovereignty, so Ethiopia was forced to safeguard hers. Both his organic interest in the events of the San Domingo Revolution, which prompted his research, and the events of imperialist aggression unfolding on the world stage propelled James into the Pan-African movement. In addition to wanting to narrate history as it unfolded, James hoped to harness the power of theater to these events and mobilizations. Indeed, "drama was a form for which James had a particular feel. His life long interest in Shakespeare was based on the dramatic quality of the work; and James recognized that theater provided the arena in which to explore 'political' ideas as refracted through human character" (*Reader* 6).

Having emigrated to England from Trinidad in 1932 at the age of thirty-one, James had distinguished himself at home as a literary scholar, cricket journalist, and fiction writer. In 1927 he completed *Minty Alley*, which would be picked up by London's Secker and Warburg Press in 1936. Earlier, in 1932, a press in Lancashire, England, published his biographical study, *The Life of Captain Cipriani*. *Minty Alley* and *The Life of Captain Cipriani* are important precursors to James's work on the San Domingo Revolution. In *Minty Alley* James portrays Trinidad's middle classes and their relationship with working-class communities. In Trinidad, James was a member of the *Beacon* Group—an interracial group of local, middle-class, male intellectuals who, inspired by a turn-of-the-century precursor, the All-Jamaica Library in addition to the Harlem Renaissance and the Russian Revolution, took up as their mission the idea that the working classes, romanticized as the "folk," were best able to articulate a "true" Caribbean voice. To portray West Indian life realistically and unflinchingly, to use local idioms, and to stop imitating European literary conventions were all priorities of the group. The group was unconcerned about offending the middle and upper classes and often published political viewpoints as well. In addition to writing *Minty Alley*, James published short stories and helped to launch two literary magazines *Trinidad* and the *Beacon*. When he left Trinidad for England he assumed it was to develop further as a writer. But James was to become an activist, and the 1936 publication of *Minty Alley* represented the conclusion of James's public career as a fiction writer.

Cipriani's examination of the relationship between a labor leader and the Trinidadian industrial workers he helped to organize in their struggle for better working conditions suggests how it was a likely blueprint for James's work on *JacobinsH* (Worcester, *James* 22). *Cipriani* was also an occasion to celebrate "Cipriani as an outstanding West Indian political personality and the overall readiness of West Indian society in assuming self-rule"; further, "the book bases its perspective on the vindication of the West Indian soldier and his achievement in the Great War" (Hill, "In England" 64). This agenda again emphasizes the larger project of recovery of Caribbean resistance movements as ammunition for anticolonial agitation attended to by James. A portion of *Cipriani* was excerpted as "The Case For West Indian Self-Government," published in 1933 by Leonard and Virginia Woolf's Hogarth Press, and circulated widely (more widely than the longer *Cipriani*) in both Britain and Trinidad.[2] Thus, during the six years of 1932 to 1938 James had distinguished himself as a novelist, an anticolonialist, a cricket journalist, and a historian of the Communist International, the Haitian Revolution, and black revolutionary struggle in general.[3] Looking back to his life before England, we can credit James's Oxbridge training in Port-of-Spain as important to his development of an awareness, called "heteroglossia" by Mikhail Bakhtin, of the multivalenced, unstable significations attached to the narration of history, and specifically discourses of the Caribbean and the black diaspora, all of which point to the logic of two *Jacobins* texts.

With Hitler's armies gathering in Germany, Mussolini preparing an attack on Abyssinia, Franco in power in Spain, Stalin in power in Russia, Trotsky expelled and living in exile, widespread labor disputes and strikes in the Caribbean where sugar prices were at rock bottom, and a general worldwide economic depression, the 1930s saw James responding in full to a rapidly changing, convulsive world. James's doubled *Jacobins* can be understood as an articulation of the profound, transparent precariousness of the historical moment. By combining orality with the written word, by valuing both European historiographic practice as well practices that derived from the griots of West Africa, James acknowledges the instability of narrative as well as narrative's dependence upon both reader and audience for its shifting meanings. In examining James's different narrations, we are also exposed to how meanings shift for him as well.

James's writings about the Haitian Revolution complicate fixed definitions of history and literature as well as the categories of writing we would place under such headings. These "complications" are rooted in the notion of creolization and its resistance to binary constructions of meaning, identity, and development in specific Caribbean geopolitical contexts. James's play and history demonstrate how creolization can help us more accurately and more expansively analyze Caribbean revolutionary activity as well as its mythmaking enterprises. Consequently, we adjust our modes of interpretation and relinquish fixed definitions of history, literature, and myth and enter fully into his aesthetics of creolization.

James further suggests a creolized paradigm for understanding Caribbean revolutions: they combine and revise West African and Western European military theories and are prompted by the specific New World experience of the slave trade and plantation economy. It would follow, then, that James would also resist the notion that Caribbean history parallels a European notion of history or that it can be effectively remembered from a singular cultural perspective. Thus, when both *Jacobins* are read together, a principal gain for the reader is an amplification of James's skilled braiding together of what European historiography would separate as myth and history. Each of James's narratives juxtaposes the role of Vodun with the role of French Jacobean Republicanism in San Domingo's successful defeat of Napoleon's armies.

James's narratives also achieve several political goals. In the history, for instance, he uses a Marxist framework to structure his analysis of the revolution. James grounds the revolutionary activity of San Domingo both in the folk cultures that the blacks brought with them from Africa and also in the French and European traditions they learned as slave citizens of the New World. James makes a case for recognizing the San Domingo mobilizations as proletarian in nature and as actually predating the French Revolution specifically and European working-class consciousness and militancy in general. That James identifies the Haitian masses as *proletarians* is a radical act, which challenges Marxist and non-Marxist views alike. Whereas Marx expected that proletarian uprisings would begin in industrialized (that is, European) centers, James makes convincing claims for understanding the sugar plantation as a particularly modern industry. The play and the history then both serve as vehicles through which James is able to crystallize his political beliefs as a Trotskyist. Grimshaw identifies the political ideology at work in both *Jacobins* when she writes,

> James wrote both . . . while he was an active member of the Trotskyist movement. His analysis was deeply marked by his particular political allegiance, though a number of the ideas central to interpretation of the 1791 slave revolution raised, implicitly, a challenge to certain assumptions which were commonplace on the revolutionary Left. First of all, he cast doubt on the assumption that the revolution would take place first in Europe, in the advanced capitalist countries, and that this would act as a model and a catalyst for the later upheavals in the underdeveloped world. Secondly, there were clear indications that the lack of specially-trained leaders, a vanguard, did not hold back the movement of the San Domingo revolution. (*Reader* 7)

James claims an eighteenth-century Anglo-European and Anglo-American rhetoric of freedom and liberty for the impulse felt and articulated by West Indians, not learned by them through an Anglo-European or Anglo-American model but rather derived from their own peculiar experience as racialized instruments of labor. In "The Making of the Caribbean People," James identifies the desire for liberty as constant and immediate from the moment of capture and enslavement. That moment of capture and enslavement is also the moment when Africans were transformed into West Indians.

> But when we made the Middle Passage and came to the Caribbean we went straight into a modern industry—the sugar plantation—and there we saw that to be a slave was the result of our being black. A white man was not a slave. The West Indian slave was not accustomed to that kind of slavery in Africa; and there in the history of the West Indies there is one dominant fact and that is the desire, sometimes expressed, sometimes unexpressed, but always there, the desire for liberty; the ridding oneself of the particular burden which is the special inheritance of the black skin. *If you don't know that about West Indian people you know nothing about them.* (*Spheres* 177; emphasis in original)

In both the play and the history, James is involved in a project of what Sandra Paquet might call "transgressive meaning production" (*Pleasures* viii). James's essentialist aim to delineate the cultural specificity of West Indians nevertheless crucially distinguishes them from Africans because of the intertwined discourses of labor and race within the slave systems of the Americas. Exemplified in his Toussaint to Castro trajectory, James claims West Indians "have been the most rebellious people in history" (*Spheres* 177).

In a 1967 speech, "Black Power: Its Past, Today, and the Way Ahead," James discloses what he believes to be obvious in the text of *JacobinsH* itself: "I had studied Lenin in order to write *The Black Jacobins*, the analysis of a revolution for self-determination in a colonial territory" (*Spheres* 233). This disclosure reminds us that for James, while colonial revolution was partly motivated by economics and the metropolitan revolution, as John La Guerre reasons, it was equally motivated by the desire for self-determination, which the slaves brought with them from the African continent (220). James's developing Trotskyism helps to explain his interest in a history that does not submerge or segregate the effect of culture. It is James, however, who, in both versions of *The Black Jacobins*, poses the culture question as one that encompasses both the effects of a value-laden metropolitan colonial culture and a proportionately devalued creolized Caribbean culture.

Finally, James's Marxism structures his idea of revolution as a cultural process. For a cultural assessment of revolutionary mechanisms are exactly what an orthodox Marxist would segregate out of his study, and signal James's authorial logic in writing two complementary texts. Reading the play with the history illuminates those "cultural moments" that are deliberately embedded in the history but that do not define it the way James's perceptions of the cultural apparatus of the Haitians overtly defines and structures the play. In effect, he puts culture in both *Jacobins* but with a heavier emphasis in the play. James's attempts to understand the role of culture in proletarian political movements aligns him with other political and cultural theorists such as Antonio Gramsci, W. E. B. Du Bois, and Jean Price-Mars.

The play highlights James's need to identify cultural mechanisms as an integral aspect of political action. James's awareness of the different audiences each medium would attract is an example of his theoretical insight into how the narrative process is linked to political mobilization: the conversation between *JacobinsP* and *JacobinsH* can be viewed as a metaphor of James's ideology and as a reflection of the refractions back and forth of James the Pan-Africanist and James the Marxist. We can understand James's coterminous writing projects as a Marxist attempt to demarcate and interrogate how Caribbean identities are informed by political action and self-determination. The slave revolution led by Toussaint L'Ouverture raised the same sorts of questions James was confronting in the twentieth century—how the nature and course of revolution itself (that is, the changing relationship between leaders and the people) was dually affected by the dynamic of the struggles situated at the peripheries and those located in the metropolitan center. It was a question that turned up in different forms throughout James's career: at times it was posed as what is the relation of proletariat formations within imperialist nations to proletariat formations within colonized populations; at other times James asked how are different struggles within a population group to be connected (*Reader* 5).

In James's studies of the San Domingo Revolution, culture and political action intersect most forcefully through the iconography and imagery of Vodun. Both *Jacobins* validate and discuss this integral though often grossly stereotyped part of Haitian culture. James shows how Vodun provides the political organization and ideological apparatus the San Domingo rebels needed to achieve independence and abolish slavery.[4] In the play, Vodun is a pervasive context for both the characters and the action. While James asserts the significance of Vodun as the essential unifier and as particularly African in both, in *JacobinsH* he portrays Vodun as a collective action and organization that functioned only as a prelude to the revolution. This discrepancy is one of the principal reasons for reading the texts together, because the centrality of Vodun in the play induces us to pay more attention to its significance in the history.

Representing Vodun

At almost every critical juncture of the three-act play, the stage accommodates the ordinary people of San Domingo, and they are usually engaging in Vodun drumming, dance, song, or in all three, as an expression of solidarity with or in opposition to their leaders. In his opening stage direction, James insists that "in the Play it is possible that crowds may assemble at the back and be spoken to from the back of the main central area. Crowds say little but their presence is felt powerfully at all critical moments. This is the key point of the play and comments cannot, must not, be written. It must be felt, dramatically, and be projected as essential to action in the downstage areas" (*Reader* 68). This stage direction attempts to balance the importance of charismatic leaders, including Toussaint[5] and Dessalines, with the greater force of a people united in resistance. James's admonition that the power and presence of the crowds is "the key point of the play" speaks directly to his growing sense of the limited benefit of an intellectual vanguard. On the other hand, the fact that these powerful crowds "say little" and directors are instructed to resist scripting lines for them problematically suggests "the masses" have little to say. James seizes upon the theatrical currency of Vodun, however, and successfully uses it as a medium that brings to the fore the people and non-European traditions as twin elements that, when combined with Jacobin revolutionary forms, contribute to San Domingo's eventual triumph.

At the beginning of act 1, for instance, when Toussaint, still a general, slyly defeats a Spanish leader who betrays the blacks, James constructs a scene (after Toussaint exits) in which the chorus takes over and enters into an elaborate Vodun ritual in celebration of Toussaint's "underdog" victory. The meticulous stage directions suggest James's desire for an authentic representation of Vodun. The extended nature of these directions (I only quote a portion of them below) further confirm the importance of the upcoming scene.

A shout goes up, out of which comes a joyous "La Marseillaise." Drummers enter to accompany the rocking anthem as the men begin to jump up ad lib. Offstage men start a chant that cuts through the repeat of "La Marseillaise" completely as more sing the former and less the latter. . . . A priestess enters with a voodoo container . . . and three women dancers enter with a new chant, "La Liberté," in counterpoint to the men's chant. Each woman brings in a jar with which they appear to sprinkle the floor. They converge on the priestess and deposit their jars in her container . . . and the drums and chanting stop suddenly. A new rhythm starts immediately. . . . As banner-bearing slaves move across upstage, the chief houngan with a cross stuck in the mouth of a gourd floats through a curve upstage right and down. . . . A woman has entered dancing behind two candle bearing attendants. . . . Celestine spins into the centre of the stage and there she sees Dessalines. . . . She moves towards him tempting him to follow her movements. (*Reader* 78)

Some of the symbolism of this interlude is immediately clear: "La Marseillaise" was the anthem of the French Jacobins; by introducing it (and then drowning it out with African drumming) James acknowledges French influence and intermittent solidarity with the San Domingo revolutionaries. But by drowning out both "La Marseillaise" and "La Liberté" with the ritual Vodun drumming, James anchors the political posturing of the masses in African custom and ritual memory, which suggests a hesitancy on James's part to understand fully the revolutionary activity as a creolized formation and foreshadows the diplomatic isolation inflicted on Haiti after its self-liberation.

James further describes an extended ceremony in which both the dancers and the bystanders respond to the machinations of the drummers, the priestess, and the chief houngan. The principal dancers, Celestine and Dessalines, urged on by the chief drummer, work themselves into a state of possession, for which James provides choreographical instruction. (In Vodun, possession is a method through which individuals are able to access and receive instructions from particular gods.) Without having enough information to determine which god or gods are being communicated with in this ceremony, we can infer much from the identity of the principal dancers, Celestine, a minor character, and Dessalines, one of Toussaint's generals. When, at the end of the dance sequence (and scene) Dessalines is seen in a pose of domination over Celestine's outstretched body, James foreshadows Dessalines's rise to power and despotic reign over Haiti. Unlike Toussaint, who negotiates with various European leaders until his death, Dessalines, who succeeds Toussaint and is crowned emperor of Haiti, builds a political platform against coexistence and negotiation with the whites whom he believed to be inherently traitorous. After Toussaint's capture, Dessalines carries on the Revolution and drives the Europeans out of San Domingo.

In this long scene without speech dialogue but with an obvious call and response between the drummers and the dancers, James makes a clear statement of value in appreciation of an African cultural system that combines the spiritual and political and that, he seems to say, is controlled and utilized by the ordinary citizen. As is to be expected in a play, James's stage directions dictate but do not articulate or analyze the particular actions in the ceremony.

The juxtaposition of Toussaint's tactical victory over the Spanish official and Dessalines's significant participation in a celebratory Vodun ceremony also underscores a tension set up in the play between the written word and the spoken word. The play consistently constructs Toussaint as an intellectual with book learning and Dessalines as crude and illiterate. This opposition is then doubled through the minor characters of Moise and Marie-Jeanne. Again, James's position is easy to discern. As intellectuals, both Toussaint and Marie-Jeanne are foiled in part because their literacy is European-based. Dessalines and Moise, in contrast, do not "read" anything other than the will of the people.

James can thus be understood as straddling contradictory positions. In his effort to emphasize African cultural retentions and to suggest their importance to the Haitian revolutionaries, he literally "drowns out" the equally influential European cultural formations. He thereby implies that creolization in this historical context has little lasting value or effect. At the close of the play, stage directions indicate a continuing conflict: Dessalines's coronation coincides with the news of Toussaint's death in a French prison. To mourn the latter, "the crowds" begin to sing what James calls the "Samedi Smith" song. (Baron Samedi is one of the most powerful figures in the Vodun pantheon. He is associated with death and funerals and is said to guard grave sites and cemeteries.) To drown out this Vodun melody and to celebrate his own triumph, Dessalines orders a minuet be played. The play closes with a spotlight on Dessalines and Marie-Jeanne dancing forcibly to the sounds of this minuet. Dessalines then betrays the people too, as this last aesthetic choice symbolizes. The historical record shows that during his reign over Haiti Dessalines tried to make the nation as "French" as possible and, as in this scene, distanced himself from both the masses and from Vodun.

The creativity of revolt, the notion, attributed to René Dépestre of "I rebel, therefore I am," is at the epicenter of both the play and the history. African-derived folk traditions are recognized as the source of both revolution and creativity. However, James expresses the centrality of these traditions most forcefully in the play perhaps because of the greater opportunity for artistic expression by the actors and sensory perception by the audience. Despite the signifying line I quote as my second epigraph to this chapter, which James has Dessalines speak—"In France they write plays. But listen, listen. This is San Domingo. We can't write plays about voodoo!" (106)—James finds both a way and a reason to write "voodoo" into his script. It functions as a benchmark against which the "leaders" are measured and as an issue upon which they rise and fall.

In his history, James portrays Dessalines's betrayal of the revolutionary agenda by constructing him more overtly as the pawn of others. James describes the coronation where Dessalines is flanked by England and America and becomes a showpiece of capitalism and neocolonialism:

> On October 10, 1804 he had himself crowned Emperor. Private merchants of Philadelphia presented him with the crown, brought on the American boat the *Connecticut*, his coronation robes reached Haiti from Jamaica on an English frigate from London. He made his solemn entry into Le Cap in a six-horse carriage brought for him by the English agent, Ogden, on board the *Samson*. Thus the Negro monarch entered into his inheritance, tailored and valeted by English and American capitalists, supported on one side by the King of England and on the other by the President of the United States. (370)

James's contempt for Dessalines is specifically critical of his inability to transfer successfully his insurgent military triumphs to his role as head of state.

Representing the Masses

James's discrete focus in each *Jacobins* text is clear. Explicit mention of Vodun and Vodun imagery is absent from the above passage, although Dessalines's corruption is perhaps more obvious. James's general use of Vodun in *Jacobins*H is consistently couched in economic and more exactly Marxist revolutionary terms. Rhetorically, these passages are marked by James's use of words like "masses," "mobilization," "slave system," and "conspiracy."

In *Jacobins*H James establishes two important incendiary moments for the masses of San Domingo: first, their initial large-scale mobilization orchestrated by the one-armed Mackandal, a slave from Guinea and a maroon leader who utilized poison to destroy the whites; second, the inauguration of the Revolution by Boukman, a Papaloi (high priest of Vodun), and his followers just before Toussaint joins the uprisings. James identifies the significance of these mobilizations as the rise of the Haitian proletariat. After setting up a Marxist description and analysis of the slave system and French colonial enterprise in San Domingo in chapters 1, 2, and 3, James uses the fourth chapter, "The San Domingo Masses Begin," to describe the mobilization of the slaves under Boukman. "Voodoo," James writes, "was the medium of the conspiracy" (86). Linking the specific work conditions of the San Domingo blacks with the practice of Vodun, James enthusiastically celebrates their organizational skills: "working and living together in gangs of hundreds on the huge sugar-factories which covered the North Plain, they were closer to a modern proletariat than any group of workers in existence at the time, and the rising was therefore, a thoroughly prepared and organized mass movement . . . in spite of all prohibitions, the slaves traveled miles to sing and dance and practice the voodoo rites and talk; and since the French revolution, to hear the political news and make their plans" (86).

James's attention to the Vodun belief system as an explicit mode of empowerment for the black insurrectionists marks another departure from orthodox Marxist ideology; he would recognize similar forces of empowerment and grassroots mobilization accessed through Christianity by black Americans. In a passage notable for its lack of referencing, James belies his affinity for the inherent dramatic spectacle of Vodun. He reconstructs a midnight gathering of the insurrectionists during which Boukman delivers a rousing speech in the midst of "a raging tropical storm with lightening and gusts of wind and heavy showers of rain" (87). Boukman, recounts James, also performs a Vodun ritual of animal sacrifice and exhorts the thousands of gathered rebels to heed "Our God," who "created the sun which gives us light, who rouses the waves and rules the storm, though hidden in the clouds, he watches us . . . Our God who is good to us orders us to revenge our wrongs. He will direct our arms and aid us" (87). The reader is given no footnote or reference as to how James managed to get such a "transcript" of Boukman's very "subaltern" voice. The connection of the weather to the subject suggests another sort of creolization as James adopts/adapts the Western literary device of "pathetic fallacy." By connecting the weather to the thunderous speech, James evokes magical and fearsome aspects of Vodun. But I would suggest that he does so in admiration of an effective leader and also as a means of representing the concrete forms in which African cultural formations, though now creolized in Vodun, were retained by the Haitians. In short, James's explicit references to Vodun in *JacobinsH* seek to counter lies perpetrated through racist, colonialist, white European representations of black people. In chapter 1, "The Property," he refers to "the intelligence which refused to be crushed, these latent possibilities which frightened the colonists as it frightens the whites in Africa today." Discussing the Middle Passage, he asserts, "Contrary to lies that have been spread so perniciously about Negro docility, the revolts at the port of embarkation and on board were incessant" (8). Within the political economy of slave revolt, Vodun was the currency with which the Haitians brokered their initial revolutionary successes. And, as stated earlier, James also uses the creolized belief system to chart a revolutionary trajectory encompassing the San Domingo masses and the Ethiopian resistance to Italy's 1935 invasion.

James desensationalizes Vodun, popularly misnamed as voodoo, through its presentation as a political mechanism and as a context for San Domingo's revolutionary effort and success. He values it as much more than an unusual cult or spiritual backdrop to Haitian culture. A consequence, however, of presenting Vodun as a demystified, practical political tool is that in the rest of the text, after chapter 4, references to Vodun diminish; it is relegated to the background as James moves on to descriptions and analysis of the more sophisticated military stratagems employed by what he significantly terms the revolution's "true" leader, Toussaint L'Ouverture. Vodun can be understood then in both the play and the history as a signifier of collective action. In the history, however, James shifts his focus away from a collective enterprise after the opening chapters and begins to emphasize the leadership of Toussaint.

Representing Toussaint

James's understanding of Toussaint as a creolized man is indicated by his attention to Toussaint's formation under the influence of specific European texts as well as by the material realities he experienced as a slave. This combination, making Toussaint exceptional, facilitates James's focus on Toussaint's individual military genius and achievement. Though James gives detailed facts about hundreds of supporting cast members and events, these simply serve to make Toussaint more distinctive. James deliberately calls attention to Toussaint's literacy and literariness, and the act and context of his writings. Key chapters of the text are devoted to Toussaint's voice, speeches, and letters as well as to the critical aspects of his campaign against the French Republic and, later, Napoleon. This privileging of Toussaint as a singular hero, strategist, and writer is less prominent in the play.[6]

Together the play and the history illuminate a typical Jamesian ambivalence (shared by many black intellectuals from Du Bois forward): throughout his life James will struggle with the role of an intellectual vanguard in relationship to proletarian movements, and thus, another crucial divergence between these two texts is James's characterization of Toussaint. In *JacobinsH* James writes Toussaint as a figure who tries but fails to combine his position in an intellectual vanguard with a commitment to the mass movement. The Toussaint of the history is one who dazzles James with his intellectual prowess. There are three progressive situations in which James recognizes "Toussaint's superior intellect" at work; each situation is demarcated by a literary and a scribal moment or series of moments. In the first instance, Toussaint's entry into the revolutionary struggle is catalyzed by reading a key text by the Abbé Raynal. In the second instance, in the midst of the Revolution and after assuming a leadership role, Toussaint authors and sends a key letter to the French Directory. It functions as a praise song of sorts in which he warns the Directory of the Haitian blacks' resolve to prevent the reinstitution of slavery. Finally, after Toussaint's penultimate rout and imprisonment by Bonaparte, James focuses our attention on Toussaint's key final efforts to attain leniency from the French emperor through a letter-writing campaign. In fact, these actions correspond to the beginning, the middle, and the conclusion of San Domingo's war with France. James is unambivalent about his final critique of Toussaint: the great man's fatal flaw is engendered in the very literacy that distinguishes him. Toussaint tumbles from leadership because his *idea* of intellect and literacy is exclusively grounded in the value system of the colonial metropolitan center. Eschewing creolization, his European cultural literacy occludes his ability to draw strength from and build coalition through a cultural literacy of Vodun together with the Haitian masses.

Toussaint did not join the revolutionary activity at first, but when he did, according to James, the disparate uprisings began to gain a certain coherence. James asserts, "From the moment he joined the revolution he was a leader, and moved without serious rivalry to the first rank" (91). James recounts that the Abbé Raynal, "a literary opponent of slavery," wrote the text that catapulted Toussaint into revolutionary action. The text, *The Philosophical and Political History of the Establishment and Commerce of the Europeans in the Two Indies*, was "famous in its time and it came into the hands of the slave most fitted to make use of it, Toussaint L'Ouverture" (24–25). The following line of Raynal's text is used in both the play and the history: "a courageous chief only is wanted. Where is he?" (25). Toussaint reads this line and the text over and over again and, according to James, experiences a transcendent, almost religious, moment of inspiration. The power of the text along with the context of slavery transform Toussaint into a revolutionary actor upon a world stage. A text galvanizes Toussaint while Vodun inspires the masses. Herein lies Toussaint's tragedy.

In the history, James goes into particular detail regarding the development of Toussaint's intellect: he read *Caesar's Commentaries,* which "had given him some idea of politics and the military art and the connection between them." He "read and re-read the long volume by the Abbé Raynal on the East and West Indies" and thus gained "a thorough grounding in the economics and politics, not only of San Domingo, but of all the great empires of Europe which were engaged in colonial expansion and trade" (91). This description of Toussaint's critical thinking abilities—he not only read, but he reread; he not only read history and politics, he read cross-culturally and in various disciplines—underlines James's understanding of why Toussaint as a member of the oppressed group (the slaves) and as a quickly formed/forming intellectual was uniquely poised to assume leadership of the revolutionary movement. But significantly, Toussaint read while the masses acted. In the play, Dessalines, who will oversee San Domingo's assertion of independence, is repeatedly described as being illiterate and "rough."

In 1794, the Republic of France abolished slavery. In 1796, there were clear indications that the merchant and planter constituencies might succeed in having slavery restored. This pivotal moment in the San Domingo Revolution was seized by Toussaint, now a general, in his famous letter to the French Directory, an impassioned treatise protesting the return of slavery in the colonies. Declaring the letter a milestone in Toussaint's career, James expansively compares it to "Pericles on Democracy, Paine on The Rights of Man, The Declaration of Independence, and The Communist Manifesto [sic]" (197). Compared to the writers of these other documents, Toussaint was virtually "uninstructed," and yet, James says, "in one respect he excelled them all . . . these masters of the spoken and written word," for "owing to the class complications of their society, these Europeans too often had to pause, to hesitate, to qualify. Toussaint could defend the freedom of the blacks without reservation" (198). This is just one of the instances in the text where James's Marxist ideology is clearly articulated: the role of the intellectual as part of the vanguard is significant only as far as that intellectual is connected to the proletariat movement/experience, as Toussaint was at this moment in his career.

In the following excerpt from the letter to the French Directory, Toussaint's prose style immediately reveals what James identifies as "a strength and single-mindedness rare in the great documents of the time":

> It is for you, Citizens Directors, to turn from over our heads the storm which the eternal enemies of our liberty are preparing in the shades of silence. It is for you to enlighten the legislature, it is for you to prevent the enemies of the present system from spreading themselves on our unfortunate shores to sully it with new crimes. Do not allow our brothers, our friends, to be sacrificed to men who wish to reign over the ruins of the human species. . . . Blind as they [the French Government are]! They cannot see how this odious conduct on their part can become the signal of new disasters and irreparable misfortunes, and that far from making them regain what in their eyes liberty for all has made them lose, they expose themselves to a total ruin and the colony to its inevitable destruction. Do they think that men who have been able to enjoy the blessing of liberty will calmly see it snatched away? . . . . If they had a thousand lives they would sacrifice them all rather than be forced into slavery again. (195–96)

Rhetorically, Toussaint couples the Citizens Directors to the Haitians. Politically, this is an enactment of "permanent revolution" to be advocated a century and a half later by Trotsky. Additionally, it reveals Toussaint's tenacious posture of dependency—this letter is an exhortation, but it is also a plea. It is a warning, but it is also an attempt to "save the colony." Ultimately, it is not a confident assertion of independence.

As the historical record shows, while slavery was not restored, once Toussaint realized that emancipation and Haiti's colonial status were incompatible, it was too late. Before Haitian independence was won, Toussaint was captured and imprisoned in the Jura mountains of France, where he soon died. However, Toussaint's faith in the power of so-called reason, democracy, and French patriotism would not die at all. James details how Toussaint's last, cold, horrible days were consumed by writing pleading letters to Napoleon, who did not respond. In the end, these acts of writing, his conception of intellectual reasoning, the very culture of France that he admired and to which he wanted Haiti to aspire failed Toussaint and exposed what James calls "the limitations of his political conceptions" (364). Toussaint's reliance on "intellectualizing" obscured his sensibility as one of a revolutionary multitude. Speaking generally of Caribbean *belles lettres*, Sandra Paquet observes that "the emerging discourse invests specific cultural authority in the written word as an agent of colonization and also of decolonization" (xvii). The nuance that Paquet identifies is lost on Toussaint in James's history. In a classic example of using the master's tools to attempt to dismantle the master's house, Toussaint's leadership and military successes are generated in large part from his aptitude for learning and appropriating their European forms. However, Toussaint's inability to successfully negotiate multiple strategies and his failure to creolize his multiple literacies ultimately separate him from the men and women whom he led in a phenomenal campaign for emancipation and nationhood. And while Dessalines is initially grounded in the culture and belief systems of the majority of San Domingo people, in both versions of this story, James explains Dessalines's eventual failure and death as a result of his deliberate separation from his cultural and political base.

A month after the revolution broke out in full force, as engineered and inspired by Boukman's activities in July and August 1791 (burning the plantations and killing the whites), Toussaint joined in. Of this delayed entry, James comments, "like so many men of better education than the rank and file, he lacked their boldness at the moment of action" (90). It seems clear, however, that he also lacked the spiritual force inspired in "the rank and file" by the offices of Boukman and the ritual of Vodun. Both educated and Catholic, Toussaint begins his revolutionary career as he ends it, separated culturally and spiritually from the very people to whom he was devoted.

Theorizing Myth and History

James's two narratives of the San Domingo Revolution exist as parts of a larger discussion of myth and history engaged by other Caribbean theorists and writers. In his article, "History, Fable, and Myth," Wilson Harris states, "in the absence of a historical correlative to the arts of the dispossessed, some kind of new critical writing in depth needs to emerge to bridge the gap between history and art" (125). In an anticipatory stroke, James uses Vodun to pursue such a "historical correlative to the arts of the dispossessed," and in the process develops the sort of the bridge Harris demands. In *Caribbean Discourse*, Glissant both calls for and questions such reformulations. Glissant extracts from the myth/history dialectic questions about collective memory, the valuation of the written over the spoken when preserving history, and what spoken cultural processes ensue when histories are written down. Glissant understands history and literature as "inherited categories" in the Caribbean and cautions, like Derek Walcott and Harris, that as such they "must not . . . be an obstacle to a daring new methodology, where it responds to the need of our Caribbean situation" (Glissant 65). James's methodology revalues "conventions of (Western) analytical thought" by resisting unitary definitions of history and art (Glissant 65).

"Myth" and "history" remain hotly contested terms in Caribbean discourse, and the fertile slippage between their connotations has been addressed by nearly all of the region's writers and cultural theorists since James.[7] The distinctions I make between history and myth do not hinge on ideas of fact or fiction but rather consider the ways in which the cultural discourses of revolution become entwined with its critical discourses. James resists the notion of a singular history or a history that can be recorded accurately from a singular cultural perspective. James is well aware of popular misconceptions of Vodun as "black magic," or superstition; therefore, it is possible to read his inclusion and acknowledgment of Vodun's role in the success of the San Domingo revolution as deliberately subversive. He effectively de-exoticizes Vodun. In *JacobinsH*, Vodun prefaces an extraordinary mobilization of revolutionary forces. In the play Vodun articulates the pageantry, the faith, but, most important, the attentiveness to political events by the masses. James's uses of Vodun cleverly manipulate Western European configurations of myth and history where these terms exist as virtual opposites and carry strict denotations of fiction and fact. For instance, the *Oxford English Dictionary* defines *myth* as "a purely fictitious narrative usually involving supernatural persons, actions, or events, and embodying some popular idea concerning natural or historical phenomena." Conversely, it describes *history* as a "written narrative constituting a continuous methodical record, in order of time, of important or public events, especially those connected with a particular country, people, individual, etc."

Not surprisingly, these *OED* definitions delineate Western Eurocentric values for narrative representation and clearly privilege the "written record" of history over myth's "popular ideas" concerning past events. But in the Caribbean, as Glissant argues, "myth not only prefigures history and sometimes generates history but seems to prepare the way for History, through its generalizing tendency" (83). Myth and history, rather than being distinct, can easily dovetail into a singular enterprise. Equally unsurprising, the *OED* definition of myth does not accommodate the ways that myth functions within African and African diaspora communities of oral transmission and oral history, where mythic figures and mythic representations are often quite "historical" and "true," and as such become part of the cultural apparatus of the community. As Barbara Webb writes in her book *Myth and History in Caribbean Fiction,* "In an effort to escape the alienating effects of New World history, some Caribbean writers have turned to the archetypal patterns of myth . . . myth and history are not mutually exclusive modes of literary expression" (3). While myth may be an antecedent to written historical documentation, it garners no less value because of that. Whereas James is not writing or even reproducing myths in the OED sense of the word, he is actively engaged in the construction of a Caribbean self-identity. His near-mythical portraits of the likes of Boukman, Toussaint, and Dessalines in both *Jacobins* situates that self-identity squarely within a new combination of narrative traditions and values that selectively incorporate colonialist values and forms.

In a Negritudian gesture, the two *Jacobins* offer compelling evidence of James's desire to establish the humanity and self-reliance of Caribbean peoples through historical precedent. He uses the written word simultaneously to evoke an African past, chart a historical trajectory, and bridge the rupture of the Middle Passage. And while the overt gesture is a rejection of European imperialist propaganda that always constructs black as other and as less than, James discerns how the written word can function (as reading does for Toussaint) to affirm the humanity and intelligence of blacks *and* inspire revolutionary action. This seems to imply a type of double consciousness—James himself will conduct a lifelong love affair with the written word, but he will remain aware of how this is a medium of communication that often cannot reach members of a worker-led mass movement, that it is a medium that has been used to malign and misrepresent black people, and that it is a medium that, through literacy, can function as a sign of elitism.

In 1962, James adds a third part to his doubled narrative of the San Domingo Revolution when he writes a thirty-page appendix to *Jacobins*H. His narrative of Caribbean cultural formations via the play, the history, and the appendix thus comment on three distinct time frames: the 1790s, when the Haitian Revolution took place; the 1930s, when both the history and the play were originally written; and the 1960s, when the appendix, "From Toussaint L'Ouverture to Fidel Castro," is added to the history. While this chapter has teased out the dialogue between the play and the history, in the appendix James arrives at a forthright articulation of the revolutionary, anticolonial consequences of understanding literature and history as intersecting and as mutually informing one another. By discussing a group of Caribbean writers to cement his redefinition of historical narrative and mythical narrative in West Indian contexts, he simultaneously evokes a sense of regional unity. James evinces a Brathwaitian desire to imagine the pieces whole even as he anticipates Glissant's assertion quoted in my first epigraph that, in Caribbean contexts, "History and Literature form part of the same problematic." James uses the appendix to declare the primacy of the creative endeavor (often literary) as a political tool in the Caribbean.

The fact that James chose 1962 to revisit *JacobinsH* can be attributed to a number of events. Of great importance was the emergence in the 1950s of a particularly talented and large cadre of West Indian authors who took it upon themselves, as cultural and political ambassadors, to continue what James and others had begun decades before, that is "to write" the Caribbean from a Caribbean perspective. Among those writers was George Lamming, whose 1961 text, *The Pleasures of Exile*, liberally acknowledges and celebrates James and *JacobinsH*. Additionally, in 1962 Trinidad and Tobago gained its independence from England. There was also the short-lived West Indies Federation (1956–58). Most important of all, however, was probably the success of Castro's revolution in Cuba in 1959. Castro represented in rhetoric, as well as action, the continuation and organic properties of the Caribbean revolutionary personality. Castro's grassroots victory over the corrupt, U.S.-backed Battista dictatorship paralleled San Domingo's eighteenth-century ouster of France and Napoleon. And, unlike Toussaint, Castro envisioned a new, *Caribbean* economic and political system for his country. In a speech quoted by Eric Williams, Castro declares, "This is true Marxism-Leninism as we see it, but it is not Communism as it is practiced in Russia, Eastern Europe or China. We are working out our own Cuban system, to meet our problems and satisfy our people" (486). In the Caribbean of the early sixties, James could see a community coming of age and "bursting at the seams" ("Kanhai" 166). All of these factors contributed to James's restructuring and more confident assertion of how Caribbean historiography differs substantially from that outlined by European theoreticians.

The appendix identifies West Indian creative writers as those in the best position to carry on the work begun by the two *Jacobins*. In 1962, that work was to make the connection between the political moment of Caribbean independence movements with the region's long history of revolution and, more important, of self-determination and self-narrativization. "The West Indian writers," James wrote, were the ones who could make the populace aware of this very important cultural process and political continuum. "They have discovered the West Indies and West Indians, a people of the middle of our disturbed century, concerned with the discovery of themselves, determined to discover themselves. . . . to be welcomed into the comity of nations a new nation must bring something new. The West Indians have brought something new" (417). When James refers to the newness of the Caribbean contributions, we are again reminded of Brathwaite's creolization model. James cites some of the principal creative writers in whom, he feels, rests the ability to tease out and reveal this Caribbean national identity. By grouping twentieth-century writers such as Aimé Césaire, George Lamming, Wilson Harris, and V. S. Naipaul together with his discussion of Toussaint L'Ouverture and Fidel Castro, he raises them, in turn, to Toussaint's and Castro's political stature. Indeed the calibration of Caribbean identities has been figured within a revolutionary paradigm by a large and diverse group of Caribbean writers. Independence and awakening as the core of Caribbean identity is an important component in the work of the region's many revolutionary intellectuals. Thus, at the end, revolution in his doubled texts comes to mean not only an uprising and overthrow of colonial domination but the concomitant and ongoing act of bringing something new onto the world stage.

Revolutionary mobilization is contrasted in James's narratives of the San Domingo revolution with the solitary but crucial act of reading, generated and emphasized by the Raynal phrase, "a courageous chief only is wanted." Because the play and the history were crafted together, we are able to read them as an extended meditation by James on the subject of the San Domingo revolutionaries, the foot soldiers, the leaders, and the culture of self-liberation. Both texts value the solitary act of reading as a frequent impetus for political action in Caribbean contexts. But James's dual narrative also makes a powerful statement against individualistic and vanguard movements that interfere or stymie action at the collective level.

In the next chapter's discussions of James's novel, *Minty Alley*, we observe an earlier, "fictional" exploration of how to represent the individual and the community. Drawing liberally from his own life experiences and adapting the bildungsroman form to a critique of the middle classes, James can again be seen transgressing the conventions of genre.

FRAMING**COMMUNITY**

MINTY ALLEY, LA RUE CASES NEGRES, AND CLASS CONSCIOUSNESS

> Whitman emphasized that he wrote as an individual. That is not accidental. Bourgeois society is essentially the production of individuals. Today the individual can be individual only so far as he is a member of a collective unit. The individuality of today is a higher individuality but it rests on a very conscious collectivity. Everywhere you see it. A worker in 1860 had as his highest aim to become his own boss. That was the American dream. Today he may say that in words (though he rarely does) but his aim is through his union to gain collective benefits. No one can sit down and write verse expressing that. But to see it and feel it, and understand it makes a poet write in a different way.
>
> C. L. R. James, *Special Delivery*

The relationship of the individual to the community characterizes many twentieth-century Caribbean novels and is fundamental to the bildungsroman (coming-of-age novel); it is also a central concern within James's fiction and nonfiction writings. The creative history making that James undertakes in his two narratives of the San Domingo Revolution and his particular focus on Toussaint in the history both have precedent in his novel, *Minty Alley*. As the *Jacobins* texts seek to advance a black revolutionary trajectory, *Minty Alley* seeks to disrupt the cultural norms of respectability of early-twentieth-century Trinidadian society as well as some of the conventions of the bildungsroman form. The critique of the Trinidadian middle classes that Minty Alley undertakes shows James's early imperative to use a creative narrative genre to convey aspects of his developing political and social theory.[1]

The novel's narrative struggles, engaged by both author and characters, elicit standard Jamesian frictions: do bourgeois voices overtake the popular? Does the in-depth focus on the individual overpower a portrait of the collective? The reader, in turn, is left to contemplate what type of radical messages can be derived from within the conservative ideological boundaries set up by the bildungsroman form. In this chapter, I tackle these questions and introduce an analysis of the film La Rue Cases Negres (1985) as a means of fully comprehending the dynamics of class and gender at work in James's novel. The film confirms Minty Alley's lasting influence even as it offers a productive critique of its conceits. Both texts' creolizations of the bildungsroman are realized through discourses of "folk" culture located within the community as well as through each protagonist's meticulously marked achievement of class consciousness.[2]

James's engagement of class issues in Minty Alley creates a paradigm for much of his later work. Minty Alley reveals one of James's primary intellectual contentions in its developmental stage: his contention that a revolutionary and/or radical narrative could be fashioned from within a white European, bourgeois form, in this case the coming-of-age novel. James's creolization of the novel, what I read as a radical impulse, is manifest in his emphasis on vernacular Trinidadian speech, working-class characters, and his consistent attempts to make the community as important as the protagonist. In this text, James's desire to give voice to "the masses"—which makes Minty Alley a major Beacon period text—falters when his bourgeois viewpoint and English Standard English narrative voice are allowed to maintain narrative primacy. In her book, Radical Representations: Politics and Form in U.S. Proletarian Fiction, 1929–1941, Barbara Foley identifies the bildungsroman as "the classic form of the bourgeois novel" (321). She goes on to remind us that "theorists of the bildungsroman generally concur that this genre is privileged to articulate bourgeois individuality" (322). So even though D. Elliot Parris, Hazel V. Carby, Kenneth Ramchand, myself, and other critics recognize and applaud the interest Minty Alley has in portraying the working classes, the novel nonetheless revolves around its middle-class protagonist, Haynes. I turn then to Euzhan Palcy's cinematic interpretation of Joseph Zobel's 1950 novel, La Rue Cases Negres, for a realization of "the higher individuality based upon a very conscious collectivity" that James admires in Walt Whitman's poetry and political practice and in literature more generally. The film is more successful than *Minty Alley* in destabilizing the notion of a centralized protagonist. Both Palcy and James use their works as part of a movement toward Caribbean self-definition and self-determination, a common characteristic of Caribbean literature of the 1930s-1970s.

Minty Alley's gesture toward radical representations of Trinidadian culture, by which I mean James's recognition of women, orality, and the working class as important if not primary markers of Trinidadian identity in the late 1920s, are tempered by James's more stereotypical and conservative depictions of "vulgar" working-class characters and a "refined" middle-class character. This polarized view of his society in which he frequently genders vulgarity as female is informed by James's own location as an adult within Trinidad's Victorian-identified middle class. While Palcy's *La Rue Cases Negres* shares some of *Minty Alley*'s prejudices, it is simultaneously able to critique its own class and gender biases in ways James cannot. Therefore, when read against *La Rue Cases Negres*, *Minty Alley* can be characterized as a gesturing text; it anticipates the direction of a radical narrative but cannot wholly be one itself.

Zobel's novel shares several key features with James's novel, and Palcy's cinematic vision maintains these features. Like *Minty Alley*, *La Rue Cases Negres* is set in the 1920s and engages issues of class consciousness and gender entitlement. Each text pairs its male protagonist with a female friend who in turn represents and is inseparable from the community. As representatives of middle-class individuality and as alter egos of their authors, the male protagonists of *Minty Alley* and *La Rue Cases Negres* occupy positions of privilege and education. Yet, underlying both narratives is the clear sense that the potential to transform society resides most forcefully in the larger community and not in the individual. Paradoxically, this sensibility does not lead to the depiction in either the film or James's novel of women as more revolutionary or as possessing more revolutionary potential than men. Perhaps, because of this shared shortcoming, the film acts as an excellent counterpoint to *Minty Alley* inasmuch as, unlike *Minty Alley*, it seems conscious of how it often privileges a gendered (male) position; it grapples with the decision to value the individual over the community and therefore male over female. The urban microcosm of the yard depicted in *Minty Alley* is also a point of connection with *La Rue Cases Negres*. Zobel's novel and Palcy's film both focus on a small, insular community that is rural and dependent upon sugarcane labor. As the novel/film's protagonist, José, advances in his self-development, the transition to city life occasions a host of contrasts that are absent from *Minty Alley* but that anchor *La Rue Cases Negres* in the bildungsroman form. These contrasts involve José's interactions with his guides along his journey of development.

My interpretation of *Minty Alley* emphasizes the historical contexts (both private and public) in which James was writing as especially pertinent to the evaluation of the text's representations of class and gender dynamics. In the 1920s and 1930s, the Caribbean was host to a groundswell of political action characterized by widespread labor strikes and demands for wage reform in the sugarcane and oil fields. These events were eventually recognized as key pre-Independence collective actions. James, not yet a radical, was a member of a loosely formed association, subsequently called the *Beacon* Group. This group of young male writers and intellectuals from Trinidad's educated ranks were inspired by workers' movements taking place internationally. They determined that cultural autonomy (in opposition to British colonial influence) was a key component in the fight for political rights and set about publishing and producing an indigenous and proletarian literature. The *Beacon* era in West Indian literature was framed by the appearance of two magazines, *Trinidad* and the *Beacon*, which, though both had short publishing runs, had an enormous impact on the creative expression in Trinidad and across the Anglophone Caribbean.[3]

Literary contributors to each of these journals were intent on disrupting and revising (European) colonial interpretations of Caribbean life. Hence, the *Beacon* writers chose characters from the lower classes, especially the inhabitants of Port-of-Spain's slums, or barracks yards (a term that describes the architecture of much lower-class Port-of-Spain housing), in an attempt to locate and then celebrate "authentic" local (as opposed to metropolitan) culture. They thereby flaunted previous literary conventions by ignoring what was acceptable to the small West Indian elite and the British. Carby connects these *Beacon* developments to similar literary acts expressed within the Harlem Renaissance and the Russian Revolution. They all, she states, "turned to the working class and to realism for a 'new literature,' shorn of European and colonial conceits" ("Proletarian" 46). Gillian Whitlock further describes common novelistic techniques used by James and his colleagues: "'realism' was interpreted as a focusing upon the life of the lower classes, which was seen to be more distinctively 'local' than the culture of the British-oriented middle and upper classes, and a means whereby a national literature could be nourished 'in the very earth of a new land.' So the barrack-yard was a frontier... the *Beacon* barrack-yard stories... incorporated elements of the oral and folk traditions of the calypso tents" (43). In the barracks yard of No. 2 Minty Alley, James, the novelist, constructs his vision of Trinidadian society through what we can now recognize as a "miasma of privilege,"[4] elevating the folk in an impulse informed by class position and a cultural orientation that was both West Indian and European. But even as James and the *Beacon* Group presented a romanticized and schematized depiction of "the folk," they also developed a concomitant schematic for the depiction of "the" middle classes. *Minty Alley*'s attention to the developmental possibilities for its middle-class character, therefore, can also be read as an admonishment and critique of the novel's presumed audience: Trinidad's bourgeoisie.

Often the texts produced by *Beacon* writers, like *Black Fauns* (1935) by Alfred Mendes, centered around what literary critic Rhonda Cobham describes as "the lifestyle of at least one lower-class female character, where the woman's independent spirit is generally played off against her sexual and economic needs" ("Women in Jamaican Literature" 197). Cobham's study reveals that this tendency to focus on working women is evident in earlier West Indian works as well, such as *Jane's Career* (1913) by Jamaican writer H. G. De Lisser. From the turn of the century up until the 1940s and 1950s, working-class women were considered by male middle-class writers to be primary representatives of local colonial communities and what was romantically referred to as "folk culture."[5] James makes similar presumptions in *Minty Alley*.

Gendered Class Representations

The sojourn of Haynes, the protagonist of *Minty Alley*, at No. 2 can be seen as a period of socialization during which his understanding of his middle-class position and its attendant privileges is made complete. Of particular interest is how James genders this rite of passage: women are the chief arbiters of this socialization process. James's bourgeois Trinidadian viewpoint is perhaps most tellingly revealed by the fact that at the end of the text Haynes is more firmly rooted in the patriarchal discourse of colonial subjectivity and, after facilitating that rootedness, the women and the working-class characters return to the margins of his life.

Minty Alley charts two years in the life of twenty-year-old Haynes and his daily interactions with an urban, working-class, predominantly female community he unexpectedly finds himself a part of. The untimely death of his mother has left Haynes in financial hardship and acts as the catalyst for his departure to

Minty Alley. This crisis in the first pages of the novel alerts the reader to Haynes's inexperience and his inability to take care of his own basic needs. He moves to Minty Alley at the suggestion of his house servant, Ella. His mother's wish for him "to be independent" and her acknowledgment that "in these little islands for a black man to be independent he must have money or a profession" (22) clearly announce Haynes's class position and aspirations; his mother intends for him to become a doctor in England or America. When the narrator states, "ever since Haynes had known himself, he had known and accepted her plans for his future" (22), the reader is further made aware of Haynes's willing subordination to authority while his "independence" is presented as an individualized male quest. Thus, the first chapter briskly introduces the notion of privilege, class, and difference as well as a bourgeois desire to maintain the status quo. But instead of charting Haynes's pursuit of "independence" as a journey to the "mother country," James chooses to "grow" Haynes on home soil.

Mrs. Rouse, who runs a bakery from her kitchen and also rents out her extra rooms, presides over No. 2 Minty Alley. Her yard community is made up of black, mixed-race, and East Indian servants, bakery workers, and tenants. Benoit, Mrs. Rouse's business partner and philandering, common-law husband of eighteen years, and Maisie, her seventeen-year-old niece, are significant players in Haynes's journey of self-development. Minty Alley becomes the site and creole community that collectively ushers the contemplative and sheltered Haynes through a process of creolization.

Haynes represents the isolated and self-absorbed existence of the colored middle classes, which is blatantly illustrated by the fact that although the distance from Haynes's family home to Minty Alley is less than two hundred yards, he had no idea the street existed. Over the course of the narrative, James steadily brings his characters to the brink of class encounter, but Haynes consistently fails to increase his understanding or awareness of the community he has ostensibly joined. Haynes remains on the outside and consistently "others" the creolized Minty Alley community; James writes this perpetually dichotomous relationship through the conceit of a mind/body split. Haynes and his mother try and fail to avoid his own "corruption" by the lower classes; thus the maintenance of his distance from them can be understood as a desire for purity, at several different registers.

As other critics have noted, the titillation of encountering the real and metaphorical "body" of the yard entices Haynes to stay at Minty Alley despite the awkwardness of his first days there (Carby, "Proletarian" 48). He decides to stay after catching a glimpse, through a peephole in his bedroom wall, of Benoit making love to one of the bakery workers. Haynes steadily enlarges the peephole and view of the "vulgar" yard bodies, until his connection with them is developed through real contact, friendships, and his relationship with Maisie—with whom he has his own first sexual encounters. While Maisie can be understood as a minor character, her body actually synthesizes James's use of a mind/body split and becomes, by extension, a fleeting representation of Trinidad's capacity for social and political transformation. Over the course of the novel, because she is covertly shown to possess an acute intellect in addition to an independent spirit, Maisie briefly exceeds her role as Haynes's girlfriend. Nevertheless, the overarching use of a mind/body split as played out through Maisie and Haynes keeps that separation, and James's interpretation of class and class difference (as a means of representing creolization) omnipresent in the text.

James's explicit use of the concepts of refinement and vulgarity to distinguish Haynes from the working-class "folk" of Minty Alley feeds into his equally problematic but typical notion of "the folk" as merely bodies and Haynes as a "thinker." Establishing these patterns of demarcation through the types of work the two groups engage in, James juxtaposes Haynes's quiet and often solitary job as a clerk in a bookshop with Minty Alley's physical, collective, and odorous business of making cakes. Haynes's sexual innocence is contrasted with details of the sexuality or sexual exploits of nearly every other resident. Almost all of the residents of Minty Alley become sexualized at one point or another in the text. This includes but is not limited to Mrs. Rouse, Benoit (who tries to sleep with everyone and tells Haynes to take advantage and do the same), Nurse Jackson (who has two bold affairs, the first with Benoit, the second of which ends up in the courts), Maisie (who has a host of boyfriends and eventually seduces Haynes), and Miss Atwell (a "kept" and eventually abandoned woman). This conceptualization of "folkness" is not unusual in its stereotype and derives most directly from Trinidad's bourgeois Victorian colonial value system. James subconsciously redeploys class binaries between the elite and the folk based on European models of a peasant class and an aristocracy (Roberts 65). Maisie, working-class and female, is distinguished by her sexual maturity and her storytelling performances and contrasts with Haynes's innocence, intellectualism, and formalized literacy. By writing Haynes as a thinker and by writing the Minty Alley residents as flesh, specifically through Maisie, James inscribes his own class bias. Throughout the novel, Haynes's position as a (more) morally pure person of intellect is strengthened because he is usually figured as a passive observer—he is someone to whom sex happens. Indeed, Maisie eventually seduces Haynes while allowing him to think he orchestrated her seduction. Haynes's body is situated as passive, refined and therefore representatively middle-class in opposition to Maisie's presumably degraded, vulgar, and sexually aggressive working-class body.

In the introduction to her book *Noises in the Blood* (1995), Carolyn Cooper provides a helpful explanation of how "vulgar" and "refined" are constituted in a West Indian cultural context. Though referencing Jamaica, the usages and ideological ramifications of these terms coincide precisely with the ideologies of class expressed within *Minty Alley*:

> The pejoration of "the vulgar"—the people, the language and the corpus of the culture produced—marks the high/low and Euro/Afrocentric cultural divide that is encoded in the Jamaican body politic. From the relative neutrality of the Latin *vulgas*, "the common people," the vulgar becomes "coarsely commonplace." The vulgate—"of language or speech: Ordinary, vernacular. Now arch. 1513" (OED)—becomes the sign of illiteracy. The vulgar body of knowledge produced by the people—"common or customary in respect of the use or understanding of language, words or ideas 1553 . . . commonly current or prevalent, generally or widely disseminated, as a matter of knowledge, assertion or opinion 1549" (OED)—is devalued. In all domains, the "vulgar" is that which can be traced to "Africa;" the "refined" is that which can be traced to "Europe." (The quotation marks are intended to foreground the constructed nature of this ideology of essential cultural difference.) In the domain of language and verbal creativity, English is "refined" and Jamaican is "vulgar"; oral texts are "vulgar"; written texts are "refined." (8)

The coincidence and overlap of the body and the written word in the etymologies of vulgar and refined, as defined by Cooper, also occur in *Minty Alley*. Haynes is admired and respected not just because he is seen to belong to the middle class but because he cultivates a life of the mind; initially more comfortable as a voyeur, he reads; he works in a bookshop; indeed, he has a public relationship with the written word. Maisie, on the other hand, as the primary representation of the vulgar body of Minty Alley, is sexually active, a skilled storyteller, an impressive performer, and preserver of the (West African) art of the spoken word. As Cooper's ideas suggest, there is never any question in the novel about which way of knowing—through the written word or the spoken word—is more highly valued or which relationship to sex and the body is equated with respectability. However, James's hierarchy, which situates Haynes on an upper tier of aesthetic value and Maisie at the bottom, is not fixed. Haynes is not just a refined person of some intellect; he is also a pathetic, colonized adolescent. Haynes, unlike James, who was also titillated by his real-life barracks yard experience, lacks the self-reflexive *capacity* to recognize the false dichotomy of positing the middle classes as smarter or better than the working classes. Throughout the text, even as Haynes acquires and consolidates the power of influence over the yard community, his bumbling inadequacies are simultaneously revealed.

For example, James questions the presumed privilege of the middle class after Haynes has been resident at Minty Alley for many months and has assumed a place of authority at No. 2. The clout, status, and uselessness of Haynes's formal education is realized most profoundly when Mrs. Rouse begins to enlist Haynes's help in making decisions. Although Mrs. Rouse is a literate, numerate, mature business woman, Haynes's presence curiously throws her abilities to reason into question. Among other things, she decides that he can do the bakery books more skillfully than she, even though he is just an underpaid clerk in a bookshop. The other Minty Alley residents contribute to this construction of Haynes as advisor and patriarch because of his perceived ability to interpret the written word. Eventually, "he was master of the house. Nothing was ever done without consulting him" (173). In short, because he possesses the stamp of the middle class—a colonial education—his interpretive abilities are collectively acknowledged as superior at No. 2.

The occasion of Haynes providing amateurish advice to Mrs. Rouse regarding a marriage proposal she has received successfully casts a more profound aura of respect and responsibility around Haynes, one that is perceivable to both himself and the yard community. Haynes realizes "that whatever he said would carry weight with them and with this realisation came a sense of responsibility and increasing confidence" (154). That realization and exchange with Mrs. Rouse each constitute crucial steps in Haynes's ideological preparation to inhabit fully his role within the bourgeoisie. But the circumstances of these incidents of socialization simultaneously reveal the charade of Haynes's presumed and then assumed abilities: at the end of the day, Haynes is not helpful, and at the end of the text, except for the loss of his sexual "innocence," he is no more savvy than he was at the beginning.

Haynes is doubly positioned in the text as both a representative of the middle class in conversation with the working class—an example of Trinidadian society's potential for change—and as a representative of the incompetence of the same middle class—an example of the need for Trinidadian society *to* change and especially to relinquish its dependency on colonial ideas of worth. This implicit critique of class within *Minty Alley* is often overlooked. In "Case for West Indian Self-Government" (1933) James implicates the Crown Colony system in his critique of the ineptitude and internalized racism of the colored middle classes.[6] In reference to the only branch of Trinidadian government that nonwhite Trinidadians (the colored middle class) could serve within, James asserts, "The career of this fair-skinned man, from their point of view (perhaps also from the point of view of the Government) seems to depend to a large extent on the way, whether openly or covertly, they dissociate themselves from their own people. They have been nominated or selected for high office chiefly because along with their ability or lack of it they have shown a willingness and capacity to please their rulers . . . These men are not so much inherently weak as products of a social system in which they live" (55). For James, a principal flaw in the Crown Colony system was its overt and deliberate lack of democracy. A significant difference, therefore, between the sociopolitical context of the fictional No. 2 Minty Alley and the one of the official government that James describes in "Case" is that Haynes receives his position of authority not from the antidemocratic benevolence of a well-connected patron, but rather from the community. Considering the ways in which the Minty Alley community collectively understands the numerous leadership and social skills that Haynes lacks, their "election" of him to a position of authority should be understood as a dialectical process that exposes a clash of separate forces that shape Minty Alley's assessment of Haynes. The Minty Alley community is decisively shaped by a set of social practices that activates a deference to colonial authority, and by virtue of his class position Haynes is as synonymous with colonial authority as he can be as a "nonwhite." However, Minty Alley's deference to him does not prohibit their understanding that within their self-activity they can simultaneously see and articulate Haynes's deficiencies. It is both at the same time.

This reliance upon and deference toward Haynes prompts H. Adlai Murdoch to note that "the novel may be read as a barometer of colonial life, a microcosmic re-presentation of the forces underlying the fragmentation and hierarchization of a society made subject to colonial discourse" (62). He continues, "subjection to the discourse of colonialism has been inscribed in the text. This inscription is represented through the character of Haynes who, by virtue of his paradoxical position as a member of both the ruling and the oppressed classes, may be said to mediate a simultaneous identification with the ideological position of the colonizer as well as participation in the fragmentation and dislocation of the colonized" (65).

By the end of the novel, Haynes's social position is not so much altered as it is embossed and ratified by his immersion in the Minty Alley community, an immersion that ultimately emphasizes his apartness. A telling textual example of his apartness occurs towards the end of the novel. Critical of the bad temper which he often observed in Mrs. Rouse, Haynes doesn't understand it until he finally experiences her work environment:

> Nearly a year after he was living in the house, he went into the kitchen for the first time. As soon as he was fairly inside, he felt that he was in the mouth of hell. The big three-decked stove was going, the coal-pots with food, the concrete below so hot that he could feel it through his slippers, and above the galvanized iron roof, which the tropical sun had been warming up from the outside since morning. He could scarcely breathe and involuntarily recoiled. Mrs. Rouse came to the door smiling as usual.
> "You find it hot, Mr. Haynes?"
> "How can you stand it, Mrs. Rouse?"
> "Poor people have no choice, Mr. Haynes . . ."
> He stood at the kitchen door wondering how any mortal could stand that for so many hours every day for so many days. (187)

Although the bakery is the main activity of the yard, Haynes has managed to pass an entire year without entering the kitchen. This is not terribly different from Haynes walking past Minty Alley most days of his life before he moved there and being oblivious to its existence. Haynes's myopia is generated from that "miasma of privilege" that clings to him. Mrs. Rouse's simple statement, "poor people have no choice, Mr. Haynes," pinpoints their continued class stratification and difference. When he leaves Minty Alley after two years, Haynes melts back into the middle-class morass, epitomized by the fact that he does not object to or even question the fact that Maisie still addresses him as "Mr. Haynes" after they have become close friends and lovers. James writes Haynes as a perpetual outsider within the Minty Alley community, and his outsider status cannot shift because he cannot circumvent or change his class position.

James creates two Minty Alleys: the one that Haynes inhabits and the one created and lived in by the fluid membership of Mrs. Rouse's extended household. Reading No. 2 from Haynes's perspective, it is a static community disconnected from a larger political context.[7] This perspective also highlights a major difference between James and later Caribbean novelists who would use the bildungsroman form to great success as a metaphor of nationhood; James does not parallel the development of his protagonist with the political development (toward colonial independence) of the nation.

Noting the leadership conferred upon and assumed by Haynes, Murdoch contends that "patriarchy is the overriding trope governing relations between Haynes and his fellow colonials"; this in turn assists Haynes's "assimilation of his role to one that replicates the colonial paradigm" embedded in the novel's structure (68). Murdoch also observes that since Haynes is the main mediator of information in the novel (to the reader), the colonial subject, in this case the yard residents, are prevented, as in other colonial discourses, from speaking for themselves (66). But with this point I disagree. When we examine Minty Alley as fashioned by and through the creative coherence of its working-class residents, language becomes a site and a mechanism through which a sense of history *is* conveyed. Like his counterparts within the Harlem Renaissance and his colleagues within the *Beacon* Group, James recognized the saliency of writing the vernacular when writing "the folk" into the literature.[8] In this Minty Alley, Maisie becomes the repository of a historical and political consciousness, which she articulates in a loud and irreverent voice despite her characterization as a troublesome minor.

Through the force of Maisie's voice the reader is made aware of how working-class women use the spoken word in localized insurgent activities. Though Maisie is disenfranchised because of her class, race, and gender, she is not completely without agency. Illustrating the importance of orality to the understanding of who she is and where she has come from, Maisie unifies or merges the mind/body split, allowing the subaltern to speak, to paraphrase Gayatri Spivak. Maisie utilizes what Glissant calls a "natural poetics" to counteract her own disadvantage within the social order of the yard. Glissant posits that "even if the destiny of a community should be a miserable one, or its existence threatened, these poetics are the direct result of activity within the social body . . . the most violent challenge to an established order can emerge from a natural poetics, when there is a continuity between the challenged order and the disorder which negates it" (121). Thus, despite the value attached to Haynes's literacy, the ability to *tell* a story competes within the text with the ability to read or write one.

Maisie's actions as an individual remind us that the insurgent vocality of Trinidadian women has a historical and overtly physical context. In her 1987 preface to the slave narrative, *The History of Mary Prince, a West Indian Slave, Related by Herself* (1831), Ziggi Alexander recounts an origin for women's vocal insurgency: "Evidence does exist to suggest the likelihood of female rebellion was greater than historians have led us to believe so far. For example, the Governor of Trinidad maintained that slave women were 'the most prone to give offence,' and soon after in 1823, another government official complained that female slaves more often deserved punishment than males, for they used to great effect 'that powerful instrument of attack and defense, their tongue'" (xi).

There is a pivotal moment in *Minty Alley* where Maisie's powerful voice is most clear and where the discourse of a mind/body split as articulated along lines of gender and class is unified. The moment, a dramatic battle of words and fists between Mrs. Rouse and Maisie, centers on Mrs. Rouse's terror that Maisie will degrade her and "tell" Mr. Haynes she has accepted Benoit back, so she tries to threaten Maisie. Maisie responds with a magnificent speech. She declares to Mrs. Rouse, "'Why don't you see after the nurse and Mr. Benoit? They do you worse than me. And to besides, woman,' said Maisie, changing from her calm and speaking without passion, but with a deliberately assumed pretense of mere irritation, 'the days of slavery past. My tongue is my own to say what I like.' She walked from the mango tree towards the centre of the yard. 'I not going to let an old blow-hard like you frighten me'" (217). In fact, Mrs. Rouse does (slightly) frighten Maisie and is most immediately the established order that Maisie attempts to negate. Using language in her violent challenge to Mrs. Rouse's authority, Maisie, more than any other character in the text, is aware of the power of her voice and the historical attempts to silence it. She reminds both Mrs. Rouse and the gathered audience that "the days of slavery past." That same utterance functions as what John Beverly calls "testimonio" and "evokes a polyphony of other voices," the voices of women oppressed by class and race (16). Because of the disorder that her voice creates Maisie is often scapegoated as the source of No. 2's misfortune, and Mrs. Rouse and Haynes expend an enormous amount of energy to silence her. The impossibility of silencing Maisie—recalling the frustration of the British governor—is an articulation of the tension and struggle for power within the local political structure of Minty Alley. The "natural poetics" of Maisie's "my tongue is my own to say what I like" speech, in its rejection of a mind/body split, also evokes a broader political signification of localized struggle and social transformation. Finally, albeit inadvertently, Maisie's speech historicizes the class stratification as enacted bodily and verbally throughout the novel.

At the end of *Minty Alley*, Maisie makes the decision to leave Trinidad for America. While this decision could be read as a further manifestation of her resistance to her marginalization within the barracks yard community, her announcement is presented flatly. The narrative does not convey her decision as an event that will change her life. Not surprisingly, the focus is on the heartache experienced by Haynes the last night they see each other: "There was a harshness and determination behind the casual air with which she spoke that stunned him into acceptance . . . 'You sorry I am going Mr. Haynes?' Haynes was choking and could only nod." (226). St Louis evaluates this departure as conservative: "In leaving the barrackyard for America, Maisie does not radically transform the social and political structures that she is to exist within. Her presence as an individual is indeed powerful but it does not translate into a revolutionary alteration of her social reality. At best she may have replicated her level of disenfranchisement in America" (C. L. R. James's Social Theory 178). I concur with St Louis's comment that "James's narrative does not indicate that Maisie's leaving is a *revolutionary* act" (178) and would add that there is also no place for Maisie to be in James's conception of Trinidad. Nor is there a new concept of community created for Haynes, who, at the novel's close must also step backwards into his old life. Finally, the suggestion that Maisie may have to prostitute herself to get to America (as a means to earn the ocean passage fee) greatly qualifies the agency she realized and expressed within her actions and articulates in her "My tongue is my own to say what I like" speech; the very suggestion of prostitution resituates her as a one-dimensional physical and sexual being. And since she represents the entire Minty Alley community, it too remains sexualized and one-dimensional.

The Camera's Representations in *La Rue Cases Negres*

In 1950, Joseph Zobel published a novel that directly descended from the tradition James helped to establish in the 1930s. Euzhan Palcy's 1985 cinematic interpretation of that novel helps to focus the rest of this chapter. Although Zobel's novel was published after the *Beacon* period, it shares the group's goal of using literature as a tool for Caribbean cultural self-definition and self-determination. The film is faithful to the cultural politics of the written narrative in its articulation of class difference and class socialization and diverges from *Minty Alley* in several key ways. Whereas *Minty Alley* is mostly interested in "reportage" and does very little questioning or interrogation of Haynes's position of privilege in relationship to the other Minty Alley residents, the film is able to critique colonialism's use of education as an exclusionary tool that only allows for one or two people to access it to "open the door to a better life," as one line of the film goes. This self-reflexivity exhibited within the film is connected to its choice of first-person narration. José Hassam (Gary Cadenet), the young protagonist, provides an "insider" viewpoint. The fact that he originates as a member of the working-class community whose story he partially tells and has existed within the same poverty and oppression as they have creates a space within which becoming an outsider is recognized as a process and does not become normalized as it does through Haynes's characterization in Minty Alley. The film adopts the conventions of a bildungsroman novel, but, in contrast to Minty Alley, it does not utilize a Caribbean bourgeois perspective and does not *exclusively* endorse colonial bourgeois education and individualism as normative or unproblematized experiences. At key junctures, however, the film does valorize the individual male protagonist, José. Class is gendered, then, but it is *not* sexualized as it is in Minty Alley. The notion of vulgar bodies is absent from the film and, by extension, José's story of development is not concerned with sexual maturation. A further significant distinction between the film and Minty Alley is that Rue Cases Negres's concept of "folkness" derives from West Africa, not Western Europe, and this concept is explicitly articulated, as opposed to functioning as a presumed aspect of the narrative as in Minty Alley, through Monsieur Medouze's lectures and through several community gatherings.

The use of the close-up and the panoramic, or pan, shots as employed in La Rue Cases Negres, are central to the film's privileging of the individual and need to be considered as key aspects of cinematic bildungsroman. The dialectics of La Rue Cases Negres' desire to articulate the oppressed majority's acquisition of class consciousness leading to potential radical self-activity coexists with the film's often sentimental depiction of José as an individual whose advancements and triumphs are generally realized at the expense of the majority, and which work to splinter the seemingly more radical masses. This tension emerges through the film's interplay between the pan and the close-up.

José is a very poor orphan of about ten being raised by his grandmother, Amantine (Darling Legitimus), an elderly canecutter with great ambitions for her grandson. The film is set in a fictionalized rural community of Martinique in which the economic and social relationships of slavery and French colonialism are securely intact and revolve around sugarcane production. The surest escape from cane labor is the acquisition of a formal education (an attribute of many types of colonialism), and thus, the film quickly introduces José's love and aptitude for learning. As is usual with the bildungsroman form, José has several guides along his journey of development, including his schoolteacher, Stephen

Roc (Henri Melon). Roc often articulates colonialism's controlling ideologies via such phrases as the one he dictates on the first day of school, "Education is the key which shall unlock the second door to our freedom." Roc, of course, is referring to formal, schoolhouse, textbook education. The elderly Monsieur Medouze (Douta Seck), another guide, offers José a counterpoint to Roc and the colonial curriculum with folktales, riddle sessions, and lectures on history, slavery, and colonialism. José's friend Tortilla (Job Bernabe), anchors him in the community and pushes him to resist critically the various ways each of his other guides fuel his individualism and the individualistic trajectory of colonial educational policies. Set in the 1920s, the film spans José's development from a village student to a city scholarship boy, a time frame of less than one year.

Two scenes that feature Tortilla and José comprehensively express the film's dialectical engagement of the individual and the group. The first one which I will discuss occurs in the second half of the film when the announcement of the school certificate winners draws all the parents to the village school. Tortilla, José, and eight other children earn the coveted prize, and Stephen Roc chooses just Tortilla and José to represent the village in the tougher, even more prestigious scholarship exam. However, Monsieur Saint-Louis (Tortilla's father) says to Roc, "I'm deeply moved by what you've told me. I can't let her continue. I can't. There are my other kids . . . And the postmistress is trying to find her a little job." Roc retorts, "Do you realize how lucky she is?" and Saint-Louis replies, "I know but I can't, I really can't." During this exchange, the camera finds and closes in on each person's facial expressions of sadness and disbelief. Roc weakly says, "I understand." Silent throughout this exchange, Tortilla looks back in sorrow as she and her father walk away.

In part because of the way the camera lingers on Saint-Louis, Roc, Amantine, José, and Tortilla's facial expressions, the viewer is also aghast at this turn of events, and presumes that dismay is also the film's authorial position. Indeed, Tortilla's total dejection, her father's sheepishness, Amantine's shock, and Roc's consternation are infectious; we empathize. But these emotions are misleading. The viewer is seduced into thinking exclusively of Tortilla's lost opportunity, an opportunity that seems all the more precious because of her father's apparent ease in denying it. In order to resist that seduction, I contend that the viewer/analyst must critique the camera's role in what I consider to be a misrepresentation: The close-up, as a metonym for the individual, enables us to forget that Tortilla is walking away *with* a school certificate in hand, the very certificate that Roc earlier calls "a great step forward for the humblest people."

We forget that, like José, Tortilla is "moving up" too and will not have to return to the canefields. Tortilla is moving up *within* the community while José (in typical bildungsroman fashion) is moving up by moving *away* from it. Although Tortilla must sacrifice, it is ostensibly so her siblings will have similar opportunities.[9]

Tortilla's trajectory, her less radical movement out of the canefields, is representative of both the type of resistance most members of her community would be able to access and the type of familial-based, community-oriented types of resistance "third world" colonized women necessarily practice or are forced to practice. Tortilla's connection to the community is reiterated by the fact that the camera represents her alone, in a close-up, only once during the entire film; at all other times she is represented as a member of a duo or larger group. Although Tortilla is successful on multiple fronts, she is nevertheless portrayed as *un*lucky when compared to José. (Indeed, for wanting to accommodate the educational potential of his other son and daughter, Tortilla's father is portrayed as shortsighted and insensitive.) As a result, the viewer has to make an effort to recall, even to see initially, how Tortilla enacts the possibility to aspire to move beyond the canefields and how she might achieve "success" without having to abandon family and community. The film thus constructs a feminist assessment and a class-based reading of the consequences of Tortilla's missed opportunities. Within the values of the bildungsroman form and of individualism she is robbed by her father and left at a disadvantage in her life prospects when compared to José. When understood within the rubric of local (versus metropolitan) organic class mobilization Tortilla is positioned to become a leader, not a loser. However, the idea of the first assessment, that Tortilla "loses," is given more prominence. In order fully to understand the impact of this school certificate scene, we must go back and consider an early scene involving José and Tortilla in the classroom.

In a typical representation of José's separation from the community in an effort to emphasize his specialness, his grandmother arranges for him to get hot lunches on school days at the house of an acquaintance, Madame Leonce. Within a day or two, however, José discovers that the arrangement is a foul one, as Leonce puts him to work washing dishes and shining shoes, which continually makes him late when class resumes after lunch. He decides to get back at her and sneaks away from Roc's classroom. At this moment, we see Tortilla approach the blackboard. The camera angle is from José's perspective, outside the classroom window peeking in; thus Tortilla is very small and we have to look past the rest of the class to see her back. The camera then follows José on his rock-throwing mission, and on his return, the camera finds Tortilla finishing her recitation at the board. She speaks two words, "The End." Stephen Roc says, "Thank you, Miss Saint-Louis, very good." Roc then turns to José, who is pouring with sweat from his work of retribution, and with a moderate close-up, we watch José give an extended vocabulary recital on the difference between "cackling" and "singing." As José is reciting he receives encouraging looks and prods from Roc and offers his own expressions of satisfaction and enthusiasm as he searches for just the right verb or adjective. When he concludes, Roc says, in a breathless voice, "Very good, Mr. Hassam, you defined the terms well but . . . such a brilliant student should not be late for school." Roc's wonderment at José's aptitude mirrors the same satisfaction experienced by the viewer.

A close examination of this second scene reveals why we react as we do to Tortilla's fate regarding the school certificate. Even as the greater story of the film identifies Tortilla as José's peer and equal, the camera pushes her to the margins. And even as the film wants us to understand José as emerging from a collective and as able to maintain that sense of collectivity, the camera and his elders elevate and separate him and thereby underscore the colonial valorization of the individual. It is easier to feel sorry for Tortilla because her life is not overtly portrayed as being rich or full. When Roc tells Tortilla's father that she is "lucky" we are inclined to believe him rather than recognize her brilliance on our own, for, we are never really shown her academic abilities, though we see José's over and over. It is easy to presume that her life will be less successful or less upwardly mobile than José's because we never actually see her work as an assistant to the postmistress or any direct results of that work. In contrast, we are shown José winning a full scholarship (from the Fort-de France school) and literally counting the mound of money (300 francs) in front of Amantine. The lingering image is of José, not the village community; they are his backdrop, his context, his origin, but ultimately not his equal. Like the community of Minty Alley and their deference toward Haynes because of his higher social status, the viewer who sympathizes with José (which is nearly impossible not to do) must also accept and value upward economic mobility realized individualistically. Tortilla's characterization consistently, though inadequately, prepares the viewer for the uncharacteristic final scene.

In what I interpret as the ultimate articulation of the film's dialectic, the final scene marginalizes José and shows how he has become marginal as it foregrounds the Rue Cases Negres community engaged in a form of political protest.

Men and women, parents and children, are all gathered in outrage at the authorities who have arrested and are physically punishing Leopold, the mulatto son of the plantation overseer. Leopold's personal crisis of not being legally recognized by his dying white father is expressed through his decision to unite with the black cane cutters. He steals the plantation ledger in an attempt to prove how the black workers continue to be cheated and exploited. José's late arrival to the scene and the strategic, sweeping pan shots that are used throughout the scene conclude the film with multiple images of collectivity. José's final voice-over, "Wherever I go, I will take Black Shack Alley with me," not only ratifies his separateness but, juxtaposed with the final scene of protest and collective support, suggests the idea that both José and Rue Cases Negres are actively involved in their self-development and self-determination. Tortilla remains throughout the film as a kind of discomfiting challenge to the film's politics. Her characterization raises a series of potential interventions into the overt values of the narrative: Would her father have been so quick to curtail her education if she had been a boy? And, while we understand that José has prospered from his education because of the film's initial structuring as a flashback, what happens to Tortilla and how might she materially gain from her apprenticeship?

James's unrealized ideal in *Minty Alley*, one which he aimed for in subsequent writings, was to effect a Bakhtinian dialogism between the individual and the collective—this is what he alludes to in the Whitman quote at the beginning of this chapter. The interactions between Haynes and the Minty Alley community are generally didactic, top down, and hierarchal. And whereas the interactions in *La Rue Cases Negres* are similarly constructed—especially in its multiple representations of the tutor and the student—the film's univocal aesthetic is formalistically mitigated by the conversation that exists between the use of the pan and the close-up.[10] The univocal aesthetic is consistently interrupted through the actions of Tortilla's character. In an early scene, as the parents go off to work in the fields, the kids get together for what is an everyday event; they pool their meager food resources and take turns eating at one another's homes. This day it is José's turn, but he does not want them to come inside; Tortilla confronts him about this. She reminds him that neither he, nor his house, is more special than any of the rest of them. Later, the kids climb an adult neighbor's fence to steal fruit. Tortilla explains why: "I don't like Twelve Toes," she says. "He keeps all his fruit for himself." And finally, when school has reopened, Tortilla asks, "José won't you eat with us?" (meaning with the neighborhood kids), and José replies, "Ma Tine won't let me." Instead, he goes off to eat at Madame

Leonce's. In each instance, Tortilla's words work to balance the message that José is getting from his grandmother—that he is both special and different from the rest of the children.

In contrast, James formally endorses Haynes over the Minty Alley collective. From beginning to end, what we know of Minty Alley is dependent upon Haynes's presence and perspective, and its story ends with his departure from it. Tortilla's connection to the "group" emphasizes José's detachment from it. But unlike the immutability of Haynes's class separation from the Minty Alley community, José's falterings gesture in a politically positive direction by highlighting the necessity and possibilities for group activity as opposed to individualized activity.

"I am just writing a story"

I have used *La Rue Cases Negres* as a counterpoint to *Minty Alley* to highlight some of the ways in which the Caribbean male bildungsroman is perhaps most useful in its depictions of gendered perspectives on class. James himself would look back at *Minty Alley* and offer assessments that help to connect these close readings back to an aesthetics of creolization and illuminate how James's overtly literary projects would shape his subsequent nonfiction and political activist work.

Whereas I have argued that the struggle to articulate a revolutionary ideology (the dialogic relationship between class and gender in colonial Trinidad) from within a bourgeois form, the bildungsroman, is evident in *Minty Alley*, James denies there exists a political template with which he created *Minty Alley*. Before a Rutgers University audience in 1973, James claimed, "This is 1928. I haven't the faintest idea of any political or social relations, I am just writing a story" (16–17). Only hindsight, he would have us think, enables him to describe *Minty Alley* (in the same speech) as "the relation between the black middle class and the black plebeian class." The idea that he was not politicized when he was seriously writing fiction is one that also gains credibility from autobiographical statements James makes in *Beyond a Boundary* (1963). But James's autobiographical voice is frequently inconsistent and untrustworthy. Indeed, before we accept James's idea of himself as a political ingenue in 1928, it is useful to remember that around the all-male, *Beacon* Group dockworkers were mobilizing, Caribbean migration to the United States, Britain, and other Caribbean islands was high, the Russian Revolution had dethroned the czars, and Marcus Garvey's Universal Negro Improvement Association (UNIA) and Back to Africa Movement had peaked in the mid 1920s. So, even though James myopically remembers himself as disconnected from an understanding of political and social relations, it is impossible to imagine that he was both unaware and unaffected by these world events, particularly as *Beacon* and *Trinidad* colleagues like Albert Gomes were more actively involved in them. In her introduction to Gomes's autobiography, *Through a Maze of Colour*, Rhonda Cobham writes that "the circle of young artists and liberals who gathered around James, Mendes and Gomes during the *Beacon* years was probably unique in Trinidad society of the time" (iii). Cobham goes on to quote Gomes, in reference to the bohemian outlook of the *Beacon* Group: "The great thing about our little *Beacon* society was the way it cocked a snook at the larger society mocking its stratified conventions in deed as well as in word.... Racial and colour barriers certainly weren't reproduced there. The only criterion was a common bond of shared convictions—and, of course, identification with the magazine and its general approach" (iii). These are the complex circumstances James existed in as he conceived and wrote *Minty Alley*.

James's political consciousness was not undeveloped or nonexistent when he was writing fiction, rather it was in the process of development, a process that would necessarily continue and evolve over his lifetime. His fictional work demonstrates *a* politics at work; a specifically middle-class political perspective pervades *Minty Alley*; this perspective is most clearly evidenced by the fact that James places himself at the novel's center: "The novel that I wrote I made the hero of the novel, not the hero but the chief character, myself at the age of about 18—knowing nothing, ignorant, my head full of books, and I go to these people who are not so much proletarian but they are plebeians, they live the ordinary life" (Rutgers 17). It is not that James was apolitical or had no ideas of politics, rather *Minty Alley*, through its specific organization as a bildungsroman, and the choice of Haynes as the central character, reflects the dialogue or interplay between James's Trinidadian middle-class orientation and his desire to enter into a conversation with the working class.[11]

Reinhard Sander identifies this early stage in James's process of political development as not only common among the Trinidad intellectual elite but also a process that begins, for this group, in childhood. In *Trinidad Awakening*, Sander charts the likely development of James's class consciousness in Trinidad:

After leaving elementary school, James would have had little direct social contact with lower-class black Trinidadians and would probably have had only a superficial knowledge of their African-derived culture. Few middle-class, black West Indians questioned the cultural bias of their orthodox education. They saw the masses of ignorant, uneducated people around them as deserving of their sympathy and guidance, but they would hardly have considered such people capable of teaching them anything in the way of moral or cultural values. When as a young man and member of the intellectual group around *Trinidad* and *The Beacon*, James began to look more closely at the lifestyle and values of the lower class, he had to deal with the inherent ambivalence in his attitude. The relationship between the educated black man and the uneducated black masses is a recurring preoccupation in his early writing. (92)

It is important to remember that in 1928 James the aspiring novelist camped out in a working-class community, had read widely, but had not yet formally encountered the doctrines of Marx, Hegel, Lenin, or Trotsky. That exposure would come later, after James emigrated to England in 1932. His understanding of how class structured his life and his Trinidadian society, therefore, was not yet as intellectually sophisticated as it would eventually become. For that reason, it is possible, though inaccurate, for him to make the statement "I am just writing a story." Clearly, the politics of class permeated his West Indian boyhood. Born into the "brown-skinned middle classes" in 1901, James was expected to become a civil servant, and he surprised many by not pursuing a university degree. His educated father and mother struggled for economic stability most of their lives. James spent his young adulthood teaching secondary school, working as a cricket journalist, and fashioning himself as a creative writer. Thus, as Sander implies, writing *Minty Alley* is part of the process of James beginning to recognize and understand his own class position and privileges as he began to engage the complexities of class-based politics.

Additionally, in order to accept as true the idea that James fashioned *Minty Alley* from an authorial position of political naivety one would have to ignore James's literary studies as a youth and as a young adult. In *Beyond a Boundary*, James declares, "I laughed without satiety at Thackeray's constant jokes and sneers and jibes at the aristocracy and at people in high places. Thackeray, not Marx bears the heaviest responsibility for me" (47). In addition to Thackeray, James read Dostoevsky, Tolstoy, Chekhov, Flaubert, Hemingway, Dickens, and Faulkner (71). These writers (and others) were James's first tutors in the ideology of literature as a means to comment upon and represent society and the foibles and crises of its social classes.

Thus, before he even sat down to write *Minty Alley*, literature (especially the novel form) was for James an expressive medium intertwined with, indeed inseparable from, the act of (political) critique and analysis of the world in which writers lived. The bildungsroman is a form James would not return to himself, yet his use and valuation of literature and narrative to make extended commentaries on class, politics, and the revolutionary transformation of society remain critical aspects of his work and must be recognized as such—what Cynthia Hamilton has identified as a "Jamesian" rejection of intellectual fragmentation (442). As a fiction writer and as a member of the *Beacon* Group, James participates in creating a new literary politics even as he is writing against the cultural politics of colonialism. As author of *Minty Alley*, however, he exposes his own entanglement in the web of colonial subjectivity: he is unable *not* to behave as a member of a privileged group; he is unaware of a need to create a multivocal or dialogic narrative. As I discuss in chapter 5, even as James develops into a political theorist and underground socialist activist, there persists in his own actions the tension between idealizing and advocating the collective and yet writing and behaving as an (elite) individual. To return to the Whitman quote I began with, *Minty Alley* establishes the Jamesian notion of literature as a form of politics and also articulates a usefully unresolved tension between acting as an individual and acting as a community. Aldon Lynn Nielsen corroborates this idea when he writes:

> The other themes that pass through all of James's texts, not only the literary works, but also his studies of history, his work in radical theory and his examinations of popular culture, are the relationships between the one and the many. . . . We will see that he always has an eye on the question of how the intellectual relates to the masses of the people, how the individual in society is formed by a culture and in turn transforms the culture of which he or she is a part . . . The most important question in all of James's work, though, is how the masses of the people form the conditions of possibility for the future. (*Critical Introduction* xxvi)

By showing how James's aesthetics of creolization works within his fiction we can begin to erode the arbitrary line of demarcation that has been drawn between James's literary and political personas. In the past, such lines of demarcation (ironically encouraged by James's own claims to have had discrete periods of development) have served as a convenient way to manage and engage James's complicated, diverse contributions to twentieth-century thought. They simultaneously suggest, however, that when James took off his fiction hat and put on his historian hat or took off his cricket commentator hat and put on his Trotskyist hat, there was no contaminating residue of one discrete category affecting the next.

Finally, we have to dispense with the notion that the 1920s were a period when all James wrote or published was fiction. Around the same time as he wrote Minty Alley he researched and wrote The Life of Captain Cipriani: An Account of British Government in the West Indies, in which, as the title suggests, he creolizes the traditional idea of biography, and makes it an occasion to examine the political apparatus of British Caribbean colonialism in the 1920s. Grimshaw describes Cipriani as a project "focused upon a local figure, Captain Cipriani, whose career James analysed as reflective of more general movements among the people of the Caribbean" (Reader 4). James's interest in Arthur Cipriani was generated both by the latter's achievements as an individual and by Cipriani's work to facilitate political autonomy for the disenfranchised nonwhite Trinidadian majority. Thus, Cipriani exists as both a biography and as a critique of the Crown Colony political system that defined Trinidad and Tobago's relationship with England. Like Minty Alley, however, Cipriani is not published until James emigrates to England. In 1933, newly resident in Northern England, James reduced Cipriani by 75 percent and published the short version as the influential pamphlet, "The Case for West Indian Self-Government." Thus, the novel and the pamphlet, conceived and published within similar time frames, exist as additional evidence that refute characterizations of James as apolitical during what has come to be known as his "literary period," the 1920s. Minty Alley's apparent lack of an internalized political and historical context is partially explained by the fact that James was "practicing" how to write a novel and simultaneously writing Cipriani. As he would later do in his studies of the Haitian Revolution, James found a way to articulate a comprehensive discourse across generic mediums.

James's subject position as a middle-class author using the working class as "material" encodes a set of silences and points out some political disadvantages of choosing the microcosmic approach in his depiction of urban Trinidadian life. The matters of colonial government, independence, nation formation—all issues of the day as Minty Alley was being written and in the eight years that would lapse before it was published—are subsumed to the interpersonal, private relations of the Minty Alley residents that reveal James's selective definition of social realism. James is unable to sustain Maisie as a character who integrates the mind and the body because of his own acculturation within the Trinidadian middle class and within the discourse of masculinity that charted thinking, and more specifically thinking as an avenue towards change, as an exclusively male activity. James falters in his attempt to critique the middle class because his questioning of Haynes's position relies upon demeaning the Minty Alley residents and narrating their inability to lead themselves; James generally portrays their conflicts as petty and internecine.

Nevertheless, *Minty Alley* succeeds in its disruption of certain cultural norms of respectability and convention as it expands the terrain of Caribbean literary production. For instance, as writer and critic Merle Collins notes, James's inscription of Trinidadian English into a literary text stands uncontested as a major transformative act within Caribbean literature. Nevertheless, James cannot ultimately free himself from the binary class oppositions imposed through a mind/body split. In 1928, James could not yet articulate how communities such as Minty Alley were implicated in even as they were disenfranchised from the formal political structures of the island. He brings Maisie and Haynes together for a relatively brief encounter within the environs of Minty Alley only to separate them more completely at the end of that encounter.

Minty Alley has received a small portion of the attention accorded other James texts; for instance, until late 1997 it was never published in the United States. To be sure, this critical neglect is compounded by the fact that fiction comprises such a small part of James's prodigious publications and collected (if unpublished) writings. But his three and a half short stories and one novel are disproportionately important. Fiction is a foundation of James the writer and the thinker. What Nielsen and others have begun and what I hope to continue is to actively connect his fiction and nonfiction; to understand his goals as a fiction writer as implicit in, rather than simply antecedent to, his development as a Marxist thinker and to the larger category of Caribbean studies. Ironically, by engaging James's fiction, his work can be decompartmentalized and emerge as a loosely integrated whole; his fiction can be seen as paradigmatic of the later studies he makes as a Marxist historian, political theorist, and cultural critic. Having delineated some of the ways in which James valued fiction and narrative exposition as a means of political praxis, we have also begun to engage James's usefully uneven aesthetics of creolization. In the next chapter I will discuss how James continues to prioritize fiction and narrative as he develops a creolist approach to leadership questions in North American contexts. Richard Wright's monumental *Native Son* (1941) is just one in a series of novels that James calls upon to help him discuss sea changes in the political landscape and development of mass-based, anti-totalitarian political formations. In chapter 5, I will discuss the citizenship debts James attempted to pay with the currency of Melville's *Moby Dick* and how that failed transaction speaks to the practical if not theoretical failure of James's creolist methodologies at the end of his American sojourn in 1953.

The quote with which I opened this chapter captures the dialectical process within which James is immersed. His attempt, sometimes conscious sometimes not, to articulate his ideas about society from his own multiple subject positions is revealed in the way he constructs *Minty Alley* from the perspective of an individual yet with a sense of the collective. The significations of *Minty Alley* as a novel also introduce a set of discourses, as opposed to a set discourse, which also usefully shift over time. Where *Minty Alley* falters we are able to glimpse the insidious dangers of form. Yet, James's reliance on the bildungsroman form can be read as analogous to the adoption of two-party nation statehood chosen by so many West Indian countries at independence. Both forms, though undeniably conservative and bourgeois, are nevertheless not impervious to subversion and sometimes produce decidedly radical and revolutionary progeny. Indeed, James's attention to vernacular language, to creolized communities, to the ways class, gender, and race shape those communities, all continue to merit the attention of Caribbean novelists, historians, and politicians alike.

FACTIONS AND FICTIONS

CONSIDERATIONS OF THE "NEGRO QUESTION"

> The novelist does not only explore what had happened. At a deeper level of intention than literal accuracy, he seeks to construct a world that might have been; to show the possible as a felt and lived reality.
>
> George Lamming, *In the Castle of My Skin*

George Lamming's words penned in the 1983 introduction to his classic novel of 1953, *In the Castle of My Skin*, speak to some of the power held by novelists writing from anticolonial positions. James recognized and called attention to that particular reservoir of power at different points of his career. In this chapter, I examine James's views on the "Negro Question," his reliance on specific narrative techniques to express these views, and his usage of a creolist methodology to compose new and revise more standard Leninist responses to the query. This discussion places James in conversation with Richard Wright, who approached the question of black struggle with a similar combined reliance on politics and fiction; who, as a friend of James, shared many of the same concerns; and who, like James, eventually chose a path that diverged from the dominant arteries of the formalized Left in 1940s America.

Citing Frantz Fanon's debt to the Marxist dialectic of subject and object in his discussion of the struggle between the colonizer and the colonized in *The Wretched of the Earth*, Edward W. Said depicts such circles of influence as "the partial tragedy of resistance, that it must to a certain degree work to recover forms already established or at least influenced or infiltrated by the culture of the empire" (*Culture* 210). In chapter 3, I demonstrated how James uses the bildungsroman, a form already established by the empire, to fashion an insurgent if not wholly radical narrative. In this present chapter's focus on the "Negro Question," I use James and, to a lesser extent, Richard Wright to observe a similar intellectual transaction: Wright and James seek to refashion (in contrast to the American Communist Party [CP] and Socialist Workers Party concepts) the ideologies of the "Negro Question" from a black U.S. perspective. I find, however, less tragedy than optimism on the part of James, and ire on the part of Wright. In pulling away from the dominant organizations of the American Left, each man articulates divergent visions for America's radical future. I argue that both James and Wright drew from their migratory and racialized experiences to and within America to construct their ideas of mass leadership and the potential of the black American masses to lead themselves. Migration as autobiographical experience for James and Wright becomes another opportunity to observe a technology of creolization at work. At the close of the chapter, I present brief, strategic detours into Lamming's *Castle* and Paule Marshall's novel *Brown Girl, Brownstones* (1959) to highlight how migration facilitates black U.S./Caribbean conversation in the 1940s and 1950s and also keeps a creolist aesthetic at work in this present project. Wright and James each provide important insight into how nation and belonging, citizenship and interpersonal relationships, in concert with radical politics and individualistic tendencies were charted through "black" masculinist personas at midcentury.

James and Wright use different perspectives to reach similar conclusions about the "Negro Question." By the time James turns to the question of the American Negro, under the auspices of Trotskyism, he has already moved through an initial critique of Marxist ideology and is therefore better equipped than Wright to recognize the specific, organic values of Negro revolutionary struggle. The personal position of James as an outsider, away from any notion of "home" himself, suggests a need to understand these movements locally as a means to articulate a theoretical home for himself within America. Wright's "insider" status as an American Negro inevitably places him on the outside of and alien to mainstream America—hence his relief at finding a community that extends beyond the confining borders/ideologies of the United States.

C. L. R. James's contributions to the subject form a key axis of his (evolving) philosophy of revolution, itself explicitly connected to Negro struggles within and beyond the Americas. In this chapter I look carefully at James's ideas regarding the "Negro Question" in relation to three things: his eventual movement away from Trotskyism and the idea of a vanguard party as necessary for the development of proletariat formations; his usages and promotion of the novel as an effective means of expressing the most progressive ideas in a society at a given moment; and finally his overall optimism about America. Embedded in his discussions of the "Negro Question" are clues to this distinctive optimism.

This chapter, as well as chapter 6, acknowledges how James's theorizations about U.S. racial politics and black identity were formed out of constant dialogues with key U.S. figures; in the 1940s one of the most significant was Richard Wright. In making such comparisons I attempt, first of all, to add to the body of scholarship that accentuates the porousness of national borders in investigations of black identities and black epistemologies.[1] More specifically, such comparisons intend to provide specific evidence of convergences in West Indian and black U.S. perspectives on North American racial politics as one way of locating transient creolist methodologies. James's presence in America during the World War II and the Cold War eras places him in conversation with a host of black male intellectuals who share concerns about Marxism, revolutionary struggle, Pan Africanism, and political organization in the United States, the Caribbean, Africa, and Europe.[2] I have chosen to read James and Wright together because of their similar political perspectives but divergent personal actions and writing projects in the 1940s and early 1950s.

Other links between Wright and James include their friendship and the friendship between their families. Another is the absence of any sort of real or manufactured rivalry between them that might have been constructed as a West Indian/black U.S. antagonism, or a CP/SWP antipathy. James and Wright met in 1944, after Wright had broken with the CP but before James left the Workers Party (WP) for the SWP (in 1947). Soon after they met they discussed at length possible collaborative projects, none of which actually came to fruition. Their friendship developed nonetheless and extended to their respective spouses; Constance Webb (James's second wife) would eventually gain Wright's permission to write his first biography. In the 1940s James's SWP political activities were equaled in magnitude only by the total obscurity of his life to American people, including black Americans. On the other hand, Richard Wright was known throughout the world. Their involvement with Pan-Africanism (although not chronologically parallel) is also integral to each man's rejection of dominant Marxist organizations as mediating devices for either their politics or their intense relationship with America.

The Background

When James went to England in 1932 his involvement in socialist politics was guided and encouraged by his friend and fellow Trinidadian Learie Constantine. Aligning himself with the Trotskyists, James quickly distinguished himself as a public speaker. In 1938 he was asked by James P. Cannon, leader of the SWP to travel to America to help organize strategy and embark upon a lecture tour focused on what was called at the time the "Negro Question." While Worcester suggests that the invitation was prompted by Trotsky himself (Worcester, *C. L. R. James* 50), Grace Lee Boggs recalls that the invitation was delivered by James P. Cannon to James at a Trotskyist conference in Europe. She writes that the tour was also to give "members a sense of what was happening in Europe and at the same time help the party develop a position on the Negro struggle" (47). One of the principle theses of *JacobinsH*, as I detail in chapter 2, interprets the San Domingo Revolution as a proletarian movement, one influenced as much by the French Revolution as the French were by it. Haiti's success, James claims, is all the more significant because it occurred without a vanguard party. James would go on to extend this idea, of an un-vanguard, to contemporary and historical struggles by black people in the United States.

During his first two years in the United States, James lectured and traveled widely from his base in New York City. Early in his visit, he traveled to Mexico for conferences with Trotsky. However, once his six-month visitor's visa ran out, James was forced underground, and his travels became more circumspect, though they did not cease. During his American period, James moved through, critiqued, and helped create new Marxist organizations. In 1940 he participated in a split from the SWP, joining the newly formed Workers Party. The split was occasioned by some members' disagreement with the Hitler-Stalin pact of 1940 and Trotsky's support for "the unconditional defense of the U.S.S.R."

Within the WP and later, in a different offshoot, the Johnson-Forest Tendency (JFT), James would, with his colleagues, conduct what Grimshaw and Hart describe as "a disciplined search for a coherent Marxist position" relevant to the realities of modern American life (*American Civilization* 11). James created and co-led the JFT with Raya Dunayevskaya and Grace Lee (later Grace Lee Boggs). Operating out of New York (and years later from Detroit), the JFT was James's home base for the duration of his American period. James's search for a "coherent" Marxism involved, among other things, an intensive study of the Soviet Union and Hegelian dialectics resulting in several coauthored publications, including *The Invading Socialist Society* (1947) and *State Capitalism and World Revolution* (1950) (*American Civilization* 12). From the beginning and nearly for the duration of his fifteen years in America, the "Negro Question" would occupy James in dialogue with his work toward reformulating Marxist theories of revolution. By the early 1950s James was fighting against deportation from a country in which he discerned great political and social potential and in which, through his family, he had an emotional investment. Conversely, Wright, taking his family with him, relocated to Paris in 1947 with a different vision of and a disinvestment from America as a place where he could function as a radical activist writer. Their opinions, in short, are characterized by a consistent optimism on the part of James—what Kent Worcester has described as "heroic expectations"—and by an equally strong pessimism felt by Richard Wright.[3]

The Negro Question

The idea of a "Negro Question" has been an aspect of American discourses of politics and change at least since the wide scale adoption of Africans as the labor force of choice in the early years of the American and Caribbean colonies. Since then, it has been notably debated as a topic of abolition movements and as a component of various ideologies voiced during the Reconstruction period after the American Civil War. As a point of specific concern within party policy the "Negro Question" was also a regular agenda item from the 1920s within the CP, the SWP, and the WP. As Cedric Robinson outlines, "In 1920, and again in 1921, Lenin had indicated disappointment in the direction and organizational priorities established by the American Communist Party. He suggested further that Blacks should play a critical role in the Party and in the vanguard of the workers' movement since Blacks occupied the most oppressive sector of American society, and were clearly to be expected to be the most angry element in the U.S." (*Black Marxism* 303–4). This is the basis for what has been subsequently referred to as "The Negro Question"—the query centered on how best to incorporate the black masses into the greater Communist plan. At the Fourth Congress of the Communist International in 1922, the Comintern presented a formalized idea about policy toward American blacks (304). At this Congress, a Negro Commission (whose members represented an international perspective) was established and a thesis on the "Negro Question" was put forth which established, among other things, "the necessity of supporting every form of Negro Movement which tends to undermine capitalism and Imperialism or to impede their further progress" (as quoted in Robinson 305).[4] This necessity then became the outline of James's duties when he traveled to the United States in 1938. His work would range far more widely than the "Negro Question," but it was an issue that he would continually circle back to and write about for at least a decade.

The foundations of James's optimism in the black masses and potential for revolutionary action within the United States permeates his writings during this period. Of course, an important antecedent for his optimism was his own development between 1932 and 1938 into a socialist and Pan-Africanist. James arrived in America with a worldview most recently shaped by collective activism of these campaigns (launched from the International African Friends Service Bureau [IAFSB] with colleagues such as George Padmore and Amy Ashwood Garvey,) by further ideological development as a revolutionary socialist, and by his individual work as a radical historian epitomized in *The Black Jacobins* and *A History of Negro Revolt* before sailing for the United States.[5] While *JacobinsH* is important for understanding James's conceptualization of the black masses as making their own leaders, *A History of Negro Revolt* crucially situates black U.S. struggle in a global context. Linking the San Domingo rebels with black soldiers who fought for their own freedom in the U.S. Civil War, James writes, "Slavery degrades, but under the shock of great events like a revolution, slaves of centuries seem able to conduct themselves with the bravery and discipline of men who have been free a thousand years" (*History* 62). Asserting how Pan-Africanism is inclusive of the United States, he writes, "Thus the San Domingo revolution, the abolition of the slave trade in 1807, the emancipation of the slaves in 1833, and emancipation during the Civil War in America, all these events are but component parts of a single historical process" (60). Wright, who was similarly optimistic about the contributions that could be made toward radical change and cultural advancement by black U.S. writers, was himself building upon the momentum (though negatively assessed) occasioned by the Harlem Renaissance and the Russian Revolution.

When James met with Trotsky for a series of conferences in Coyoacan, Mexico, the Trinidadian's recommendations proceeded from his work as a Pan-Africanist and offered a preview of the specific work on "the Negro Question" that he would conduct over the next decade. James outlined to Trotsky his thesis that independent black struggle is a powerful force of its own and in its revolutionary actions has proven throughout history that a vanguard party is not required (Buhle, *Artist* 63). He was further able to convince Trotsky to consider this concept in terms of the specifics of black American struggle. James's essay "The Revolutionary Answer to the Negro Problem in the United States" (1948) is a continuation of similar themes engaged by James in both versions of *The Black Jacobins* and in *A History of Negro Revolt*.

The Rhetoric of Autonomy

In "The Revolutionary Answer to the Negro Problem in the United States," as in his earlier discussions with Trotsky, James asserts that the most pressing task for socialist organizations in the United States was *not* to recruit black people, *not* necessarily to construct a "black platform"—as the Communist (Stalinist) party did; the most pressing task was to vigorously support but not necessarily infiltrate or incorporate black struggles but rather to allow them to develop in the organic direction they themselves had already developed and would continue to chart. In his interpretation of Lenin, James stated that by "their agitation, resistance and the political developments that they can initiate, black people can be the means whereby the proletariat is brought onto the scene" (McLemee and Le Blanc 182). James saw the independent Negro movement "logically, historically and concretely headed for the proletariat" (McLemee and Le Blanc 185). As Buhle reminds us, James insisted that "the American working class was not backward by true Marxist standards" ("Marxism" 64). In other words, in a radical departure from Marxist/Leninist doctrine, black struggle, indeed all proletarian struggle, did not require a vanguard to lead them, the black masses would, could, and should *lead themselves* through organic struggle as demonstrated in San Domingo and other rebellions in the United States. Therefore, James asserted, the work of any socialist organization was first to educate themselves about the issues that the black community defined as its most pressing and then to devise ways to be supportive of those struggles and, finally, to realize that in such a show of alliance and solidarity, not leadership or infiltration, the black masses would find their way to socialism and class struggle. James gathers these ideas together in "Revolutionary Answer."

Turning to the text of "Revolutionary Answer," I quote at length in order to highlight James's rhetoric of optimism or, as Kelley phrases it, "James's incredible faith in the masses."

We say number one, that the Negro struggle, the independent Negro struggle, has a vitality and a validity of its own; that it has deep historic roots in the past of America and in present struggles; it has an organic political perspective, along which it is traveling, to one degree or another, and everything shows that at the present time it is traveling with great speed and vigor. We say number two, that this independent Negro movement is able to intervene with terrific force upon the general social and political life of the nation, despite the fact that . . . it is not led necessarily by either the organized labor movement or the Marxist party. We say number three, and this is the most important, that it is able to exercise a powerful influence upon the revolutionary proletariat, that it has got a great contribution to make to the development of the proletariat in the United States, and that it is in itself a constituent part of the struggle for socialism. (McLemee and Le Blanc 180)

James's optimistic assessment of current independent Negro struggle assigns to it an inherent value that reaches beyond forming a contained response to the class-based oppression of blacks. James successfully implicates black people in each and every U.S.-based revolutionary movement.

The analogy that James draws between black liberation movements and the American Revolution coupled with his rhetorical strategies suggests an overt, even deliberate, link with nineteenth-century abolitionists. Using such literary devices as alliteration and repetition, James the essayist highlights the word "independent" in association with black Americans no less than three times. He uses the word "struggle" four times and, through alliteration, he focuses the reader on the words "vitality," "validity" and "vigor." Later in this piece (in a recycling of the second chapter of *A History of Negro Revolt*), James tracks black contributions to all American struggles including the Revolutionary War and the Populist movement. When he states that the independent Negro movement "is able to intervene with terrific force," "it is able to exercise a powerful influence," and finally, "it is in itself a constituent part of the struggle for socialism," he adorns black people with a mantle of authority and strength in their ongoing struggle for power and enfranchisement in the United States. In a response to both the received wisdom of the SWP and the white capitalist power structure of America, James rejects the notion of "minority" and he shirks a posture of oppression in his assessment of what role(s) black Americans might play in their own self-liberation. James's optimism about U.S. black revolutionary vitality is reiterated by other black Caribbean intellectuals. In *Black Skins, White Masks* Frantz Fanon generalizes that black Americans fought for their liberation while (with the exception of Haiti) Caribbean people had it conferred upon them. And, as I will discuss later in this chapter, the character Trumper, of *In*

The Castle of My Skin (by George Lamming), acquires his notion of black solidarity and race pride in the United States.

James envisioned a trajectory for black Americans of concrete activity leading to what Worcester calls a discovery of their collective power and eventual recognition of "natural allies" in their struggle (*C. L. R. James* 73). While these "natural" and "future allies" might turn out to be a branch of the SWP, James's deliberately open-ended prediction signals his understanding that part of the power of revolutionary activity and its potential success lies in its unpredictable workings. In this sense, we observe the force of James's rejection of vanguardism; he insisted that "the masses" would best lead themselves and in their self-activity learn what needed to be known about class politics and socialism. As Buhle and McLemee have noted, James's position on independent Negro struggles was quite radical even within the ranks of radical politics. Nevertheless it was a position that James convinced Trotsky to adopt.

Despite his articulate advocacy of independent Negro struggle within America, it was not until James arrived in the United States that he fully comprehended or confronted racism and its discriminatory effects (*C. L. R. James* 57). This relatively late exposure to America's distinctive racial politics is an important difference between James and Richard Wright and suggests a partial explanation for their respective optimism and pessimism regarding revolutionary struggle within the United States. As James's fiction, his *Beacon* collaborations, and his early agitation for West Indian and African independence all indicate, he recognized and understood multiracial alliances as an organizational advantage and while in America himself worked in the multiracial cohort of the Johnson-Forest Tendency. Able to contextualize broadly America's black/white racial divide, James theorized U.S. black struggle and nationalism from a global standpoint and interpreted the status of black struggle in the 1930s and the 1940s as part of a long history of global black revolutionary agency. Again, this standpoint suggests some of the reason that he could see the potential for a massive U.S. black revolution in the same group of people whom Wright assessed as a dormant mass in need of awakening in his 1944 essay "I Tried to Be a Communist."

The "Negro Question" in Dialogue with Wright's Fiction

Although his IAFSB experiences and authorial successes allowed James to arrive in the United States as both a catalyst and chronicler of change, as a private citizen James was at a palpable disadvantage to Wright since now, as a mature adult, he (James) had to adjust to the racist Jim Crow system within which Wright had come of age. This shift in sensibility and subjectivity was profound and "although James did not abandon his primary emphasis on class and class conflict," asserts Worcester, "his experiences in the U.S. led him to revise—more than once—his conception of the dialectics of class, race and capitalism" (*C. L. R. James* 57). That process of revision is discernible in a range of James's "American" writings but especially so in "Revolutionary Answer to the Negro Problem." Over the course of his career, Wright also progresses in a direction that gradually engages the same dialectical triad. Wright's novelistic depiction of that engagement in *Native Son* arrests James's attention; he was impressed by how well Wright understood the power of race, class, and capitalism to spark extreme self-activity among blacks. For in that novel James, like many thousands of other readers, saw placed before him an extraordinary example of the intertwined nature of racial and class oppression the American Negro was subject to.

In Bigger Thomas (Wright's protagonist in *Native Son*) James identified a "revolutionary pride" manifest in a recognition of his own free will and a determination to fight for his life against his white pursuers (McLemee, "Introduction" 58). Moreover, the work the novel accomplishes in the free market of American publishing crystallizes its metapolitical impact. In his 1941 review of *Native Son*, James opens with the following declaration: "Six weeks after publication, *Native Son*, a novel about a Negro by a Negro, Richard Wright, had sold a quarter of a million copies. This is not only a question of literature. Whatever brings a nationally oppressed minority to the notice of the oppressing majority is of political importance" (McLemee, "Introduction" 55). For James, the novel is important not just for what it says and how it says it but for whom it is able to reach. James locates Wright's achievement in the novel's acute rendition of capitalist forces acting against the black individual: "Black Bigger did the things he did because American capitalist society has made an outcast of the black man. Bigger is not the sinner. He is the man sinned against" (56).

Further using Bigger as a way of recognizing and understanding the masses of American Negroes, James continues, "The majority of them feel as Bigger feels, think as Bigger thinks, and hate as Bigger hates; but they have learnt to suppress it. The flames burn very low, but they are there. Far more powerful stimuli will be needed to make them act as Bigger acted. That is all" (57). In a different review, "Native Son and Revolution: A Review of *Native Son* by Richard Wright,"[6] James asserts with even greater force the imperative to read Bigger as a revolutionary actor and the novel as a revolutionary document explicitly participant in the American national conversation regarding, alternatively, the Negro Problem or the Negro Question. The text, says James, "forces discussion and unwilling reconsideration of the world's number one minority problem, the Negro question in America. . . . The career of Bigger Thomas is a symbol and prototype of the Negro masses in proletarian revolution" (McLemee and Le Blanc 88).

This second review reveals James reflecting upon author intentionality, an act especially relevant to the types of arguments I make regarding creolization as a resistant ethos and as a scholarly methodology employed by James. James declares "irrelevant" the question of whether or not Wright set out to "consciously epitomize Negro revolutionary struggle in the career of Bigger Thomas" (91). James goes so far as to argue that the reader brings to bear on the text his own experience and therefore can often discern meanings, "symbols, parallelism, depth and perspective unsuspected by the creator" (91). Given their similar political perspectives and growing criticism of the leftist organizations the men were connected to, an explanation of their divergent expectations for America focuses the rest of this chapter. Why is it that by 1947 Wright is so determined to leave the United States, but by 1953 James is desperate to stay? In answering this question I move from "The Revolutionary Answer to the Negro Problem" to "With the Sharecroppers" (1941) and then to Wright's "Blueprint for Negro Writing" (1937) and "I Tried to Be a Communist" (1944). Collectively these texts suggest the development of James's and Wright's parallel (although not identical) theses regarding black American revolutionary potential. Indeed, a dialogic relationship between the personal and the political emerges in each man's search for and construction of a total community, which complicates our understanding of the driving forces behind James's high expectations and Wright's profound gloom.

By the mid-1940s Wright was perhaps the country's most visible ex-Communist and its most famous black American (rivaled only by Joe Louis). Born in Mississippi in 1908, Wright grew up and entered adulthood in contexts of extreme racism and segregation; these were the American norm. Migrating to Chicago in 1927, he brought his immediate family and some extended family to live with him and for years, through a variety of jobs, functioned as their sole financial support (Wright, *Outsider* 591 Chronology). In 1933 Wright joined the Chicago John Reed Club, around the same time that he began to imagine himself as a writer. The following year he became a member of the CP. This sequence of events highlights a number of convergences with James: Although the specificities were different, portions of Wright's politicization, like James's, occurred in a revolutionary context predicated on Western European philosophy and experience. In addition, each man used the specific experience of his youth as a platform from which to critique the white Western European premises of party politics and motivate adjustments to fit the needs and history of black people. Both *Uncle Tom's Children* (1938) and *Native Son* bear the hallmark of Wright's involvement with the Communist Party. The publication of *Native Son* in 1940 earned him "instant" and international celebrity, and, although Wright remained a prominent radical, he quit the CP in 1942 because of the constraints he felt party membership imposed upon his creativity.

Like James in his assessment of the Haitian rebels, Wright was able to recognize in black Americans a revolutionary potential akin to and yet more advanced than that of their European comrades. In "Blueprint" Wright cites the historical and material conditions of black American workers as evidence of their revolutionary consciousness. In an invocation of Lenin, he asserts: "The workers of a minority people, chafing under exploitation, forge organizational forms of struggle to better their lot. Lacking the handicaps of false ambition and property, they have access to a wide social vision and a deep social consciousness . . . That Negro workers, propelled by the harsh conditions of their lives, have demonstrated this consciousness and mobility for economic and political action there can be no doubt" (Mitchell 98). In this section of "Blueprint," subtitled "The Minority Outlook," Wright contrasts black workers with the prototypical petty bourgeoisie and makes the claim for black political and social organizations as demonstrating more "strength, adaptability, and efficiency than any other group or class in society" (98). It is within "Blueprint" that we can locate key statements by Wright that sound like James in their affirmation of the potentiality of black U.S. struggles. Both this section and a later section of "Blueprint," "The Problem of Nationalism in Negro Writing," suggest intersections with James's ideas about folklore and revolutionary potential. Wright's textbook application of Marxist philosophy to the U.S. Negro experience attests to the plasticity Wright initially found within Communism and its applicability to black struggle. It also points directly at a key aspect of Wright's revolutionary ideal.

"Blueprint," however, is written to and for writers, not workers. In response to what he perceived as the frivolities of the Harlem Renaissance and the "conspicuous ornamentation" it produced, Wright offers "Blueprint" as a guide by which Negro writers might "stand shoulder to shoulder with Negro workers in mood and outlook." The worker, then, in Wright's construction of society, is more evolved than the intellectual—another point of connection with James and a common Marxist perspective. Even as Wright creates a "blueprint" and is critical of the lack of "intent and design" that have guided earlier epochs of Negro writing, he suggests that writers need to be organically connected to, and that their writing needs to develop organically from and remain devoted to, the lived realities of the black masses. Thus, in Wright's understanding of writing as a didactic enterprise, and as he opines that Negro writing must shift its presumed audience from a white one to a black one, we can discern his aims to rescue writing from a position of ornamentation and shape it into a tool of revolutionary change. As such, "Blueprint" suggests the impossibility of separating the political from the artistic; "Blueprint" itself is as much a political manifesto as it is a literary one. Wright dictates and foresees a "purposeful agency" emanating from what James Baldwin, as the voice of a younger generation, would eventually deride as "protest writing." Wright maintains: "The Negro writer who seeks to function within his race as a purposeful agent has a serious responsibility. In order to do justice to his subject matter, in order to depict Negro life in all of its manifold and intricate relationships, a deep, informed, and complex consciousness is necessary; a consciousness which draws for its strength upon the fluid lore of a great people, and molds this lore with the concepts that move and direct the forces of history today" (102).

Conjoining the exclusion of black writers from the American cultural scene and "the acceptance of this enforced isolation" on the part of Negro writers leads Wright to theorize the importance of integration. "The Negro writers' lack of thorough integration with the American scene, their lack of a clear realization among themselves of their possible role, have bred generation after generation of embittered and defeated literati" (105). He prescribes a solution that requires two points of view: "The ideological unity of Negro writers and the alliance of that unity with all the progressive ideas of our day is the primary prerequisite for collective work . . . By placing cultural health above the narrow sectional prejudices, liberal writers of all races can help to break the stony soil of aggrandizement out of which the stunted plants of Negro nationalism grow" (106).

Wright promotes a Negro nationalism as a stage; its ultimate value, however, resides within its transcendence and as a tool of self-possession for the writer and/or the masses. Wright is harshly critical of nationalism, both Negro and reactionary, if that's all there is. His discussion of nationalism in "Blueprint" points tellingly to his eventual break with the CP and to his eventual exodus from the United States. When he writes, "for the Negro writer, Marxism is but the starting point. No theory of life can take the place of life," he hints at the self-consciousness that guided both some of his later actions as well as his later creative projects (102). Indeed, "Blueprint's" inherent advocacy of a *transnationalism* anticipates one of James's key ideas in *Mariners, Renegades, and Castaways*, to the extent that Wright's invocation of the interdependency of people in modern society offers a distinctly optimistic perspective.

Whereas in "Revolutionary Answer" James writes about black people already having everything they need to revolt and to create their own leaders, Wright suggests that black writers as a group need some serious direction, so that they might facilitate societal change on the scale of a revolution. Wright sees writers and the masses as in need of leadership—a significant difference from James. But, in addition to a posture of hope and faith in the potentialities of the black masses, the rhetorical stance of "Blueprint" suggests that Wright shares with James the conviction that black struggles require both a global and a historical perspective and must work toward an ideal of integration ("Blueprint" 104).

Wright's optimism in "Blueprint" is significant for its "ideal of integration" not only because of his more numerous representations of isolation but also in relationship to his own eventual self-exile and James's desire for an individual integration into American society. Despite their rejection of isolation for integration, despite their idea that black American struggles gain power, currency, and definition from their relationship with similar struggles around the world, and despite their movement away from the binary oppositions created within American racial discourse, neither Wright nor James is yet articulating a creolization ethos.

By examining the autobiographical personas in "With the Sharecroppers" and "I Tried to Be a Communist" I am able to connect the discussion of the revolutionary potential of the black masses to James's and Wright's personal considerations of community. Their own roles as leaders and representatives, though constructed and enacted quite differently, illuminate complex negotiations between the theory and the practice of revolutionary politics as well as between public and private identities.

The Tongueless Masses

The disparity between Wright's lived experience and scribal representations is significant insofar as he is considered by his readers and wishes to consider himself as a representative voice. Despite Wright's advocacy of the black experience as an independent entity in "Blueprint," elsewhere he sees the black experience as a battered appendage of a prejudice-infected American corpus. This sensibility is particularly evident in *Black Boy* (1945), when Wright's autobiographical persona declares that blacks were never allowed to catch the "full spirit of Western Civilization" and collectively lack certain human characteristics: "Whenever I thought of the essential bleakness of black life in America, I knew that Negroes had never been allowed to catch the full spirit of Western Civilization . . . And when I brooded upon the cultural barrenness of black life, I wondered if clean, positive tenderness, love, honor, loyalty, and the capacity to remember were native with man" (45). In *Native Son,* a similar assessment is expressed: community is seemingly impossible because Negro life itself is so stunted by American racism and capitalism.[7] Even revolt seems doubtful inasmuch as the revolutionary potential is located in Max, the white communist lawyer, and not in Bigger Thomas. The short stories of *Uncle Tom's Children*, on the other hand, are less absolute. In "Big Boy Leaves Home," for instance, the community coheres in response to the threat of white racist violence. My point here is that Wright's various perspectives on the notion of black community, its existence, and its revolutionary potential are predicated on a notion of personal experience of specific or systemic white racism. The specificity of Wright's experience raises an important divergence from James's theorizations and marks a moment where the valuation of lived experience (actual or fictional) provides the crucial difference in their perspectives on black American revolutionary potential. Obviously, black culture can be at least two things at once—both barren and potentially revolutionary. Wright's peculiar vision has to do with his combined empirical perspective and historical perspective. The divergence between Wright and James further emphasizes the difficulty in attempting to assess black U.S. culture(s) monolithically or univocally.

Where James found American socialism to be a useful mechanism with which to extend the philosophies he was developing, Wright's involvement with Communism compounded his negative experience of U.S. race relations. Therefore, the development of Wright's lack of hope in the revolutionary potential of the black masses was related to his pessimism regarding *white* racism and was nourished by his bitterness toward the white American majority population.

Wright's essay "I Tried to Be a Communist" describes his initial attraction and eventual disaffection with the Communist Party. While in "Blueprint" Wright would state that "it is through a Marxist conception of reality and society that the maximum degree of freedom in thought and feeling can be gained for the Negro writer," he found the opposite to be true for himself by the time he quit the CP. If we look at "Blueprint" as the theory and "I Tried to Be a Communist" as the lived experience, there remains nonetheless a consistent appreciation by Wright of a collective ethos and a sense that collective action by black people is possible; a similar possibility existed for coalitions with likeminded white people. A significant difference in the two texts is the narrative stance. The use of the first-person autobiographical voice in "I Tried" signals an important shift from the third-person voice of "Blueprint" and reflects a change in Wright's perspective regarding his chosen role as racial spokesperson. In "I Tried" Wright recalls: "It was not the economics of Communism nor the excitement of underground politics that claimed me; my attention was caught by the similarity of the experiences of workers in other lands, by the possibility of uniting scattered but kindred peoples into a whole. It seemed to me that here at last, in the realm of revolutionary expression, Negro experience could find a home, a functioning value and role" ("I Tried" 157). Suggesting the provincialism of U.S. racism, Wright anticipates his own physical move away from the United States and acquisition of a global, Pan-Africanist outlook. Wright credits Communism as revealing a global community in which Negro experience would be valued and nurtured. The revelation is framed not by the needs of the race, as his comments in "Blueprint" are, but by his personal needs; the voice does not assume an authoritarian didacticism as in "Blueprint"; instead it substitutes an overtly personal viewpoint.

Recognizing a palpable naivety in hindsight, "I Tried" contextualizes Wright's goals upon joining the Communist Party. He set himself "the task of making Negroes know what the Communists were," and since he perceived the Communists "in their efforts to recruit black masses" as having "missed the meaning of the lives of the masses, and had conceived of people in too abstract a manner," Wright decided to "try to put some of that meaning back" (121). He determined he would "tell Communists how common people felt" (120). Thus Wright constructed himself as a liaison between blacks and Communists and failed each of these two constituencies. His failures in negotiating these groups reinforced his own ideas about the greater virtues of individual achievement, noting, once he split from the CP, "once again I told myself that I must learn to stand alone" (157). His sense of and need for isolation points to ways in which he found community to be a paradoxical concept, both within and beyond American borders. Indeed, the formation of community was a difficult waterway to navigate simultaneously with radical political formations. For even as Wright surmises that "standing alone" is perhaps his own best bet, he is nonetheless impressed by what the CP was able to do for the incomprehensible Russian folk. The arrogance of the following statement about the Russian masses is mitigated by the sincerity with which he seems to be saying it. He perceives that population as having been "tongueless" before the Revolution: "Of all the developments in the Soviet Union, the way scores of backward people had been led to unity on a national scale was what had enthralled me. I had read with awe how the Communists had sent phonetic experts into the vast regions of Russia to listen to the stammering dialects of peoples oppressed for centuries by the czars. I made the first total commitment of my life when I read how the phonetic experts had given these tongueless people a language" ("I Tried" 130). Wright perceived the Negro masses in America as similarly voiceless and sought to represent them in his writing. Wright functioned more as a representative spokesperson for black America than James would ever have the opportunity to be recognized for. Wright was constructed as a race representative by the majority American culture and also took the role upon himself. Often, because of the constraints of writing under pseudonyms, James functioned more anonymously as a facilitator whose goal was to assist the masses in speaking for themselves.

While Wright was marveling over the "tongueless" masses or trying to explain the Communists to black Americans and vice versa, James, himself a chronicler of the tongueless masses of sorts in *Minty Alley*, had the occasion in 1941–42 to travel to Missouri to cover a local strike action for the Workers Party newspaper. James ended up spending several months in Missouri "engaged in strike support work once the Workers Party had made contact with a handful of black sharecroppers and union activists" (Worcester, *C. L. R. James* 71). James helped these workers to produce a pamphlet, "Down with Starvation Wages in South East Missouri." Of that collaborative effort James boastfully recalls the following:

This is a wonderful piece of work. I'll tell you why. I went down to Missouri and decided that the only thing that we could do, after I'd discussed with them, was to have a strike; the sharecroppers should have their own strike, and it was very successful in fact. But the pamphlet has an importance that must be noted. When the time came for us to have the strike, I called some of the leaders together and said, "We have to publish something, for everybody to read about it." They said yes. So I sat down with my pen and notebook and said, "Well, what shall we say?" So (I used to call myself Williams) they said, "Well, Brother Williams, you know." I said, "I know nothing. This is your strike. You are all doing it, you have to go through it. I have helped you, but this pamphlet has to state what you have to say." . . . And I went through each of them, five or six of them; each said his piece, and I joined them together. (*Spheres* 89)

Despite evidencing the "validity, vitality and vigor" of black American workers fighting for themselves, it is important to take note of the leadership role that James subtly assumes here. *He* is responsible for uncovering the organic power and voice of this group of sharecroppers. *He* literally "joins them together," with the pronoun "them" signifying the workers as well as their words. The attention that James calls to his anonymity, along with the prevalence of the pronoun "I" in his account places a concurrent emphasis on James's role as leader. This is a tendency that attaches to many if not all of James's American "collaborations."

The different sequence of when James and Wright became involved in Pan-Africanism is crucial to understanding their divergent understandings of America's revolutionary potential. Worcester emphasizes the links between Pan Africanism and Marxism as being important to James because "by its very nature Pan Africanism was concerned with linking movements across the diaspora, and with the exchange of ideas, personnel and tactical advice across national and regional boundaries. In this sense Pan-Africanism shared an internationalist character with Marxism" (*C. L. R. James* 37). Whereas James entered the United States with a Pan-Africanist perspective, a perspective that contains a broad notion of community, Wright did not fully gain a Pan-Africanist perspective until he left. Nevertheless, as I have noted in the above discussion of "Blueprint," as early as 1937 Wright recognizes the importance of the black writer avoiding either ideological or nationalistic isolationism. Wright's Communist Party experience contributes to his decision eventually to leave the United States.

Wright's images of hopeless, routed black masses has, over the years, received more critical attention than James's ideas of independently empowered revolutionary masses. The revolutionary potential that James located in U.S. black people was prophetic: the Civil Rights movement and the chain reaction of activism it sparked was a version of the revolution James foresaw (Buhle, "Marxism" 70). Perhaps it was this view of America's revolutionary potential and expectation that made James want to stay in the United States beyond 1953 despite the Cold War and the dashed hopes of many of his comrades and despite a U.S. government that was openly hostile to his ideas and ilk. But James also wanted to stay for highly personal reasons: his second wife and son were in the

United States. Thus, the preservation of a personal community is equally important to James's need/desire to stay in the States. Given Wright's hesitation to recognize any kind of organic future promise in U.S. blacks, it is not surprising that America was a society he finally had to leave *and* one with which he could not help but remain in conflict. This is especially true once we recognize Wright as nonetheless part of a revolutionary movement and as an advocate of a radical agenda; he was a man with a militant vision of black culture and history much like James. While we might read Wright's ideas as trapped in the toosmall compartment of a black-white racial binary, James too is impacted by America's racial dualism. He was transformed into a racialized being; no longer just a radical, he was a *black* radical. James's development is charted differently, perhaps because of his Caribbean background, or his Pan-Africanist and socialist training (a crucial combination) and previous experience of forming alliances across race, class, and gender boundaries. As strategically critical as that background no doubt was, the struggle against colonialism in the Caribbean did not necessarily invoke the same social dynamics as the struggle against racial segregation in the United States.[8]

James and Wright conceptualize America from two variable points of outsiderness; race and nationality inform their divergent understandings of what America is and how America gains meaning. Wright's and James's differing geographical and intellectual migrations affect their understandings of America. They each lay claim, as individuals and as intellectuals, to certain mythologized American tendencies even as they debunk or are betrayed by other such tendencies. An investigation into these events, writings, and occasions for writing show James to be working not in isolation and show his ideas as relevant because they are part of a larger articulation of midcentury intellectuals dealing with the crisis of a rapidly changing society. For James and Wright that change is experienced at the macro-level and group level through such mass phenomena as the CP and migration northward from the South (Wright) and through radio, the comic strip, and Hollywood (for James). It is also, significantly, experienced at the micro-level, in their own personal development. For James, this is figured through his uneasy negotiation of a personal life with Constance Webb and his "professional" family life with the Johnson-Forest Tendency. For Wright, the micro-experience of change is epitomized in his move from South to North and the profound disappointment that move culminates in, in direct opposition to the myth of the American dream of opportunity. The ambivalence these two men express toward leftist politics as a means to alleviate certain injustices and changing society to operate within more humanistic and inclusive registers is at once a formidable connection even as their articulations voice very different critiques. The endpoint, or an endpoint, is a fuller understanding of Wright's pessimism and James's optimism regarding the future of America and the possible fate of the masses and the black masses within it.

Novel Endings

On the frontispiece to the first American edition of George Lamming's debut novel there is the author's name, the announcement of an introduction by Richard Wright, and an epigraph by Walt Whitman that reads, "Something startles where I thought I was safest." In later editions, the introduction is dropped and the epigraph appears on a page to itself and so the reader loses the immediate sensation of seeing Lamming, Whitman, and Wright's names juxtaposed. This shared space tempts the reader with the suggestion of several overlaps and circles of influence, which are in fact elaborated on in the novel: the Caribbean and the United States, the nineteenth century and the twentieth, poetry and prose. Not surprisingly, the reader will not be alerted to the fact that in their commitment to politics and craft, Lamming, Wright, and Whitman are all writers whom James admired and relied upon deeply.

Wright's brief words of introduction capture a key aspect of Lamming's work while connecting the preceding threads of my argument about representation, identity, and self-activity as theorized by Wright and James:

Notwithstanding the fact that Lamming's story, as such, is his own, it is, at the same time, a symbolic repetition of the story of millions of simple folk who, sprawled over half of the world's surface and involving more than half of the human race, are today being catapulted out of their peaceful, indigenously earthy lives and into the turbulence and anxiety of the twentieth century.

I, too, have been long crying these stern tidings; and, when I catch the echo of yet another voice declaiming in alien accents a description of this same reality, I react with excitement, and I want to urge others to listen to that voice. One feels not so much alone when, from a distant witness, supporting evidence comes to buttress one's own testimony. (vi)

Here, Wright is remarking on the global experience of colonialism and a beckoning postcolonialism while reiterating his position that these phenomena be looked at and engaged together, not nation by nation, or even writer by writer. Wright recognizes in Lamming's protagonists (both the characters and their village) a portrait not of Barbadian Negroes or even West Indian Negroes but of "the" Negro in the Western world, as outsider, riven by a Du Boisian twoness and spurred forward by a cruel rationalism:

> Without adequate preparation, the Negro of the Western world lives, in *one* life, *many* lifetimes. . . . The Negro, though born in the Western world, is not quite of it; due to policies of racial exclusion, his is the story of *two* cultures: the dying culture in which he happens to be born, and the culture which he is trying to enter—a culture which has, for him, not quite yet come into being; and it is up the shaky ladder of all the intervening stages between these two cultures that Negro life must climb. Such a story is, above all, a record of shifting, troubled feelings groping their way toward a future that frightens as much as it beckons. (vi, emphasis in the original)

While James may have disagreed with Wright's notion of "ill-preparation," Wright implies that leadership, or even self-direction will operate in fits and starts, and necessarily "grope" toward new models best suited to new unknowable identities. In *Castle* Wright identifies an eruptive crisis of creolization that situates Western blacks between the Scylla and Charybdis of interculturation and acculturation as interwoven by "racial exclusion."

I would like to conclude this chapter with a brief excursion into Lamming's novel and a later work, *Brown Girl, Brownstones* (1959), by Paule Marshall, to excavate an ongoing discourse of creolization that links U.S. and black West Indian notions of black identity with responses to the "Negro Question." Of particular interest is the way these novels discuss how creolized black identities are forged out of the materials and experiences made available through the interaction of black Americans and black West Indians with one another. For both Marshall and Lamming, these fictional representations echo lived realities and portend new types of revolutionary activity at the grassroots level.

In the last pages of *Castle*, when Trumper, a childhood friend of Lamming's protagonist "G," returns to the island from America, he returns with a transformed consciousness regarding matters of race and speaks to G of having found "his people." Confused, G asks "Who are your people?" to which Trumper replies "The Negro race." His confusion compounded, G narrates, "At first I thought he meant the village. This allegiance was something bigger. I wanted to understand it" (295). Allowing his character slowly to comprehend the magnitude of Trumper's discovery, Lamming meanwhile casts that discovery almost as a material resource that Trumper has appropriated and might now exploit: "My people, . . . or better, my race. 'Twas in the States I find it, an' I'm gonner keep it till thy kingdom come. . . . 'Course the blacks here are my people too, but they don't know it yet. . . . None o' you here on this islan' know what it mean to fin' race. An' the white people you have to deal with won't ever let you know" (295). Crudely yet aptly delineating the nature of British colonialism from American racial politics and policy, Trumper's new racial consciousness is artistically represented and emphasized as the passage continues via the invocation of Paul Robeson, or, as Lamming puts it in his 1983 introduction, "The voice of Paul Robeson becomes his weapon" (xlii). "The spool finished and the music followed low and sad at first but rising gradually to a kind of ecstasy. Then the music thinned out and a voice came through deep and beautiful in its controlled resonance. Trumper sat steady, his head bowed close to the box. I had never heard anything like it before. I couldn't remember this spiritual, but I was more concerned about the voice" (294). The last words of the song are repeated by Trumper after the tape has finished, allowing G (the "I" of the passage) to comprehend the words obscured for him by the power of "the voice": "Let my people go." The voice, reveals Trumper, belongs to "One o' the greatest o' my people": Paul Robeson (295). Reinterpreting both his own work and Wright's introduction thirty years later, Lamming affirms and confirms the hopes and predictions James held out for the masses, especially the black masses in America: "Turbulence is at work everywhere, but anxiety does not adequately describe what has been happening with that half of mankind since Richard Wright wrote his introduction. The catapulted ones have become the subject of their own history, engaged in global war to liberate their villages, rural and urban, from the old encirclement of poverty, ignorance, and fear" (xlvi).

Again writing in the 1983 introduction, Lamming muses, "It is interesting for me to reflect on the role which America was to play in shaping essential features of the novel" (xl). America existed as a dream, "a kingdom of material possibilities accessible to all," and yet what Trumper, a migrant laborer returns with is "the startling discovery that his black presence has a very special meaning in the world" (xli). While there is little new about the cross-influences of the Caribbean and America in the contexts of migratory, cultural, and political black communities, the historical moment of midcentury, and the vitality of that moment as perceived by the likes of James, Wright, Marshall, and Lamming, explicitly connects the notion of creolized communities and creolized methodologies to the dawning of the postcolonial, independence, and Black Power movements. It is all the more curious, therefore, and ironic, that this is the moment that race is less centralized in two major works by James, *American Civilization* and *Mariners, Renegades, and Castaways*, and that this is the moment that he is forcibly returned to England. The particulars of this shift in focus and return and the light it sheds on creolization are raised in chapter 5.

In *Brown Girl, Brownstones*, Marshall depicts the lives of Barbadian immigrants to Brooklyn and their lived experience of the Depression, World War II, and the American Dream. At several junctures, but one in particular, Marshall engages the idea of black subjectivity by exploring the conflict and confluences between the tightly-knit immigrant community, their American-born children, and the larger black U.S. community.

At a meeting of the insular, business-minded "Barbadian Association" immediately after the end of World War II, an incident highlights the specific relationship of the association to the U.S.-born black community they have defined themselves in contrast to ("we are destroying the picture of the poor colored man with his hand always long out to the rich white one, begging: 'Please, mister, can you spare a dime?'"). An intense debate is sparked by a member's speech that radically advocates a certain solidarity with black Americans. Claiming a need to change what they call themselves, he cries: "You need to strike out that word *Barbadian* and put *Negro*. That's my proposal. We got to stop thinking about just Bajan. We ain't home no more.... Our doors got to be open to every colored person that qualify" (222, emphasis in the original). This suggestion, by Sealy, does not go down well at all. The association sees itself as providing a refuge for its members, themselves subject to racism and discrimination. It also means to provide its members with a sense of collective purpose and, most important, at least a piece of the American Dream. Such access and collectivity ironically seem to require exclusions of their own. While some members interpret Sealy's words as a form of group betrayal, another member curiously casts his inclusive impulse as an endorsement of Communism (223). The larger point is, however, that Marshall shows this group of ordinary Americans struggling with the "Negro Question" from an angle and subject position that announces its more complex significations even as it reveals discourses of outsiderism and belonging that resonate with those expressed more overtly by Wright and James.

As representative midcentury texts that engage the idea of black U.S./black West Indian cross influences in everyday life, *Brown Girl* and *Castle* join the conversation already in progress between James and Wright about the way West Indian migrants and immigrants to the United States shift the possible meanings of black identity in the United States even as the U.S. encounter simultaneously shifts how identity is understood in the Caribbean. This manifests within theories and practices of leadership in each of the novels and reflects a way in which C. L. R. James appears to have been processing his own ideas about leadership in the United States.

The passage in Marshall's novel crystallizes the central concern of this present chapter, principally: the need to understand C. L. R. James's theorizations on the "Negro Question"—a concern for many decades in the twentieth century of various socialist and Communist organizations—as emblematic of a methodological and transnational creolization reflecting his own struggle to develop new, nonstatic Marxisms.

In their convergent responses to the "Negro Question," James, Wright, Lamming, and Marshall use the novel form to "show the possible as a felt and lived reality." Their fiction and nonfiction constructs the possibility of understanding the "Negro Question" as answerable within several different, progressive registers, at least one of which meshes ideologies of cultural creolization with broadly conceived socialist ideals of the radical self-activity of the masses.

FAMILY**MATTERS**
NATION, FEDERATION, INTEGRATION

We are more and more aware of writing as a place in itself, a destination in art arrived at by way of art. And yet an urge persists to enquire into the inspiration and foundation which place affords in the creative process.

Seamus Heaney, *The Place of Writing*

Seamus Heaney's statement announces the outline and concerns of this chapter: America is a text that James sets out to read; America also affords him an entry into new families that provide him with a series of foundations.[1] In addition to existing as a text and community for James, America becomes the locus out of which he, and his JFT associates, develop a revolutionary Marxism. In "writing" America James "writes" himself; he exposes to his reader his own vulnerabilities alongside his trenchant critique of America's systems of power.[2] In 1953, at the end of his stay in America, James paradoxically arrives at a point of departure from the different families he attempted to construct and negotiate for fifteen years.

In this chapter I continue my discussion of creolization as a methodology employed by James and how it can be understood particularly in *Mariners, Renegades, and Castaways: The Story of Herman Melville and the World We Live In* (1953) as a resistant methodology. Drawing on some of Barbara Harlow's criteria for resistance literature, I contend that *Mariners* "requires both historical referencing and a politicized interpretation" (81). At the same time it "expands the formal criteria of closure and continuity which characterize the ideology of traditional plots" (81). Although Harlow is specifically thinking of narrative fiction, her theories can be extrapolated outward to include *Mariners*, an excellent example of a text that redefines form and defies categorization; its formal peculiarity represents a resistant, creolist construction and conception. "*Mariners, Renegades and Castaways*," writes Anthony Bogues, not only signaled a return to literary theory for James but "also affirmed the new contours of his political theory which were grappling with the new issues from the standpoint of social relations rather than an orthodox Marxist political economy" (154). The struggle for happiness is the specific social relation Bogues refers to, and, indeed, "the struggle for happiness" was the title James intended for *American Civilization*, the unfinished, posthumously published, parent-text, if you will, of *Mariners*. Together, *Mariners* and *American Civilization* will focus my discussion of "family" and "nation" and James's struggle for integration into both of these bodies.

The parallelism of James's consideration of the national family (America), which I extract from *American Civilization*, and his construction of and his participation in his political family (the JFT) and his private family (Constance Webb and their son Nobbie) connect and amplify the structures and theories of James's American period. The obstacles, failures, and disappointments alongside the successes and triumphs of his involvement with these various "families" offer a compelling vision of how James negotiated his individual identity with the identities of the various communities to which he was attached and, eventually, involuntarily detached from. Bogues writes, "James's vision confirms that self-actualisation of the individual was only possible within the context of a relationship to the community and, as he argues, the success of totalitarianism derives from its superficial construction of this total community" (166). In chapters 2 and 3 I outlined the development of the individual within his/her community through the two versions of *The Black Jacobins*, *Minty Alley*, and *La Rue Cases Negres*. At present, my discussion of the individual and community becomes explicitly framed by the paradoxes of James's lived experiences and the linkages those experiences provide to the development of his political and social theories. Arguing against totalitarianism for fifteen years, this brief selection of James's American writings sheds light on his difficulty in constructing a genuine total community for himself.

Initially I focus on one section of *American Civilization*, "Negroes, Women, and the Intellectuals" in order to situate some of James's theorizations of the

American "nation." I then move to a discussion of *Mariners* and James's statements and ideas regarding the concept of "federation." In the face of his theses regarding state capitalism and his recognition of fascism, "federation" appeared to James as a revolutionary process of self-activity without a vanguard. Federation is recognizable in Melville's famous *Pequod* crew and within detainees on Ellis Island, and anticipates the near future of the West Indies. I close this chapter with a discussion of James's ultimate failure to become "integrated" in the national family as a citizen, and I suggest some connections to his changing relations with the JFT and his eventual marital split from Webb. Indeed, what came to be seen as the project of his American sojourn—the integration of the political and the personal lives—does not reach fruition for James (*American Civilization* 14).

Reading the Nation

American Civilization is a book that James never finished and did not intend to publish in the form to which readers now have access. He wrote it quickly, between 1949 and 1950, and circulated it among a small circle of associates, often inserting into the text notes to his readers about ideas that would be expanded or overviews that would eventually become particularized. He wanted it to be a text accessible to the everyday man or woman, a text "no longer than 75,000 words," and a text that could be consumed during a Sunday afternoon (*American Civilization* 278).[3]

Despite the unfinished nature of *American Civilization* readers can still appreciate the vitality of experience from which James drew in order to compose it. In "C. L. R. James in America," Bill Schwarz presents a lyrical summary of the contours of James's life in America that captures the diversity of events, publications, and social activities in which James participated: "When the 1938 cricket season closed James embarked to the USA believing that he'd be back in England the following spring in time for the new season. . . . In the US his existence as a Trotskyist tyro continued. Audiences loved him: they found him charismatic, charming, erotic. He travelled, spoke and wrote with one exception all his published writings appeared under the imprint of far-left organizations, dictated by the immediate concerns of political debate. . . . He was active at various moments in the cultural and political life of Harlem" (178). Connecting James's lived experience to the diversity of James's publication, Schwarz sees *American Civilization* as premised on James's particular insight regarding paradoxical truths. James, Schwarz writes, recognized "that the structure of American Civilization is composed on the one hand by the imperatives of 1776 and the cult of individualism; and on the other, by Fordism and the system of mass production. The crux of his argument is the suggestion that these have now become indistinguishable: happiness has become entirely dependent on mass consumption and thus on mass production" (180).

James reached his conclusions as much from research as from observation and his own experience. In the penultimate portion of *American Civilization*, for instance, there is a deliberate revisioning of his responses to the "Negro Question." Clearly, James was faced with the imperatives of his life circumstances, most acutely his surveillance by the FBI, and made a conscious choice to remove any overtly Marxist language from his analyses. The result is a startlingly different formulation. Cast not as a problem of SWP leadership or strategy, indeed stripped bare of all such organizational baggage, the "Negro Question" becomes a new universal, "the number one minority problem in the modern world" and a "sort of touchstone" (201). America itself is constituted by James as a new universal, and its occupation of a series of powerful contradictions at midcentury propel his analysis throughout the text. "Never before in human history," writes James, "has the antagonism between the sexes; the antagonism between racial minorities; antagonism between the 'educated' and the 'noneducated' been so great as it is today. It is precisely because this is so after a century of 'progress' that modern man is so bewildered" (200).

Whereas James's response to the "Negro Question" as formulated previously was about the independence and vitality of Negro struggle on its own, James's partial assertion of authorial freedom from the exigencies of the party line allow him to frame his response from another angle—the positions of Negroes as unfairly excluded from the American body politic. While this angle is implicit in James's meticulous attention to the history of Negro revolutionary struggle in the United States, the straightforward articulation of this view underscores *American Civilization*'s covert autobiographical contexts; unlike sections of the later *Mariners, American Civilization* does not employ an autobiographical voice. Nevertheless, the narrative reveals the refraction of James's own exclusion from the American body politic, especially in lines that describe what is here formulated as "the Negro problem" as "a question eating at the heart of the American people, not only at its morale and its confidence, adding to the sense of frustration and impotence" (201). Grace Lee Boggs recounts that in America James was subject to "a discrimination much crueler and cruder than anything he had known either in the West Indies or Europe" (56).[4] The desirability of James to the American government is important to understand as derived from his position as a socialist *and* as a black activist, though he might have quarreled with such designations.[5] Indeed, despite James's underground life and status as "pseudonymous radical intellectual" he was much in the public eye. As Nielsen recounts, in America James "wrote regular columns for such leftist newspapers as *Labor Action, Socialist Appeal* and the *Militant*, . . . made frequent speaking tours, sometimes . . . appearing in news items in the black popular press" (160).

But understanding the tensions of James's life and negotiation of the U.S. federal government and leftist political organizations as presented through the concerns of *American Civilization* is not my primary aim in looking at "Negroes, Women, and the Intellectuals." This section of *American Civilization* is important in itself but also as a key element within James's narrative of nation and nationalism. As I will discuss later in this chapter, James makes crucial distinctions between various types of nationalisms. In *American Civilization* he eloquently links America's cult of individualism with its history of a variety of class antagonisms, whether these are classes named as Negroes, women, or workers.

The shift from the "Negro Question" as a query demanding the attention of political organizations wishing to reform society to the "Negro Problem" as a plague that cripples and deforms the nation, and thus demands the attention of the whole populace, stealthily lifts the idea of black people and revolutionary thought from the margins of American consciousness and situates it at the center. By further recognizing the "problem" as generated not from black people but rather as generated from America's inattention to its own Constitution and deliberate failure to redress the "problem," James understands the "Negro Problem" and the inability to solve it through legislative means as perhaps the loudest, most alarming indictment of the bankruptcy of American government at midcentury; and it was on display for the world to see and critique for themselves:

> The Negroes do not seek any special privileges, constitution or statehood. All they demand is freedom and equality. . . . The American government sent segregated Negroes in the army all over the world . . . and thus placed the Negro question squarely before the people of all nations. . . . The Negroes are Americans. There never was a minority which was so much flesh of the flesh and blood of the blood of the majority. . . . To raise the problem of color alone as a barrier to Americanism is to alienate the greater part of the population of the world. (201)

In the powerful imagery James employs in this passage, he succeeds in conveying at once the vulnerability of the American corpus in the context of international scrutiny even as he situates the position of Negroes in America as a broader "question of human relations" (202). Equally evident alongside James's indictment of the American government (and the language in the above passage is muted compared to other sections of *American Civilization*) is James's sense of hope in the ability of the American people, Negro or otherwise, collectively to shift the country in another, more progressive direction. The dialectic of that shift would be the crushing weight of state-sponsored oppression. James's studies of America call attention to potential revolutionary self-activity across a range of American constituencies both fictional and real.

Federation and *Moby Dick*

James wrote *Mariners* in his own defense while jailed on Ellis Island for un-American activities, the culmination of a long period of surveillance. James uses the rhetorical occasion of *Mariners* (his internment on Ellis Island) to offer a veiled critique of U.S. fascism; further, he uses Herman Melville as a nineteenth-century prophet of twentieth-century doom. Read as a continuation of James's optimistic discourse on America, Ellis Island becomes a place where the formation of a genuine total community is possible, even in the face of totalitarian tendencies. At the outset, we can assert that whatever its aesthetic and critical shortcomings, *Mariners* effectively delivers a typically Jamesian optimism regarding the potentiality of working-class struggle and in doing so anticipates the ways in which American grassroots efforts overcome and persist in spite of the Cold War and develop into the Civil Rights movement. *Mariners* can further be understood as a typical James piece in its overt conjunction of his personal experience and desires within broader political contexts and occasions.

Mariners has generally been perceived as among James's least successful works. Indeed in the surge of James scholarship that occurred in the late 1980s and the 1990s, there are but a handful of sustained readings of *Mariners*.[6] James's impulse to turn to canonical literature suggests at one and the same time a continuity of method on his part and a curious meeting point of the various developments in his life between 1938 and 1953. His movement backwards to the nineteenth century for an understanding of the twentieth is a typical expression of James's need for historical context. Such a move also reiterates his reliance on earlier forms (especially those of nineteenth-century dominant cultures) as a way of interpreting his present.

In the slender volume of *Mariners*, James discusses virtually all of Melville's works but spends three of seven chapters on *Moby Dick*.[7] The later chapters, 4 and 5, sweep through Melville's corpus and include discussions of *Mardi*, *Typee*, *Bartleby the Scrivener*, *Pierre*, and *Benito Cereno*, as James charts Melville's creative progression and concern with similar themes throughout his career. *Moby Dick* and its characters remain James's focal point, however, in each literary critique and extensive synopsis of the other texts. In the eighth chapter, "A Natural But Necessary Conclusion" (excised from some later editions), James describes the specific circumstances and hardships of his internment on Ellis Island. As Nielsen phrases it, "out of the crucible of his internment on Ellis Island James created a testament to his own Americanization" (162).

Early in the text James reveals how and why he is drawn to Ahab and sees *Moby Dick*'s 1851 publication date as a lens through which to view the world in 1952. The connection he makes between Stalin and Ahab, the attention that he calls to Stalinism, and the anti-Communist project of *Mariners* in general all alert the reader to the crisis of 1851 as homologous to the crisis of 1952—that is, as a crisis of civilization on the brink of major "change" (*Mariners* 7).[8] In the context of 1952, this is a matter of state nationalism, which James critiques through a reading of the 1952 McCarran Immigration Bill. In doing so he marks the link between fascism and nationalism and emphasizes how nationality becomes racialized. He writes:

> The political organization of Modern Europe has been based upon the creation and consolidation of national states. And the national state, every single national state, had and still has a racial doctrine. This doctrine is that the national race, the national stock, the national blood is superior to all other national races, national stocks and national bloods. This doctrine was sometimes stated, often hidden, but it was and is there, and over the last twenty years has grown stronger in every country in the world. Who doubts this has only to read the McCarran Immigration Bill of 1952, which is permeated with the doctrine of racial superiority. (10–11)

James deliberately yokes the McCarran Bill with the Nazi master race conception as a way of critiquing Western Civilization as a whole (10). Hitler's "final solution," as a theory and an act, asserts James, could be put forth in any and all countries that endorse the type of nationalism described above.

For James the fatality of individualism occurs when it manifests as isolationism; this is Ahab's tragedy: "Ahab is a doomed man . . . Having the highest technical and social achievements of his age under his command, he is completely isolated from them except as they serve his purpose . . . In this final crisis his isolation becomes so complete that he no longer has any sense of relation with other human beings at all . . . He will be soul and brains and spirit, and the rest of mankind will be arms and legs. It is the elite theory of totalitarianism" (70–71). James's aversion to existentialism, expressed so clearly in his assessment of Ahab's "tragedy," underscores his indefatigable desire to exist within a politics that can accommodate individual happiness.

James attempts to read Ellis Island and its prisoners/detainees as analogous to Melville's *Pequod* and crew. He states, "The whole of the world is represented on Ellis Island. Many sailors, but not only sailors; Germans, Italians, Latvians, Swedes, Filipinos, Malays, Chinese, Hindus, Pakistanis, West Indians, Englishmen, Australians, Danes, Yugoslavs, Greeks, Canadians, representatives of every Latin American country" (159). As James continues to draw an analogy between Ellis Island and the *Pequod*, the word "federation" enters his discourse, which is significant in terms of contemporaneous discussion going on in the Caribbean about West Indian Federation.

How can we best understand James's personal desire for individual happiness and an integrated life? The notion of the individual and the community as it is erratically sketched in *Mariners* serves as its own microcosm of James's erratic negotiation of his various individual selves and relationships with communities throughout his American sojourn. I am thinking here of the ever narrowing splits of the SWP; the overwhelming need once he arrived in America to integrate race more overtly into his personal life and political praxis, a project in which he suggests he was aided by Richard Wright as a friend and as a novelist; and his relationship with Constance Webb inasmuch as it offered up its own paradox of "togetherness" as something to be realized emotionally, after a long courtship, though rarely to be realized, at any point, as a physical reality. *Special Delivery*, the collection of James's letters to Webb, suggests how for long periods James and Webb shared a mostly epistolary relationship. There is a homologous relationship between *Mariners* and James's life. The example of *Mariners* suggests that James defined Americanness as a sort of dialectical belonging, in which one's *un*belonging, or outsiderness, becomes a means of integration, a technique of naturalization.

Mariners suggests James had four authorial aims. In order of increasing significance the first three of these aims were acknowledging the brilliance of Melville as a writer, stating the relevance of the themes Melville wrote about in

1851 to the world of 1952, and voicing the contemporary dangers of bourgeois individualism and nationalism, as they engender totalitarianism. Nielsen helpfully points out that James's recognition of the possibility of the development of totalitarianism in America echoes the interpretation of other Melville scholars at the time: "Like many cold war liberals, James tended to read Ahab as a premonition of the totalitarian psychology that has terrorized the twentieth century" (*Critical Introduction* 44). Collectively, the exposition of these three ideas advance the fourth aim of *Mariners*: they implicitly proclaim James's own (acquired) "Americanness" and patriotism. The logic of *Mariners* proceeds from the following set of assumptions: James's ability to recognize the brilliance of one of America's greatest authors, his ability to critique various forms of nationalism and fascism emanating from within the United States as well as from abroad, and finally his ability nevertheless to see America as a country of great revolutionary and social potential would coalesce positively to influence the Immigration and Naturalization Service. (Toward that end, copies of *Mariners* were sent to members of the U.S. Congress.) Nielsen suggests that James's final aim is to present *Mariners* as a kind of primer for Americanness: "The end of James's book on Melville . . . argues that the Melvillian text has made of James an insider, so much so that he produces his readings as evidence of his Americanness, and he believes Melville can serve this function for others as well" (*Critical Introduction* 38). Unfortunately, the random availability of *Mariners* for general consumption virtually eliminated the possibility of it effectively spreading the word of Melville. It is equally ineffective as documentary evidence of James's own Americanness.

While at Ellis Island (a total of nearly six months) James suffered badly from his recurrent stomach ulcers as well as from a distinct fear of his fellow prisoners who were Stalinists. "A Natural but Necessary Conclusion" offers an extended discussion of James's personal hardships as an Ellis Island detainee paired with an astute discussion of different types of nationalisms. The following quote suggests how he understood nationalisms differently—that is, nationalism as an arrogance of "super powers" and totalitarianism, and nationalism as an important component of anticolonial movements (demonstrating there do exist positive and radical nationalisms for James). Connecting the debased nation-state to the unnecessary and cruel exacerbation of his ailment, James writes, "There was not a single person on the island who could not see how ill I was . . . But for Mr. Shaugnessy I could have stayed there until I was once more perforated. Then perhaps would have been the time to consider whether maybe I should be sent to the hospital after all. I was an alien. I had no human rights . . . How to characterize this otherwise than as inhuman and barbarous? And what is its origin except that overweening (sic) national arrogance which is sweeping over the world like some pestilence?" (148). James takes on nationalism at both micro and macro levels by integrating his own story with that of Melville's men, Ahab and Ishmael, and with those narratives of his fellow inmates on Ellis Island:

> This is my final impression. The meanest mariners, renegades and castaways of Melville's day were objectively a new world. But they knew nothing. These know everything. The symbolic mariners and renegades of Melville's book were *isolatoes*, federated by one keel, but only because they had been assembled by penetrating genius. These were federated by nothing. But they were looking for federation. I have heard a boy, a young Oriental, say that he would fight in the war on either side—it didn't matter to him. What he wanted was a good peace, however, he added almost as an afterthought, peace should include complete independence for his own little country. This then is the crowning irony of the little cross-section of the whole world that is Ellis Island. That while the United States Department of Justice is grimly pursuing a venomous anti-alien policy, and in the course of doing so disrupting and demoralizing its own employees desperately trying to live up to their principles, the despised aliens, however fiercely nationalistic, are profoundly conscious of themselves as citizens of the world. (161–62)

This quote helps connect the related discussion of this chapter and chapter 4: the "penetrating genius" at once invokes Ahab but also James himself, not as a fascist but as the organizer, Brother James, showing the Missouri sharecroppers "the way." While it is not clear that the U.S. Congress would pick up on it, James calls attention to the "irony" of Ellis Island: how the U.S. Immigration Service's attempt at breaking human beings, through fascist, unconstitutional internment, actually leads to a leaderless federation of "aliens" and perhaps even a certain solidarity amongst INS agents themselves, as an outgrowth, or dialectic, of their demoralization.

Within the specific American political context of 1953, "integration" as a key term of the burgeoning Civil Rights movement suggests other ways to interpret James's failure to "integrate." For the ideology of integration depended upon a devaluation of the specificity of blackness and a movement of the black subject into the privileged arena of a white cosmos. For a host of reasons, obvious and subtle, the national discourse of integration and its eventual implementation was not conceptualized as an activity whereby white people moved into black schools and neighborhoods or found employment within black businesses. Obversely, many black schools, neighborhoods, and businesses withered under the effects of integration and desegregation. In contrast, the federation desired by James and his fellow inmates not only rejects leadership and vanguardism but is a means whereby these "folk" can preserve the sovereignty of their small states in defiance of the superpowers' desire to subsume them. After leaving the United States, James found his way back to the West Indies and eventually became the secretary of the West Indian Federal Labour Party (WIFLP), working to keep the possibility of Federation alive. This ideal of federation was entertained by the British West Indies between 1956 and 1958, but the tensions between the two "big islands," Trinidad and Tobago and Jamaica, along with other circumstances, made the West Indies Federation a short-lived experience.

To extrapolate broadly outward, then, we might wish to believe, first, that James's desire to stay and be officially integrated into America was delusional and ill-advised. And second, we may wish to believe that James's deportation from the American body politic and expulsion from its shores was an act that helped to preserve his particular creolized identities and his personal autonomy. Unfortunately, neither is true. Even though the gradual dissipation of the JFT and his split from Constance Webb (in 1950) postdated and predated James's exile from America and both had other causes, his forced departure was not helpful to either relationship.[9] Attending to the totality of James's migrations over his lifetime, I am left to agree with St Louis's insight that "James's migration proved both a productive and a sterile experience, with continual relocation ultimately rendering the vernacular rhythms of specific societies inaccessible" ("Perilous 'Pleasures'" 356).

Despite its productive political commentaries and links, in its last chapter *Mariners* is puzzling to the reader. James's particular circumstances as an illegal alien, an individual, and an intellectual at loose ends, at the mercy of a Cold War superpower, collectively make it difficult to comprehend his undiminished ideal of America and the potentialities he perceives harbored within the American masses. *Mariners, Renegades, and Castaways* can be read as the uneasy marriage of the political—in its critique of nationalism, totalitarianism, and individualism—and the personal. It is other things as well; indeed it is most overtly a text of literary criticism, yet this is neither its strength nor, in my opinion, its primary relevance. Its political critique fits into James's corpus alongside texts like *State Capitalism and World Revolution*, *The Black Jacobins*, "The Case for West Indian Self-Government," and "The Revolutionary Answer to the

Negro Problem." In its autobiographical aspects *Mariners* is related to the far more successful *Minty Alley* and *Beyond a Boundary*. But none of those texts convey an immediate urgency comparable to that which motivates James to write *Mariners*: his desire to stay in the United States, close to his family, as well as close to his political family, the JFT.

Family Matters

Whereas Lamming would write about the "pleasures of exile," James's deportation in 1953 from the United States seriously hindered his ability to be a member of his political and private families and exacerbated preexisting fault lines within those relationships. In the best, most proximate of circumstances, his participation in these families often derived from an unreconstructed masculinity, and, as such, gender becomes a useful aspect of identity from which to analyze further James's conceptualizations of citizenship and Americanness; indeed much of the content as well as the context of *Mariners* relies upon negatively feminine constructions of subjectivity. Gender, then, is the means by which I will circle back and conclude my discussion of the relationship between James's "productive failure," his peculiar negotiation and imagining of community within the United States.

James's autobiographical persona in *Mariners* is overtly feminized and curiously domesticated. Although this process is obscured in the first six chapters' discussion of nationalism and Melvillian masculinity, the eighth chapter continues the discussion of totalitarianism and nationalism but filters it through the particular circumstances of James's ill health and detainment on Ellis Island. The tone of the chapter suggests the very cultural stereotype of white middle-class women that James voices in "Negroes, Women, and the Intellectuals": because of his ill health James is in a position of dependency and frustration. In *American Civilization* James characterizes American middle-class white women as not only incapable of radical self-activity because of their biology and the physical constraints of modern metropolitan life but also as wracked by a "personal frustration and anxiety" that never ceases (219). Those emotions more accurately describe the James revealed at the end of *Mariners*, someone himself frustrated and anxious, dependent and powerless to effect the desired shift in his situation. In a letter James wrote to Webb in 1943 we glimpse his future self and concerns: "I have aged a little—grayer in the temples; a little thinner . . . a little more serious, a few lines in my face . . . my hands are more nervous than before, but I am much the same, quieter externally, more explosive inside; and very, very sure of what I am doing politically—of my self as a person, doubtful and more than a little worried as to my future" (*Special Delivery* 71).

While Melville's characters are stereotypically male in their quests and explorations of the world as a means of configuring their individual and national identities, James's desire for incorporation into the American national body is a desire to "stay home," indeed to be granted the domestic spaces of America to call his home, to supersede his status as visitor, outsider, alien. In *Mariners* his desire for incorporation into the national body requires that he re-vision and reconstitute himself as unraced and to a certain extent as demasculinized. It specifically requires that he momentarily disengage from the racial politics he had worked for and within while in America. He needs to deemphasize his own racial subjectivity in order to promote himself instead as "Joe Immigrant" as he petitions the "Land of the Free, Home of the Brave." James's public position of essentially being a supplicant to the state he so consistently critiqued is perhaps responsible for amassing negative critical opinion of *Mariners* as a failed text. His very neediness, which could be read as part of a dominant negative discourse of femininity, does the additional damage of masking the radical and rather virulent critique of American totalitarianism that he writes into the preceding chapters of *Mariners*. This is one of the ways in which James's discourse of the national family is connected to the more intimate discourse of the nuclear family; both beckon to James yet require a difficult and never wholly complete assimilation.

The broader contexts of *Mariners*—James's leadership of the JFT and his relationship with Constance Webb—invite such consideration of James's gendered voice and gendered subject position. The arenas of his political and personal families provided numerous opportunities for James to resist the structures of patriarchy and divisions of labor based upon gender. Notwithstanding his coleadership of the JFT with Raya Dunayevskaya and Grace Lee Boggs, and the scope of the love and work he shared with Webb, it remains the case that these relationships ended in part because of James's inability to intervene radically in his own masculinist presumptions. The dedication to the 1985 edition of *Mariners* alludes to his own belated recognition of his inability to reconstruct his masculinity and represents an effort to prevent his son from repeating his mistakes. In her autobiography, *Living for Change*, Boggs identifies the problematics of James's ego, alongside his leadership practices. She asserts that James's ego was an acute aspect of his split with Dunayevskaya in 1956, and the remaining fragment of the JFT in 1962: "The main reason for the 1956 split, I believe is that CLR underestimated Raya. He treated her as a subordinate, not understanding that she had always seen herself as a co-leader, both theoretically and organizationally, of the Johnson-Forest Tendency. He found it hard to accept that those whom he had mentored had to sink or swim on their own. CLR's misjudgment in this situation was not a momentary lapse. The same pattern would repeat itself time and again" (101).

When we reread *Mariners* this discussion of nation, family, and Americanness is shown to be in conversation with the letters of *Special Delivery*, in which James often struggled to knit together the conflicting strains and interests of his political, intellectual, and private lives. In the hundreds of letters he wrote to Webb he betrays one of his principal flaws: he couldn't easily transfer one of his key intellectual concerns, the importance of representing the individual and the community, to his personal relationships or the way in which he lived. A split James emerges from the letters—one that further connects James to Haynes (of *Minty Alley*) and to Toussaint L'Ouverture—reminding us that as a socialist, revolutionary historian, James nonetheless retained the cliched baggage of a middle-class, West Indian man. Because it only reproduces James's letters to Webb and not Webb's letters to James, *Special Delivery* symbolically casts the relationship as noncollaborative. What James was able to do as an underground activist—act and theorize progressively—he could not achieve on the domestic front, and his marriage to Webb seems to have failed in large part because of his crushingly conventional and patriarchal attitudes toward domestic relationships and home life. My discussion in this chapter of James's efforts at total community has attempted to delineate how James's various political and personal American failures can indeed be read as productive, but the paternalism he expressed and practiced is not so easily papered over.

James's 1953 return to England sets in motion a new series of diasporic wanderings and further encounters with the paradoxes of exile: he will go back to Trinidad, return again to the United States, and visit Africa. In his 1963 essay "Roots" Edward Kamau Brathwaite asks, "So what happens then on this rediscovered island? Does the exile returning to his home find new faith, his roots, some faith in the future?" (*Roots* 33). James's rediscovery of Trinidad, his return "home," is perhaps most productively realized before he arrives, in the discursive return occasioned by writing *Beyond a Boundary*.

James is deported from America but will eventually return many times over.

I most closely connect James's desire for integration into the United States with Brathwaite's vision of creolization enabling the construction of a "whole." Brathwaite's examination of the conflicting and contradictory aspects of the colonial encounter show how *Boundary* also anticipates some of Brathwaite's findings. The "contradictory omens" of James's actions and affiliations in the United States, along with his unmitigated failures, lead nonetheless to the production of a body of work that is more often collaborative than not and facilitate a series of transformative if unsustainable relationships.[10] In this sense James's failures are productive and remain connected to Brathwaite's theorizations through their optimism and goal of transforming society.

While some critics assert that *Mariners* fails as a literary critique of Melville's texts and others note that *Mariners* fails to influence the INS decision to deport James,[11] this chapter is aimed at broadening such assessments of "failure" that are often attached to *Mariners*. Within a creolist model and in the assertion of dialectical development and movement, failure cannot be understood as an absolute and static condition.[12] Not only is the "failure" of *Mariners* relative, when placed in the context of James's other work on America, such as *American Civilization* and the "Negro Question," but James's antitotalitarian discourse in the guise of Melville criticism should be also be understood as a continuation of his goal to make Marxism relevant to its particular historical setting.

Federated but Not Creolized

James frequently articulates his vision of the United States' unique capability to generate massive revolutionary change as a crisis of modernity. James considers America's midcentury multinational and multiracial citizenry (combined with America's industrial and technological strength) as peculiarly equipped to carry out such change. His discussion of this potential (particularly in *Mariners*, but also in *American Civilization*) suggests a theory of creolization that anticipates Brathwaite's notion of acculturation and interculturation combining to create a new and powerful society. This philosophy permeates *Mariners*. On the other hand, James's attempt to insert and acculturate *himself* to American society, his literal desire to be "naturalized" by the government, exposes an arrested, nonreciprocal, oxymoronic creolization. This chapter has described how creolization as a theory of revolutionary social formation does not successfully migrate to the United States inasmuch as the politics of repression occasioned by McCarthyism and the Cold War prevented it through the nationalist policies and ideologies of "good" citizenship, internment, and naturalization. In this chapter, then, creolization's "failure" underscores the fragmentation and exclusion engendered through discourses of nationalism and totalitarianism. The erratic nature of James's American creolization, however, does not succeed in diminishing his faith in America.

METAPHORS OF NATIONALISM

MUSIC, SPORT, AND RACIAL REPRESENTATION

> Special cultural and political relationships have been created in the Atlantic "triangle" of the African diaspora. They are the outcome of long processes in which the cultures of Africa, the Americas, Europe and the Caribbean have interacted and transformed each other. Their complex history . . . has involved struggles that dissolve the separation between politics and cultural expression. They have been concerned with the abolition of slavery and the acquisition of political rights for black Americans, the independence of colonial countries and the solidarity of diaspora blacks with movements for the destruction of racist settler regimes in Africa . . . These struggles have been signaled through the transnational power of black musics which have reached out beyond the boundaries of the nation-state.
>
> Paul Gilroy, *Small Acts*

In *Beyond a Boundary* (1963) James makes two principle claims about cricket: it possesses a particular and discernible aesthetic value as high art and, in its West Indian articulations in the early and mid-twentieth century, functions as an instrument of a developing resistant nationalism. I see both of these functions as part of James's most sophisticated, if flawed, epistemological foray into creolization theory. Writing during the same period, Ralph Ellison uses several essays both to claim and to showcase jazz as a composite artistic form that best signifies Americanness.

This chapter relies upon Gilroy's notion of "special relationships" and "the dissolved separation between culture and politics" as I consider the very different yet overlapping discourses of mixture and collaboration used by Ellison and James to investigate constructions of Caribbean and U.S. American identities and black artistic cultures. I center my discussion on *Beyond a Boundary* (1963) and Ralph Ellison's discussion of Americanness through jazz in *Shadow and Act* (1964), and I argue that these texts seem to enact a similar discourse of resistance in their insistence on recognizing cricket and jazz as "high art."

Ellison and James's discussions of cricket and jazz as acts of cultural nationalism incorporate and refigure aspects of Enlightenment ideologies of aesthetics to yield a porous, fluid ideology of (racial and political) subjectivity for black people in the Americas. That is to say, in their very different types of discussions of cricket and jazz, both James and Ellison subscribe to similar notions of art, artistic excellence, and artistic beauty as singular and definable even as their chosen subjects—jazz and cricket—are put into service to *deny* the possibility of pinning down a singular cultural identity or even national identity. The simultaneity of their contradictory discourses, connected by structure, ideology, and rhetorical style, provides a provocative opportunity for both specifying the ideologies of creolization and contributing to a discussion of comparative black subjectivities.[1]

Ellison and James's articulations of how cultural signifiers such as cricket and jazz enter into political discourses, and specifically racialized political discourses, both anticipate and bear witness to Gilroy's assertion that the African diaspora's "complex history . . . dissolves the separation between politics and cultural expression" and suggest within the specific historical moment of the early 1960s a "black Atlantic" concern with narrating complex identities. Both Ellison and James problematically delimit such cultural complexity, even as they are trying to express it; they attempt to read art and aesthetics as racially transcendent yet potentially representative of national and cultural identities reliant upon racial paradigms. Analyzing these efforts I see them as connected to larger ambivalences about a need for agency realized through the fiction of stabilized identities, encouraged by slavery, colonialism, and imperialism. Adding yet another layer of contradiction, Ellison and James inhabit a similar position that seeks to critique the essentialisms of the Black Power movement.

In addressing how creolization and attendant theories of hybridity and multiculturalism complicate our understanding of "blacknesses" within specific historical and geographical contexts, I am building upon similar discussions initiated by scholars such as Paul Gilroy and Michael Dash, in terms of "black

Atlantic" cultures and comparative creolization theories, respectively. My own contribution to these discussions comes in the form of two contentions. I assert that *Beyond a Boundary* is itself a creolized text and at the same time deploys creolization as a theory through its use of dialecticism and aesthetics. Through a comparison of Ellison to James, I attempt to discern the difference between creolization or a creolist culture and one, like the United States, which calls itself a melting-pot culture, where the ideal is unitary rather than multiple, homogeneous rather than heterogenous. I am also keeping in mind how *Boundary* developed out of James's self-exile and particularly his fifteen years in the United States; these American years significantly helped to shape the 1963 text. I am less concerned with identifying the specific cross-fertilization of ideas that transpired between Ellison and James; rather I am compelled by the coincidence of their attention to issues of art and national identity, at the same historical moment and against the backdrop of colonial and racial oppressions, and thus the juxtaposition of cricket and jazz. I am not the first to compare Ellison and James. Nielsen traces connections between the essays of these two friends and their contemplations on America in *C. L. R. James: A Critical Introduction*: "Both writers read an American body of texts whose structuring tensions were built from the very beginning around the difficulties of reconciling a commitment to the freedom of the individual with the democratic ideal of majoritarian governance, around the dramatic conflicts of individual conscience and the political repressions of the masses, around the tasks of rescuing a possible democracy from the legacy of a governing apparatus that oppresses minorities" (43). Nielsen identifies the shared concern of Ellison and James with the relationship of the individual to the mass in the contexts of democracy and political expression. In *Boundary* and *Shadow and Act*, Ellison and James confront the same issues in the arenas of art and artistic expression.

James's theory of creolization is articulated in *Beyond a Boundary* through the specific relationship he charts among nineteenth-century literature, English and West Indian cricket, and West Indian independence politics. On one level James's theory of creolization suggests that by understanding the interrelationship of these three one gains an awareness of what the Anglophone Caribbean is in 1963 and how its ongoing process of becoming can be charted. Read as such, James's theory of creolization appears didactic and closed, like Brathwaite's. Indeed, James effectively promotes a sense of different Caribbean identities separated by European language because of his inattention to (in

Boundary) Caribbean societies where the British, cricket, and nineteenth-century British literature held no such influence as James claims it had in the Anglophone territories.

Boundary conjoins aspects of James's autobiography, aspects of Trinidad and Tobago's social history, and aspects of the history of the development of cricket in England and its colonies. Crucial to Boundary's expression of creolization is James's argument that cricket as an art form and social formation is a pivotal aspect of Trinidad and Tobago's agitation for independence from England. This theory of creolization allows James to locate West Indianness as a productive mixture of cultural ideologies gleaned from England, Europe, and ancient Greece, as well as from political and social systems introduced through colonialism, African slavery, Indian indenture, trade unionism, and organized sports.

As one of James's most extensive discourses on individual and collective identity, Boundary is also one of his most contradictory. As with the texts discussed in chapters 1 through 5, Boundary centralizes notions of the individual and the community. But these subjects find both a more diversified and a contrary expression within Boundary. Quite often the individual is represented by James's autobiographical voice, but just as often the individual is a local cricketer, a historical figure, or an anonymous community member; Boundary's autobiographical structure is inconsistently reflected in the text's perspective. Such vagaries of structure and point of view are two of the ways Boundary emerges as a creolized text. Other moments of creolization that surface in the text are equally divided between instances where James's discussion of individual and collective identities intersect and moments where James's playful layering of forms can be understood as an endorsement of hybridity and mutability.[2]

Cricket and Reading

James uses the pages of Boundary to interpret how the cross-cultural effects of colonization—specifically the ways in which creolization realized through the game of cricket—created and influenced the continued development of West Indian society. James uses cricket to discuss class relations, racial politics, and high art. His postulations of West Indian social and cultural formation repeatedly suggest Brathwaite's creolization model and Bhabha's ideas about hybridity. In short, Boundary is itself a discursive act that exposes the boundaries of colonial domination: James shows how cricket was transformed by the West Indies into something of its own. In the process he attends to the instability of subjectivity and identity. By contradicting the doctrines of colonization and modernism, which thrive on myths of stable subjects and identities, James's ideas about cricket are easily linked to other types of "New World" performances, especially Carnival, which, like cricket, are mimetic, recreative, and political. James manipulates hybridity as part of his creolization theory and claims it as an original and productive concept.

It is difficult to read about cricket without the benefit of also seeing it played, and so I venture the briefest of explanations here. Developed in the eighteenth century in England, it is played professionally in many areas of the world once dominated by the British. This includes the West Indies, Sri Lanka, Australia, South Africa, India, Pakistan, and New Zealand. Test matches and World Cup competitions—two arenas for international play—ironically allow the Commonwealth to live on, even as England's dominance in the game has long since faded (much like its stature as a world power has). To the outsider, cricket can appear to be maddeningly complex with its peculiar vocabulary, extensive scoring system, and dizzying array of possible strokes to be made. And yet, certainly to the untutored (American) eye, cricket can seem to be straightforward, the object being to hit a ball with a bat in order to pile up as many runs as one can. The distant relationship to American baseball is evident: there is a batsman and a bowler (baseball's pitcher) and ten additional players per side.[3] Non-cricketing readers might approximate the significance of cricket in James's discourse by thinking about how sports teams come to represent communities, whether it is a small town's little league baseball team or an Olympic side playing for gold.

One of the key ideas that James imparts in *Boundary* is that it is the *structure* of cricket, from the role of the spectator or sponsor to the execution of a particular series of strokes, that is far more relevant than the final score or whether that score indicates a victory or a loss for a particular side. As such, it is like the jazz jam session, which has a definite beginning and end but which values the unpredictability of the improvisations, solos, and riffs that will occur in between that beginning and that end. As with cricket, certain parameters and structures of the jam session are expected, standard, and presumed by the artist and the audience alike. For James, the spectator's appreciation of and position within the structure of cricket is what makes it an art: "The glorious uncertainty of the game is not anarchy. It would not be glorious if it were not so firmly anchored in the certainties which must attend all successful drama. What matters in cricket, as in all the arts, is not finer points but what everyone with some knowledge of the elements can see and feel. It is only within such a rigid structural frame that the individuality so characteristic of cricket can flourish" (197–98).

James's Trinidadian childhood centered around reading and cricket; he experienced both as part of the British colonial curriculum. The local school was a site of indoctrination, but consequently its curriculum also became the vehicle through which minor acts of resistance were instigated. James details how that same curriculum and British "code" of morals fed his personal rebellions and his development into a Marxist. He also discusses how that code in turn prepared Trinidad and Tobago for its twentieth-century advance toward independence.

His discussion of the dialectical process of his education asserts how it generated creative and subversive tendencies from within a structure and curriculum meant to reinforce a British viewpoint and disciplinary politics. Explaining the hegemonic relationship he recalls, "our school masters, our curriculum, our code of morals, *everything* began from the basis that Britain was the source of all light and leading, and our business was to admire, wonder, imitate, learn" (38–39). Uninterested in discarding British and European "culture" despite his political opposition to their colonial and imperial conquests, James celebrates and intertwines cricket and literature, using them to destabilize the very absolutes that they were to convey and that were supposed to make him into a "good" colonial subject. James recounts his "resistant ideology" as a project deeply reliant upon the master's tools. Nowhere is this more evident than when he declares, "Thackeray, not Marx, would bear the heaviest responsibility for me" (*Boundary* 47). As a child James read Thackeray's *Vanity Fair* almost casually because it happened to be available and because he was an avid reader. In retrospect he makes the connection between cultural colonization (the naturalized act of reading) and the material and historical circumstances that placed particular books (and countless others) in his hands, in his school, in his home, and on his island.

James transferred his skills of reading back and forth between literature and cricket. Both were texts to be fathomed on multiple levels, as was, eventually, the Caribbean itself. (For James, Anglophone Caribbean cultural identity was to be understood as a resistant nationalist identity from whence a cultural identity could spring.) James also writes about the individual cricketer and how his performance contains layered meanings and how his "stage" is more than just a sports ground to play upon, it is a site upon which political conflict and debate could occur as well. "I was reading cricket and looking at it critically so early that casual experiences which would have passed unnoticed stayed with me and I worked at them as if on some historical problem" (44). To James, great cricketers and great writers had the super-ordinate ability to filter both culture and politics through their respective artistic mediums. Using great writers to codify and canonize great cricketers, European and American literary frames become a way to read the "West Indian" cricket of bowler George John. James writes: "If Spenser is the poet's poet, John was the fast bowler's bowler . . . If he had been an Italian of the Middle Ages he would have been called Furioso . . . Almost every ball he was rolling up his sleeves like a man about to commit some long-premeditated act of violence . . . Like the whale doing its business in great waters, he came up to breath periodically" (81). By laying claim to European, particularly British, literary cultures as components of West Indian culture, James presents a comprehensive outline of and makes a successful argument for what he calls New World societies and what Brathwaite would popularize as creolization.

James pairs his literary memories with several studies of what he calls "the personality in society." The particular example of Matthew Bondman, a neighborhood character and cricketer during James's youth, is frequently cited in discussions of *Boundary*. Bondman, like Rebecca Sharpe of *Vanity Fair*, gives lie to the myth of stable identities and rigid class positions. Bondman is "a ne'er do well. . . . good for nothing except cricket." James outlines Bondman's cricketing skill and technique, his personality, and his position in the community. The Bondman narrative can be read as the colonized subject rejecting a stabilized identity; Matthew Bondman is both a vulgar person and a gorgeous cricketer. James's puzzlement at how Bondman can be both creates a frame for the entire text by highlighting James's desire for stable identities: he needs but can find no definitive "place" for Bondman. In this instance, James's puzzlement is conveyed as a narrative of class position; Bondman's skill as a batsman interrupts his ferocious contempt for self-improvement. "It is only within very recent years that Matthew Bondman and the cutting of Arthur Jones ceased to be *merely* isolated memories and fell into place as *starting points of a connected pattern*. They only appear as starting points. *In reality they were the end, the last stones put into place*, of a pyramid whose base constantly widened" (7, emphasis added). Whereas Rebecca Sharpe would not be held down in her class aspirations, Bondman refuses to be pushed up. Hence his importance to James's understanding of the multiple ways colonial and capitalist hegemonies can be resisted and possibly challenged. James continues with Bondman's description:

He was a young man already when I first remember him, medium height and size, and an awful character. He was generally dirty. He would not work. His eyes were fierce, his language was violent and his voice was loud. His lips curled back naturally and he intensified it by an almost perpetual snarl. My grandmother and my aunts detested him. For ne'er do well, in fact vicious character, as he was, Matthew had one saving grace—Matthew could bat. More than that, so crude and vulgar in every aspect of his life, with a bat in his hand he was all grace and style. (3–4)

James's description of Bondman, which has captured the attention of several scholars,[4] conveys the impossibility of stable identities even within one person. (Even so, the description serves as a good example of James's reliance on binary oppositions as a point of departure for the depiction of complex understandings of Caribbean societies.) James goes to great lengths to oppose Bondman's "vulgarity" in society with the "grace" Bondman could realize in the execution of a particular stroke on the cricket pitch.

However, rather than reifying the binary constructions of colonial racist ideologies, throughout the text James attempts to turn them on their head. *Boundary* establishes cricket as a signifier that articulates the unstable and contradictory nature of colonial, colonized, and postcolonial identities.[5] One cannot have a purity without a debasement, and yet the interactions of these opposites yield something higher: the art of cricket as interpreted by Caribbean artists. The actions that create instability or that can be read as resistant to colonial hegemonic forces are themselves indebted to an aesthetics of grace, beauty, and technique derived from the same hegemonic structures, derived, that is, from the West.

Cricket, Class Antagonisms, and "Community"

Another memory that James relates from his childhood demonstrates more specifically how and where he finds creolization at work in colonial Trinidad. I quote at length a passage that depicts the evolution of an anonymous Chinese shopkeeper from his status as an unassimilated colonial immigrant to a qualified inclusion within Trinidadianness. That evolution is achieved via the shopkeeper's cultivation of an appreciation of the game of cricket. This particular evolutionary process also reveals James's continued interest in how national subjects are formed out of immigrants and other insider/outsider oppositions (such as I focused on in chapter 5) of "the personality in society."

A Chinese would land in the island from China unable to speak a word of English. He would begin as a clerk in a grocery store in some remote country district. He and others like him would pool their monthly salaries and, turn by turn, set up a small business in some strategic spot, usually in the midst of some village populated by Negro agriculturalists. These Negroes worked on contract. They were given a piece of land which they cleaned and cultivated. After five years they got so much for every mature cocoa tree, and then handed back the land to the owner. Naturally such a cultivator would be very hard up for cash, and very often by the time his five years were up he had pledged most of it to the Chinese shopkeeper. He, on the other hand, lived at the back of his shop, saved his money and in time sold not only foodstuffs but shoes and clothes and gadgets of all sorts. This often made for bad blood between the Chinese and his creditors. But this man, after about fifteen years, would be seized with a passion for cricket. He did not play himself but he sponsored the local village team. He would buy a matting for them and supply them with bats and balls. On the Sunday when the match was to be played he provided a feast. He helped out players who could not afford cricket gear. He godfathered very poor boys who could play. On the day of the match you could see him surrounded by the locals, following every ball with the passionate intensity that he gave only to his business. All night and half the day his shop was filled with people arguing about the match that was past or the match that was to come. When the team had to travel he supplied transport. The usual taciturnity of the local Chinese remained with him, except in cricket, where he would be as excited and as voluble as the rest. You could find people like him scattered all over the island. I didn't find it strange then. Today he and such as he are as intriguing as any of my cricket memories. I don't believe that, apart from his business and his family life, he had any contact whatever with the life around him except his sponsorship of the local cricket club. (63)

This narration posits cricket as a mechanism of synthesis that both cements a sense of cultural community and mends particular rifts of class antagonism in the postslavery Trinidadian community. Within his Chinese identity the shopkeeper is outside Trinidad, blackness, and the class of agricultural laborers. Upon arrival, the Chinese shopkeeper inserts himself in a middling sphere of the capitalist hierarchy whilst the black "agricultural workers," shown to be powerless, stagnate within cyclical contract work. That blacks often end up completely in debt to the Chinese shopkeepers after five-year cycles suggests a significant tension, but this tension, according to James, is relieved not by a revolution of the proletariat but rather once the shopkeeper realizes his affinity for cricket.

In this scenario the tensions of class difference are alleviated at the very moment the shopkeeper is "seized by a passion for cricket." The cricket competition as well as the preparation for the competition create spaces and expanses of time when the racial and class stratification imposed on the community through British capitalism and colonialism are subordinated to such a degree as to facilitate a sense of "community." This creolized community, riven as it is by language, race, and unequal economic relationships, is nevertheless synthesized (at least in James's memory) by a collective and passionate engagement of an organic cultural manifestation: the sport/art of cricket. The formation of such a community is important to James because into it he both casts and extracts organic revolutionary potential—a politics of resistance eventually to be realized in the particulars of Trinidadian independence and more generally in the overthrow of capitalism by proletarian communities around the globe. The shop, originally a site of oppressive capitalistic enterprise between its owner and creditors, is now also a meeting house "filled with people arguing about the match that was past or the match that was to come" (64). Importantly, the shop does not cease to be a shop; the creolization process does not erase that economic specificity, rather the specific revolutionary needs of the community are etched on top of the shop's commercial identity.[6]

This long anecdote about the Chinese shopkeeper precedes two often quoted lines in *Boundary*: "Cricket had plunged me into politics long before I was aware of it. When I did turn to politics I did not have too much to learn" (65). In retrospect James understands the cricket pitch as, to use Carby's phrasing, "a representational landscape that can embody the world of politics" (*Race Men* 126). Cricket is a site of creolization at both a personal and a collective level. James's "Chinese shopkeeper" represents the shifting identity that eventually subverts colonial discourses of power at several different nodal points: he arrives in Trinidad as a refugee of British colonialism in China to inherit a debased form of monopolized capital; fifteen years later he emerges as the unintentional instrument of pre-revolutionary activity and consciousness. For there can be no doubt that James understands the West Indian appropriation and transformation of cricket from Britain as revolutionary *in itself* and as a pre-activity to anticolonial organization. Carby makes an important observation about James's personal transition from cricket to politics, which is usefully extended to his representation(s) of Trinidad's analogous transition. She writes, "The transition was seamless precisely because ideologies of masculinity, whether conscious or unconscious, were already shaping his understanding of the performative politics of cricket and his idea of how colonialism should be opposed" (*Race Men* 120). The "Chinese shopkeeper" anecdote gives a sense of what cricket in its specific structure—accentuated by the particulars of team sponsorship engaged in by the anonymous shopkeeper—*allows*. At the same time, however, James's assertion of cricket as a resistant discourse problematically succeeds because he relies and leaves unchallenged the stereotype of the "inscrutable Oriental"—for without that inscrutability, cricket would not necessarily be his one qualified conduit into "the community." Within a rubric of creolization cricket can acculturate "the Chinese" to a point but in the process insists upon the erasure of this individual's and his group's own cultural capital, a lack which cricket then conveniently provides. Thus the "colonized" look toward the metropolitan center is often *both* in resistance and in mimicry. What Carby calls "the performative politics of cricket," then, are disconcertingly caught up in ideologies of both masculinity and racism. Carby makes it impossible not to pair the gender politics of cricket and West Indian nationalism. And if, as Benedict Anderson states, "communities are to be distinguished not by their falsity/genuineness, but by the style in which they are imagined" (6), then the nascent West Indian nationalism inspired through cricket must be understood as an imagining transcendent of even as it is bounded by learned hierarchies imparted through British colonialism.

It is at the moment that the Chinese shopkeeper enters into and participates in the ritual of cricket, leaving the periphery to "join" the community, that the colonial use of cricket as a tool with which to build empire and comprehensively subsume colonies to the needs and cultures of the metropolitan center is further subverted. The subversion, however, is hardly "pure," attended, as I have shown, by new hierarchies and old racisms.

Much later in *Boundary*, James revisits the notions of purity and originality when he asserts that cricket's "art" is in its repetition. Because of its form, it has to repeat, but in that repetition, he claims, "is the original stuff out of which everything visually or otherwise artistic is quarried." Again, this is a lot like Brathwaite's creolization—that which in its mixture creates something new—but it also recalls Benítez-Rojo, in that the particular configuration either of the game of cricket or the archipelago of the Caribbean, the repetitions, the lack of a center yield something definitively productive. The paradox of how something that is a repetition yields that which is original, is a difficult one. The idea of striving for an integrated sensibility as opposed to a segregated one also echoes a recurrent textual theme. St Louis raises the point that in James it is not the *lack* of the center but rather the activity that revolves around the center that is important. Form and progression remain significant; the center still exists and is crucial. The center can be understood as the series of strokes in cricket or series of notes in jazz; at other times it might be understood as the colonial metropolitan center. The dialectic, what I would identify as the shifting site of resistance, is in the re-articulation of that center, not its absence or its demolition.

Read through a lens of creolization, at least two radical interpretations of cricket are possible: it transforms what we think of as art to include sport and, as such, invites a re-visioning of how "high art" is imagined, transmitted, and received. James's discussion of cricket's special aesthetic value presents him with the opportunity to engage theories of art in general. James suggests differentiated forms of "high art" and urges the spectator to seek out "high art" in nontraditional venues such as the cricket pitch. He shows how the spectator or audience of "high art" can be found in places other than concert halls and museums; places like remote villages of Trinidad on the local cricket pitch. Thus the material setting of cricket and the material circumstances of "high art" can be understood as transformative. James also deliberately reads cricket "sociologically." He represents his own brief cricketing career as the bridge he used into the world of organized politics, in much the same way that he posits cricket as a conduit for Trinidad's independence movement.

"Giving the Blues the Blues"

The 1950s and 1960s saw the publication of several texts in the United States that linked national identity, jazz music, and blackness. Ralph Ellison's essays on jazz collected in *Shadow and Act* as well as LeRoi Jones's study *Blues People* (1963) are texts in conversation with one another and, in divergent ways, with *Boundary*'s discourse on creolization and independent nationalism. An initial assessment reveals Ellison to be talking about jazz and urging his reader to consider jazz as an articulation of creolization. Ellison's privileging of the aesthetic genius of jazz music as American and therefore as a dual articulation of culture and nationalism gives his reader the opportunity to attend to the complex discourses that meet and speak within jazz performances. Ellison can be understood as looking for and wresting from jazz a culturally inclusive agency from "Americanness"—a term, an idea, and a physical place generally dependent on the marginalization of "black" peoples. But, unlike James, he does not wish to read that inclusive agency as a political phenomenon.

Ellison enthusiastically recognizes jazz as a "high art," but to him, once jazz is read sociologically or once one attempts to use or recognize jazz as politically transformative, it becomes aesthetically reduced. Such an effort, says Ellison, could "give even the blues the blues," a fault he finds in Jones's *Blues People*. In its material setting jazz does not redefine how we understand "high art," for it becomes "high art" when it ceases to be dance music and is played at Carnegie Hall. Jazz's value as "high art" is instead solidified in its purer folk expression. Ellison's comments belong to the specific moment of the 1950s and 1960s that saw the development of jazz in new directions as well as the birth of the Black Arts movement and the Black Power movement, each of which sought to claim black art and black identity in exclusive terms. And although Ellison opposed such exclusivity, wanting instead to also see black art and black identity as particularly American, his extreme anxiety about "reading jazz sociologically" belies his own overinvestment in the U.S. binaries that exalt "Americanness" and assert blackness in its material contexts and cultural expressions as inferior.

What does it mean that the terms of artistic and political engagement and agency for James and Ellison rely on different sorts of racial sublimation? Whereas Ellison claims that the blues are not primarily concerned with civil rights or obvious political protest, James asserts that cricket is a politics, at least a representation of a politics. Does "race" itself mean something different for each? I ask these questions and attempt a response because it is important to understand exactly what Ellison is marginalizing when he marginalizes race.

Ellison uses creolization and seeks to highlight jazz music as an art form that flourishes because of its intentional and eclectic borrowing. His description of "true jazz" bears this idea out. In "The Charlie Christian Story" he writes:

> true jazz is an art of individual assertion within and against the group. Each true jazz moment (as distinct from the uninspired commercial performance) springs from a contest in which each artist challenges all the rest; each solo flight, or improvisation, represents (like the successive canvases of a painter) a definition of his identity as individual, as member of the collectivity and as a link in the chain of tradition. Thus, because jazz finds its very life in an endless improvisation upon traditional materials, the jazzman must lose his identity even as he finds it. (267)

In this description Ellison is able to observe and privilege the dialectic of identity formation. He asserts jazz and artistic identity as neither singular nor stable, although they draw upon "traditional materials" in their discursivity and dialogic expression. But Ellison is unable or unwilling to use creolization theory as a wedge to dislodge the hierarchy that subsumes blackness to Americanness, or so it appears in his vociferous denunciation of Jones's *Blues People*. For while he criticizes Jones's version of the blues as "lacking a sense of the excitement and surprise of men living in the world—of enslaved and politically weak men successfully imposing their values upon a powerful society through song and dance" (286), he is unequivocal in his assertion that jazz/blues's value is located in its expansive Americanness and not its narrow blackness. Political protest and black political struggles in particular are connected to jazz in error, warns Ellison: "For the blues are not primarily concerned with civil rights or obvious political protest; they are an art form and thus a transcendence of those conditions created within the Negro community by the denial of social justice" (287).

It is on the issue and interpretation of *transcendence* that the difference between Ellison and James's use of creolization hinges. Ellison understands the transcendence of racial specificities as positive and the movement of black cultural expression into an inclusively realized national American identity as desirable and politically expedient—especially for a cultural expression recognized as "high art." Ellison can observe and applaud creolist acts in paradoxically delimited, bounded fields of discourse, as in a specific jazz jam session. His opinions are like a version of U.S. multiculturalism where difference is admired up to a point but assimilation is still the spoken or unspoken goal. Speaking from the Caribbean, James understands and enacts creolization inversely. James understands the transcendence of racial and class antagonisms within the specific frame of cricket performances as informing and nurturing a resistant nationalism. However, that resistant nationalism requires a replication of the creolist ethos inasmuch as its resistance is informed by the *retention* of racial differences (at least in the ideal), not their homogenization. To be sure, in America, the imperative to assimilate is both enforced and naturalized through hegemonic discourses of whiteness and power, which benefit from constant and diverse cultural and political utterances. Such hegemonic discourses are not absent in the West Indies but are mediated through and thus articulated differently in a least one significant way—which is by a metropolitan center or centers.

Both Ellison and James access and deploy creolization theory even as they retain Enlightenment ideals of aesthetic value premised upon universal experience. Inherent in Ellison's usage is a stabilized notion of Americanness. In James too, we could turn to other examples in *Boundary*, where his discussion of cricket as "high art" is dependent upon a problematic notion of so-called Caribbean genetics.[7]

Politics and Aesthetics

When James offers his theory of cricket as a "high art" form he draws nearer, in a philosophical sense, to Ellison's wish to emphasize aesthetics over politics when speaking of jazz. James's analysis is most compelling in its refusal to oppose high art and political formations; art and politics are to be admired when they succeed in effectively representing a social group. Over and over James asserts that cricket is a sport yet also an art form that can represent a social group as successfully as other art forms such as Greek tragedy:

> The dramatist, the novelist, the choreographer, must *strive* to make his individual character symbolic of a larger whole . . . The runner in a relay race must take the plus or minus that his partner or partners give him. The soccer forward and goalkeeper may at certain rare moments find themselves sole representatives of their sides. Even the baseball batter, who most nearly approaches this particular aspect of cricket, may and often does find himself after a fine hit standing on one of the bases, where he is now dependent on others. The batsman facing the ball does not merely represent his side. For that moment, for all intents and purposes, he is his side. This fundamental relation of the One and the Many, Individual and Social, Individual and Universal, leader and followers, representative and ranks, the part and the whole, is structurally imposed on the players of cricket. (*Boundary* 196–97)

The aesthetics of cricket are essential components to the political power that James attributes to the sport. His ideas about the representations and relationships that exist within cricket become assertions of the transformative and ultimately transgressive nature of the game. "The cricket field was a stage on which selected individuals played representative roles which were charged with social significance" (72). The idea of the cricket match as a spectacle in which roles are adopted for a prescribed amount of time in a particular way is continually emphasized. To James, the county cricket player who is brilliantly creative and famous for his skill(s) on the field yet who may afterwards return to an anonymous position in society, is as significant to the evolution of the game as its greatest professional stars. In this sense the names and events that James catalogs in *Boundary* are not dissimilar to his task in writing his "biography" of Captain Cipriani. In both cases his intention was to bring to the public attention, to an audience broader than but inclusive of the Caribbean itself, the significance of the microcosmic society of the West Indies.

The contradictions within James's theorizations of cricket are not dissimilar to the quagmire that engulfs Ellison in his own attempt to discuss the aesthetics of jazz in relationship to American identities and against the backdrop of civil rights and Black Power. To deal with James first, however, he asserts the West Indies as something new and locates its national, international, and historical significance in that newness. While James wants to use cricket to broaden the reader's understanding of colonial and postcolonial society in the British West Indies, what does it mean for concepts of hybridity and creolization to yield to a notion of singular and stabilized national identity as epitomized in the phrase "West Indian brains"—a phrase James uses to discuss cricketer Rohan Kanhai? James's use of concepts of hybridity and creolization as deployed in his analysis can be seen as constantly chafing against his competing desire to define and contain a unique and specific notion of West Indian identity.

James claims that despite the model of nationalism introduced under colonialism, colonized West Indians fashioned cricket into an art form and a political tool of resistance necessary for the articulation of an independent nationalism. He makes this claim specifically for the game when he writes, "Yet cricket is an art, not a bastard or a poor relation, but a full member of the community." This statement revises a similar one in the appendix to *Black JacobinsH* where James asserts revolution as the means by which the West Indies take their place on the world stage as nations, not colonies. In *Boundary* he elaborates that claim in his discussion of Learie Constantine (192). Constantine, friend of James, great cricketer, and eventually a member of England's House of Lords, is at the center of James's discussion of the relationship between aesthetics, cricket, and politics. By recognizing and bringing to the fore the importance of the region's creolized position James provides a blueprint for understanding the West Indies not as a "poor relation" to Europe, politically and culturally, but rather as a region rich in political ability and cultural innovation.

Constantine is positioned in *Boundary* as the individual who most overtly connects cricket to a politics of change for James. Speaking of his own viewpoint when he first arrived in England in 1932, James recalls, "In that sense Constantine had always been political, far more than I had ever been. My sentiments were in the right place, but I was still enclosed within the mould of nineteenth-century intellectualism. Unbeknown [sic] to me, however, the shell had been cracked. Constantine's conversations were always pecking at it" (113). One Constantine phrase in particular, "They are no better than we" (113), effected James's transformation and became a slogan through which to interpret cricket competitions as well as the shifting colony/metropolitan relationship; it also becomes the organizing thesis for "The Case for West Indian Self Government." Writing in 1962, James correctly identifies the interactions between himself and Constantine, both the "transcendence of their relations as cricketers" and their entrance into party politics, as a phenomenon being replicated all over the West Indies and the West Indian diaspora. The collective effect "was to initiate the West Indian renaissance not only in cricket, but in politics, in history and in writing" (111).

While there is no point when James loses sight of the fact that cricket was meant to be a tool of cultural colonization that fostered a moral code and a British ideal of excellence, there are moments when his project is hampered by his inconsistent assessment of the impact race and class had within cricket and in the manifestations of resistance that he recounts. "The authorities needed always to have one white player as captain, and one or two others in reserve in case of accidents and as future candidates. They believed (or pretended to, it does not matter) that cricket would fall into chaos and anarchy if a black man were appointed captain. (By the grim irony of history we shall see that it was their rejection of black men which brought the anarchy and chaos and very nearly worse)" (*Boundary* 76). Elsewhere James cites numerous examples to detail the way in which cricket functioned as a tool of cultural colonization. Dwelling upon the subject of captains of the West Indies team, James outlines racialized class conflicts in cricket as analogous to similar social conflicts caused by the gross inequities that sustained the colonial relationship. This particular point is made when James calls attention to the fact that (pre-World War II) captainship of any of the significant teams was reserved by and preserved for local, well-positioned whites. Thus in sport, as in politics, the local white aristocracy believed blacks could play but could not lead. James continues with several examples of the local nonwhite West Indian population protesting because a black athlete was excluded from a team or left at home because of his race. In the chapter "Patient Merit," James catalogs a series of outstanding cricketers left off Trinidad's team in the 1920s because the quota of black players had been reached. This is the type of local series of events that was repeated with greater frequency and that fed a growing movement, eventually to be defined by James as part of a West Indian nationalist and anticolonial ethos where West Indian is meant to be read as "black." For James, "the mastery of cricket, a game representing Englishness, is, ironically, the West Indian's way of speaking in the modern world" (Diawara 835). And, having established the Caribbean's role in creating the modern world, and forming independent political entities, James also uses *Boundary* to examine how cricket functions as a modern art form. Yet when James writes, "I haven't the slightest doubt that the clash of race, caste and class did not retard but stimulated West Indian cricket" and that he is "equally certain that in those years social and political passions, denied normal outlets, expressed themselves so fiercely in cricket (and other games) precisely because they were games" (*Boundary* 72), his confident "readings" of cricket as a protopolitical formation are slightly misleading. Indeed, he contradicts statements both earlier and later in the text where he either denies race as a factor on the cricket pitch or claims that cricket as art is able to transcend race and class.

In "Kanhai: A Study in Confidence," James describes cricket as a game that advanced from a copy of the original (British) to an original of its own. He then locates its originality in the apparatus of nationhood, and thus confusingly reintroduces notions of puritanism and authenticity. James clearly sublimates a creolization ideal to national identity. James asserts that moments occur when the cricketing itself, its motions and executions, articulate a *West Indian* ethos. This then becomes an example of how James negates a creolization model by suggesting the possibility of a closed system of signification regarding West Indian identity. James insists that the distinction of a "great West Indies cricketer" was that his play "should embody some *essence* of that crowded vagueness which passes for the history of the West Indies" (*Rendezvous* 166). Unfortunately, since that particular history is a history of the clash of cultures and systems of domination precipitated by colonialism, James's desire to see the West Indies as something new, through the lens of cricket, is, like the restrictiveness of Brathwaite's creolization model, flawed in its boundedness. James ends up conveying not the newness of "West Indianness" as discernable through cricket but rather a sense of how West Indian cricket preserves the memory of the British Empire even after that political apparatus has been dismantled. James succeeds in showing how even as cricket leads to a resistance politics it *also* reveals a palimpsest of colonialism itself. The voice he uses to describe the Chinese shopkeeper's entrance into the world of cricket as part of the power of cricket reveals James's presumptions of otherness as housed in the least familiar face in his own landscape.

In contrast to James, V. S. Naipaul understands Trinidad and the Caribbean in general as a "society which produced nothing, never had to prove its worth, and was never called upon to be efficient" (*Middle Passage* 41–42). Ironically, Naipaul is also aware of cricket's singular place in West Indian culture, but unlike James, he does not identify it as cultural appropriation or even creative mimesis. He is skeptical of that moment when cricket ceases to be a scrap thrown to the masses by the colonial power and when it becomes a catalyst for change. I quote Naipaul at length:

> Cricket has always been more than a game in Trinidad. In a society which demanded no skills and offered no rewards to merit, cricket was the only activity which permitted a man to grow to his full stature and to be measured against international standards. Alone on a field, beyond obscuring intrigue, the cricketer's true worth could be seen by all. His race, education, wealth did not matter. We had no scientists, engineers, explorers, soldiers or poets. The cricketer was our only hero figure. And that is why cricket is played in the West Indies with such panache; that is why, for a long time to come, the West Indians will not be able to play as a team. The individual performance was what mattered. That was what we went to applaud; and unless the cricketer had heroic qualities we did not want to see him, however valuable he might be. (42)

Naipaul raises an interesting challenge to James's Greco-Roman ideal of representation and "The One and the Many." Despite Naipaul's acknowledgment of the "heroic" stature of West Indian cricketers, his insistence that cricket existed solely as an individual endeavor by both the players and in terms of the fans' appreciation of the players directly contradicts James's theory of cricket as a unifying, politicizing mechanism. Naipaul differs from James in his analysis of cricket and of the West Indies chiefly because he identifies a residual, uncreative politics in the region, one which can only operate in reaction to colonialism. James, on the other hand, remarks upon an emergent politics of community, roused and unified, in fact, by cricket. James again is seeking to understand dialectically both the cricket and the nationalism of "the West Indies" as separated by time, space, and circumstance from the cricket and nationalism of England.

Sandra Pouchet Paquet usefully captures the idea of cricket that James presents in *Beyond a Boundary* when she states: "James chronicles the parallel development of cricket from a ritual of colonial dominance into ritualized resistance and, finally, a ritual of independent selfhood" ("West Indian Autobiography" 363). Indeed it is this exact subversion of the mechanisms of colonialism achieved by cricket in the West Indies that allows the sport to take its place in the ideology of the Anglophone Caribbean as "an instrument for the assertion of national spirit" (364). "Independent selfhood" is exactly what James saw in the cricket of Rohan Kanhai and in Naipaul's *A House for Mr. Biswas*: in each he recognized New World, Caribbean performances, but also distinctive individual performances.

The Caribbean rarely understands itself in isolation; James, particularly in the early 1960s emphasizes the "comity of nations" that the Caribbean joins. At the same time, after spending fifteen years in the United States, he appears overinvested in the potentialities of that individual nation. Regarding James's notion of the United States, Ellison suggests both an alternative and, if you will, a native perspective to contrast James's outsider's viewpoint. Ellison and James exhibit similarly paradoxical viewpoints: James constructs a monolithic notion of black West Indian identity out of examples of creolized New World communities. Ellison rejects a monolithic interpretation of black U.S. identity by asserting its linkages to a particularized though more dominant American identity. And, as the 1990s incarnation of Afrocentrism has proven, the lure of one black world still holds great appeal for a great many; my discussion of Ellison and James, jazz and cricket, has attempted to investigate what Antonio Benítez-Rojo calls "the paradox of identity," the sometimes seductive ideologies of creolization.

The idea of creolization existing in a U.S. context recedes further into the impossible because so much of America's ethos is built upon the myth not only of absoluteness but also of equality. An immense difference then, between the Caribbean and the United States is the pivotal absence, in a U.S. context, of a metropolitan center that acts as a conduit of politics, culture, and capital. Furthermore, the real and metaphorical physicality of the Caribbean as a group of *islands* and *a sea*, which Dash says "is not an inland, centralizing body of water, but one that explodes outwards, thereby dissolving all systems of centering or totalizing thought" (*This Other America* 14), is very different from the geographical formation of the continental United States. When we speak of the Caribbean we are already speaking of a multiplicity, we are automatically signifying more than one nation, language, and political system. When we speak of the United States, no matter how politically divided, legally segregated, or internally culturally diverse it seems to be or sees itself as, it is nevertheless constituted *as a whole*, not even as a fragmented whole, but a carefully delineated, constructed whole. Thus we can see creolization as an organic manifestation of Caribbeanness and therefore how it is not transferable *as itself* because of its "open insularity," to use Michael Dash's term. Speaking of Glissant, Dash goes on to elaborate this concept: "If cultural particularity in the New World is convulsive and incomplete, then the Caribbean archipelago is even more so, in Glissant's view. Here he privileges the idea of open insularity as opposed to the continental mass of North and South America" (*This Other America* 13). Urging us to pay attention to geographic as well as cultural differences, the theories of Dash, Glissant, Brathwaite, and Benítez-Rojo all tend to extrapolate outwards from the land and the water. The geographic boundedness of the United States makes it create different cultural paradigms even as it is susceptible to different prejudices than the Caribbean region. Neither James nor Ellison were as concerned with the physical as related to the cultural; diversity, difference, and confluence were more readily theorized for them within the no less rarified realm of the artistic aesthetic.

Spike Lee's film *He Got Game* (1998) offers an example of the difficulty of achieving diversity and cross-cultural relationships, as defined by Glissant, in racialized U.S. contexts. As with Lee's previous films, *He Got Game* self-consciously provides an auditory as well as visual experience for the audience. But whereas earlier films focused on black life and employed "black" musical forms (most prominently jazz, rap, and soul musics) to help anchor the stories, *He Got Game*, a story specifically about an incarcerated father's relationship with his son, and more broadly about the game of basketball and its meanings and myths "in the ghetto," boasts a soundtrack by Aaron Copeland of so-called white American music. In the film, which one reviewer calls Lee's "paean to basketball," he includes just one track by a "black" group, Public Enemy. A record store marquee in New York advertised the Copeland soundtrack, but not the Public Enemy single, with a quote from Lee saying "When you think of basketball you think of America, when you listen to Copeland you hear America." Given the continued racial stratification of the American music and film industry, not to mention America itself, Lee's crossover maneuver, linking Copeland and a "black" narrative of basketball, appears radical in a rather peculiarly American way. The result of the juxtaposition of Copeland, basketball, and America is a glossy, though momentary elevation of all three *above race*, enveloping them within a cozy, seamless cloak of Americanness.

Lee's desire to elevate basketball, music, and America above race, even momentarily, is not an unfamiliar impulse on his part, or on the part of any aesthetician. Simply put, Lee presents basketball as an art and underscores his position by linking it with the already established art of Aaron Copeland, a gesture reminiscent of James's similar linkage of bowler George John with Spenser and Melville. For Lee, it is as if the juxtaposition of basketball and Copeland can cancel out any racial specificities we may be tempted to read into each; Lee's desire to read the sport and the music as quintessentially "American" signals an attempt to downplay their racial identifiers. Indeed, to say "America" is conceived as shorthand for "melting pot." And it is here that some of the similarities between Lee's position and Ellison's as differentiated from those of James and Glissant become evident. For to say melting pot is to emphasize and value the whole. The parts of the whole are only considered great because of what they derive from the whole, from being American, not from being particularized as white or black. We can see, then, how Lee's attempted articulation of creolization is precariously situated. While there may be a constant borrowing back and forth across the American cultural landscape, an acknowledgment of that borrowing is nearly impossible: hence Lee's separate soundtracks for *He Got Game*. To emphasize Americanness is to devalue the fractures; it is at the very least a gesture toward wholeness, not unlike Brathwaite's concept of submarine unity: perhaps desirable once, but now, and specifically when read through late-twentieth-century theories of creolization, it can be seen as both naive and sentimental.

The idea that basketball—and perhaps music—can and does exist, is played, listened to, appreciated in a realm above and therefore untainted by the overdetermined idea of racial difference and antagonism (still often understood within the United States as a binary opposition of black and white) is most forcefully rendered in the opening montage of *He Got Game*. This visually beautiful and unabashedly sentimental sequence features all sorts of under-18s: boys and girls, urban and suburban, white, black, Latino/a, Asian, solo and as teams, taking their best shots on basketball courts all across America. As the narrative of the film unfolds, this rhetoric of liberal humanism in the realm of sport and black life is presented with slightly more skepticism and irony. A more in-depth review of the philosophical motivations and significance of Lee's cinematic effort are best left to a film critic. Nevertheless, I could not help but see several connections between some of the ideas Lee unleashes in the opening visual and auditory moments of *He Got Game* and my present concern with creolization, the United States, jazz, and *Beyond a Boundary*.

Whereas previous, discrete interpretations of cricket and jazz have generally used them to read the West Indies and black America within totalizing and closed discourses, my interest and usage of concepts of creolization in my discussion of Ellison's essays and *Beyond a Boundary* are attempts to reframe each as open-ended and evolving significations of identity. Using cricket, James reorients the structure of colonization. James is like Caliban, whose apprehension of English marks not only a cultural appropriation but the beginning of more effective revolts against Prospero.

One of Derek Walcott's arguments in "The Muse of History" is that it is necessary for the West Indian artist to understand "history as its own brand of fiction" (20). James anticipates Walcott's reasoning but argues against "liberation from memories." James retains Prospero's language and Prospero's books and Prospero's sport but uses them to "pioneer new regions" (or, in other words, to act as a sort of colonizer). He declares:

> I do not wish to be liberated from the past and, above all, I do not wish to be liberated from its future. Not me. Most of this book had already been written when it so happened that I revisited the West Indies after twenty-six years absence and stayed there for over four years. Greedily I relived the past, every inch of it I could find, I took part in the present ... and I speculated and planned and schemed for the future; among other plans, how to lay racialism flat and keep stamping it out whenever it raises its head, and at the same time not to lose a sense of proportion, not at all easy. (*Boundary* 65–66)

The West Indies Federation, Trinidadian independence, the December 1960 cricket test series with Australia, each inform the composition of *Boundary*. In his work, as well as in his writing, James was convinced that a knowledge of history was pivotal in any attempt to transform the present. In *Boundary*, James demonstrates an assumption he made early in his life, that a "true West Indian" begins to know himself as such only after he has left the West Indies (Buhle, *Artist* 11).

There is a certain amount of agency I admit to seeking and perhaps therefore finding in creolization theory and by extension in James and Ellison. It is an agency that Gilroy notes as a "combination of danger and opportunity," that highlights the way in which black people are both affected by and fight against the forces of oppression in "overdeveloped countries." Gilroy writes, "The vision of crisis as danger and opportunity, lived and systematic, can also give due weight to the macro-structural and economic conditions that shape the locations in which black creativity develops" (*Small Acts* 10). Why seek agency within creolization theory? The desire to test the parameters and applicability of creolization grows out of the very specific issue of comparison that arises with regularity in the classes I teach. I find myself in repeated encounters with students eager to misread "African diaspora" and "Black Atlantic" as opportunities to resurrect a mythical originary wholeness and to use the instance of comparing Caribbean and black U.S. literatures as an occasion to leave blackness undertheorized. Thus because of my appreciation of the extensive body of work regarding the notion of decentered subjectivities and destabilized identities, as provided by a host of African American, Caribbean, and postcolonial theorists, my investigation into the limits and usages of creolization theory is offered as a specific rubric with which to employ it critically and without romanticization. Creolization theory can usefully convey *individual* expressions of black subjectivities from *within* the Caribbean or the United States but often blurs the specific historic specificities when generalizations are sought.

CODA

A conclusion would be antithetical to the theoretical spirit of this project and so instead I return to the so-called beginning: In mistakenly uncovering the Americas while supposedly en route to the treasures of the East, Columbus's expedition of discovery "found" the Caribbean islands within a "New World" that lacked the divine providence, Christian ethos, and mercantilism of early modern Europe. The discovery of the Caribbean islands and the systematic extermination and expulsion of its indigenous peoples violently created a *tabula rasa* where history, subjects, and culture were not yet established but there to be made. As a result, the settlement of the Caribbean islands by colonial administrators, adventurers, planters, enslaved Africans, and indentured laborers created the distinctively modern phenomenon of creole society; a population of "settlers" committed to the land but not indigenous to it. These inhabitants of creole society developed what has since been seen as a profound awareness of the settling of their new land and self-consciously cultivated a unique perspective on their fabricated environment and novel social condition-creolization. Unlike the European dogmas of separate and distinct nations, races, and cultures, creolization recognizes the inescapable mixing of peoples and cultures as an undeniable facet of the modern world.

As a direct descendant and inhabitant of creole society, C. L. R. James used the written word and political activism to recognize the tangled circles of influence between the Caribbean, the Americas, and Europe in the formation of the modern world. James's corpus interprets the idea of creolization by illustrating the originality and complexity of the modern Caribbean condition and the delicate threads that connect it to the Americas and to Europe. Creolization is but one of many possible rubrics through which to read James and his evolving political and philosophical positions. Creolization should not, therefore, be used to privilege uncritically the Caribbean over the other ways and places he located himself.

I have presented James as a dynamic voice of contemporary creolization and exposed the insistent, international, and interdisciplinary conversations within his work. The idea of creolization embedded in his creative output as well as his consistent faith in the power of the masses to transform society offer readers compelling models of resistance and interpretation to shape and adjust to the struggles of the twenty-first century, however such struggles may come to be defined. I am confident that these struggles will be haunted by the aggressively present, if (un)welcome specters of gender, race, class, ethnicity, and sexuality and therefore I suspect that the idea of creolization will remain a valuable framework with which to examine the construction of our societies. At the same time, C. L. R. James, in conversation with new interlocutors, will continue to generate fruitful disagreements about the world we live in.

NOTES

Chapter 1

1. Whether James was born in Tunapuna or Caroni, Trinidad, is disputed by his biographers. His grave, however, is definitely in Tunapuna.

2. The *Beacon* Group is discussed more fully in chapter 3.

3. Whereas this sketch of James's life will be expanded in the subsequent chapters, the reader is also encouraged to refer to the two biographies of James, Paul Buhle's *C. L. R. James: The Artist as Revolutionary* and Kent Worcester's *C. L. R. James: A Political Biography*; Anthony Bogues's *Caliban's Freedom: The Early Political Thought of C. L. R. James* and Aldon Lynn Nielsen's *C. L. R. James: A Critical Introduction* are also both extremely useful and accessible introductions to James's work. Anna Grimshaw's introduction to *The C. L. R. James Reader* is also excellent.

4. Brett St Louis introduced me to the idea of acknowledgment as constituent to the definition of creolization. (In conversation with the author, London, July 1998.)

5. Creole as a language formation is not a topic that I cover in the present study. Nevertheless, the linguistic aspects of creolization share a close relationship with creolization's representational currency within politics and culture. In chapter 3, this overlap is broached in my discussion of orality and vernacular speech in the context of *Minty Alley*.

6. See also Ania Loomba, *Colonialism/Postcolonialism* (London and New York: Routledge, 1998).

7. I am indebted to Kevin Meehan for a series of conversations in 1994 that helped me to navigate these points of connection and convergence between creolization and hybridity.

8. There is a great deal of excellent work that has been done on mimicry. In reference to cricket, Manthia Diawara's article "Englishness and Blackness: Cricket as Dis-

course on Colonialism," and *Liberation Cricket: West Indies Cricket Culture*, edited by Beckles and Stoddart, are useful places to begin. Mimicry and performance is also an aspect of Parama Roy's *Indian Traffic*.

9. The psychoanalytic turn in Bhabha is prefigured by Glissant's constructions of creolization. For further critiques of hybridity and its lack of political efficacy see Aijaz Ahmad, *In Theory: Classes, Nations, Literatures* (London: Verso, 1992), and B. Parry, "Resistance Theory/Theorising Resistance or Two Cheers for Nativism," in *Colonial Discourse/Postcolonial Theory*, ed. Francis Barker, Peter Hulme, and M. Iverson (Manchester: Manchester University Press, 1994), 172–96.

10. Hybridity and creolization can also be understood as sharing characteristics and political resonances with the term *cultural syncretism*. According to Ashcroft, Griffiths, and Tiffin (1998), cultural syncretism is a term "sometimes used to avoid the problems some critics have associated with the idea of hybridity in identifying the fusion of two distinct traditions to produce a new and distinctive whole" (229). They suggest, however, that *(cultural) syncretism* is a term used far less frequently than *creolization* or *hybridity* in postcolonial studies because of its "strong associations with the specialist fields" of religion and theology (229).

11. See for instance, Bhabha, "Signs"; Glissant, *Caribbean Discourse*; and Walcott, "The Muse of History," and "The Caribbean: Culture or Mimicry?"

12. See for instance, Farred, "Maple Man," and Carby, *Race Men*, esp. 123–25.

Chapter 2

1. Grimshaw helpfully quotes from two reviews of the play that appeared in the *Manchester Guardian* and the *Daily Telegraph* (*Special Delivery* 33 n. 11). The revised version of the play is reprinted in the *Reader*. Grimshaw also discusses the play in her introduction to the *Reader* (5).

2. This publishing history is related in the appendix of *C. L. R. James's Caribbean* edited by Paget Henry and Paul Buhle. See especially pages 263–70, where they reprint excerpts from *Cipriani*.

3. In 1937, James published *World Revolution, 1917–1936: The Rise and Fall of the Communist International*, and in 1938 he also published the monograph *A History of Negro Revolt*, which was revised in 1969 and retitled *A History of Pan-African Revolt*.

4. Validation and celebration of nonwhite, non-European, non-middle- or upper-class cultures is also an aspect of the Negritude movement and the Harlem Renaissance, both of which are important contexts for James's work in the 1930s.

5. In referencing Toussaint L'Ouverture by his first name, and by using an apostrophe in his surname, I am following James's own practice. Kara Rabbitt notes that by using the leader's first name, James constructs a certain "intimacy" between the reader and the subject. In contrast, he consistently refers to Napoleon Bonaparte by his last name, when the opposite is the more common practice (Rabbitt 133 n. 10).

6. James's focus on Toussaint is also a parallel, or a reflection, of James himself. As George Lamming says, "James becomes completely immersed in the fortunes of his hero.

... [he] cannot overcome the bond which Toussaint's glory has sealed between the historian and the soldier" (*Pleasures* 148). The duplication of himself in the subject or protagonists of his books is something James does rather consistently throughout his career as we can note in *Minty Alley* and *Beyond a Boundary*.

7. While I have used Walcott, Harris, and Glissant here, other important contributions to this conversation about myth and history include Alejo Carpentier's *The Kingdom of This World*, René Dépestre's *Festival of the Greasy Pole*, Frantz Fanon's *The Wretched of the Earth*, and Michelle Cliff's *No Telephone to Heaven*. Wilson Harris identifies Vodun as one of two myths central to the West Indian imagination (the other is the limbo dance), and each are derived from Africa and the "Middle Passage" endured by slaves en route to the Americas. Edward Kamau Brathwaite's poem "Caliban" and his essay "The African Presence in Caribbean Literature" also suggest revolutionary (or resistance) meaning for the limbo.

Chapter 3

1. James also uses short stories to convey similar critiques. See, for instance "Triumph" and "La Divina Pastora."

2. In my study of *Minty Alley* as a bildungsroman, I am building on the fine work done in situating this genre within the Caribbean and noting how the Caribbean transforms the genre already begun by scholar Maria Helena Lima in her article "Revolutionary Developments: Michelle Cliff's *No Telephone to Heaven* and Merle Collin's *Angel*," *Ariel* 24, no. 1 (Jan. 1993).

3. Reinhard Sander is an excellent source for more information on the *Beacon* era of West Indian writing. I quote here from his article "The Thirties and Forties," in Bruce King, *West Indian Literature*, (London: Macmillan Press, 1979):

> *The Beacon*, [was] a monthly magazine published by Albert Gomes in Trinidad from March 1931 to November 1933 (28 issues). *The Beacon* superseded the pioneering literary magazine *Trinidad*, which appeared only twice in 1929 and 1930, under the joint editorship of Alfred H. Mendes and C. L. R. James. *The Beacon* devoted its pages not only to creative writing, but also participated actively in local, West Indian and world politics. In its editorials it denounced the Crown Colony form of government, reported and commented on the proposals for a West Indian Federation, followed India's struggle for independence and praised the Russian experiment in socialism. In outlook it was anti-capitalist and anti-ecclesiastical, bohemian and iconoclastic. Although it sold more than 5000 copies at the peak of its popularity, it received a hostile reception from the Trinidad middle class. (49)

4. Kimberly Murphy, a former graduate student at the University of Maryland, coined this apt phrase in response to Jamaica Kincaid's descriptions of "conquerors" in her "In The Garden" essays (Fall 1997).

5. My use of the terms "folk" and "folk culture" and my attempts to understand them in complicated ways is informed by John Roberts's analysis in his article "African-American Folklore in a Discourse of Folkness" *New York Folklore* 18, nos. 1–4: 61–77. See pages 64–65.

6. In her introduction to *The C. L. R. James Reader* Grimshaw contextualizes the perspective James expresses in "Case" both in terms of his political orientation as learned up to that point from literature and in terms of how his perspective would later change as he became more overtly engaged in politics. She writes, "James's sharp observations of the cringing hypocrisy and mediocrity among those holding position in colonial society was strongly reminiscent of the style of his favourite novelists, Thackeray and Bennett. This was not surprising, given that his essay, 'The Case For West Indian Self Government,' was rooted in the early phase of James's life; thereafter, his approach to the colonial question was transformed (shown clearly in his polemical piece, 'Abyssinia and the Imperialists') as he became swept up in the political turmoil of pre-war Europe" (4–5).

7. I agree with Kevin Meehan's recommendation to read Ralph De Boissiere's novel *Crown Jewel* (1953)—a political romance set against the backdrop of Trinidad's political transformations in the 1930s—in conjunction with *Minty Alley* as a means to counteract the political silences in *Minty Alley*.

8. James's linkage of language and folk culture suggests yet another point of connection with Brathwaite's nonfiction theorization of creolization as well as the creative manifestations of his theories as expressed in his poetry.

9. There is another, more straightforward way to read this school certificate scene: from a feminist perspective, one immediately questions whether Monsieur Saint-Louis would have denied an elder son the opportunity he denies Tortilla. There exists a double standard for boys and girls when it comes to assessing the benefits of scholarly advancement.

10. This formulation of the pan and the close-up as a metaphor or embodiment of James's concept of the individual and the collective belongs to Lee Walker as I understood it from his talk, "C. L. R. James, Shakespeare and Film," presented at the C. L. R. James Institute, Feb. 23, 1998, New York City.

11. In unpublished autobiographical writings, James asserts that Haynes is based on his own experiences in a room he rented "one summer . . . watching back street life." His observations fed his narrative, and James wrote a chapter a day. See C. L. R. James, "Autobiography: The Writing of *Minty Alley*" (undated, 1970s). Unpublished manuscript available at the C. L. R. James Institute, New York; 3 pp.

Chapter 4

1. Relevant scholarship includes but is hardly limited to that by Cedric Robinson, Hazel V. Carby, Paul Gilroy, Kevin Meehan, Belinda Edmondson, and Carole Boyce Davies. Earlier generations were led in such endeavors by W. E. B. Du Bois, Claude McKay, George Padmore, and, of course, James and Wright themselves.

2. Such people include but are not limited to Frantz Fanon, Aimé Césaire, Paul Robeson, Ralph Bunche, A. Phillip Randolph, and George Padmore.

3. Various reasons for Wright's and James's differing assessments can be located in a number of categories, each one related to Wright's and James's biographical experience and (shifting) political orientations. These categories include race, class, gender, formal

education, status as outsider and sojourner, Communism and socialism, Black Power and Pan-Africanism.

4. For a longer, more detailed analysis of the origins and contexts for the "Negro Question," I encourage the reader to consult Cedric Robinson's *Black Marxism*, a text which in its entirety is essential for a broad contextualization of figures like James, Wright, and Du Bois. Interestingly, Claude McKay was one of two black attendants at the Fourth Congress.

5. Italy's invasion of Ethiopia was an important rallying point, as Robin D. G. Kelley puts it, "virtually every self-respecting black activist, irrespective of their national origins or ideological bent, joined the Ethiopian defense campaigns" (Kelley, Introduction to *History* 8).

6. This second review, collected in Paul Le Blanc and Scott McLemee's edited volume, *C. L. R. James and Revolutionary Marxism*, appeared in 1941 in the Trotskyist press. The first review is collected in McLemee's edited volume *C. L. R. James on the "Negro Question."* Both versions are relevant to the development of James's response to the "Negro Question" during the 1940s, both are concerned with the political nature and impact of creative writing, and both contain implicit and explicit warnings to the Left as well as to mainstream America that *Native Son* is just one of the more successful vocalizations of Negro revolutionary ferment in the United States.

7. During and after his Communist days Wright cultivated an isolated artist persona, and in some ways he lived it. But at various times during his life he was part of diverse literary and political communities. This disjunction between representation and reality reminds us that Wright, like James, presents a slippery narrative persona: such a disjunction is particularly evident in the different narrative tone of *Black Boy* and *Twelve Million Black Voices* (1941). Wright himself studies black literature, attempts to write that community into the national consciousness and is friends with a wide array of black writers and activists, including Langston Hughes, Margaret Walker, Arna Bontemps, and Sterling Brown. Wright is neither ignorant, involuntarily isolated, nor apolitical, but that's often how he represents U.S. blacks. At the same time, his break with the CP shared a premise with James's break from the Workers Party: it was owing in part to "its unwillingness to confront wartime racial discrimination" (*Native Son* 557 Chronology).

8. According to other critics, James's same Caribbean background and British colonial orientation left him politically ill-prepared to fully engage and critique the complex significations of racialized oppression in the United States in the 1940s. He worked prodigiously to facilitate such an uprising, which he and his comrades felt would manifest on the heels of the brazenly capitalist enterprise of "the great war." James's critics have correctly identified the lack of contingency in the event that such a proletarian uprising (in any part of the world) did not occur or in the event that, as in the case of the United States Civil Rights and antiwar movements, uprisings occurred within differently envisaged configurations of workers and capital. On the other hand, in his engagements and discussions of class and class conflict, he did accurately predict the national conflagrations of the 1960s, especially U.S. antiwar activities. (See Surin and St Louis.)

Chapter 5

1. I am grateful to Sandra Pouchet Paquet for first calling my attention to this quote and to Heaney's text in her foreword to George Lamming's *In the Castle of My Skin*.

2. In its autobiographical moments *Mariners* offers an interesting midsection to his published autobiographical writings, sandwiched as it is between *Minty Alley* and *Beyond a Boundary*'s earlier and later autobiographical revelations.

3. Detailed information about the circumstances of *American Civilization*'s production as well as that of *Mariners, Renegades, and Castaways* is provided by Anna Grimshaw and Keith Hart in the introduction to *American Civilization*. Key points include the fact that "*American Civilization* was drafted under difficult circumstances" occasioned by James's new family responsibilities (his son was born in early 1949) and these duties "exacerbated his longstanding financial anxieties." In addition, James "was being pursued by the FBI which was seeking his deportation because of his unresolved immigration status" (22). Finally, "there was a potential conflict between publishing a highly personal document and the discipline required of him as an official member in the leadership of the SWP" (23). Grimshaw and Hart offer these facts as part of the explanation for the secrecy with which James circulated the text and for why it remained unpublished for so many years.

4. There is a moment in "Negroes, Women, and the Intellectuals" where James invokes his own experiences of Jim Crow as a black man to underscore the validity of his comments. He writes, "The writer of this as all readers of this outline know, is a Negro, and if it is thought advisable, could give examples of his own direct, personal experiences, extending from New Orleans to Memphis" (203).

5. The surveillance of James encompassed and complicated his personal life. The U.S. government would not recognize James's divorce from his first wife, Juanita Young (whom he married in Trinidad in 1929), when he then married American Constance Webb, a former model and actress, whom he courted for nearly six years. After marrying Webb in 1946 James was required to go to Reno, Nevada, in 1948 to acquire a new "official divorce decree and to establish residency" (Worcester, *Biography* 100). After the second divorce from Juanita, James remarried Webb, now pregnant with their child. This marriage ended in 1951. Worcester discusses the time James spent in Reno in detail and, referencing James's letters to Webb, identifies those weeks as depressing and difficult for James in terms of Jim Crow segregation, financial hardships, ill health (ulcers), and, not least, heartache (100). The Reno period represents an interesting precursor to James's internment on Ellis Island, in 1953. The "house arrest" of Reno precedes his eventual breakup with Webb, and his detainment on Ellis Island anticipates the long-distance relationship he maintains with the JFT after deportation. James's experience of confinement in Reno forces him to revise his positive notion of America's geographic and political "expansiveness."

6. See William E. Cain's "The Triumph of the Will and the Failure of Resistance: C. L. R. James's Readings of *Moby Dick* and *Othello*" in Cudjoe and Cain, *C. L. R. James*; Robinson's "C. L. R. James and the World-System"; Nielsen's *Writing Between the Lines*, ch. 2; and Spanos's *Errant Art of Moby Dick*.

7. *Moby Dick* assumes a primacy of position in James's revolutionary canon alongside *Vanity Fair, King Lear,* and *Native Son.*

8. St Louis makes the point that *Mariners* can be situated as both an anti-CP and a "courtship" text designed to "woo" the INS. *American Civilization,* the other often disparaged James book, also articulates James's attempt to be American and suggests a new pragmatism on his part structured through a movement from the radical left to a Social Democrat position (in conversation with the author, 1998).

9. Dunayevskaya broke from James and the group in the mid-1950s, while others, including Grace Lee Boggs, broke from the group in the 1960s. Throughout this period James stayed in close contact and attempted to lead the group from his various locations abroad.

10. Many of James's publications during this American period were collectively authored. In 1956, the JFT produced a condensed, polished version of the *American Civilization* manuscript. For a variety of reasons, mostly simplicity and my interest in making connections between James's narrative voices and his lived experiences, I have chosen not to consider these publications in my study.

11. See Cain "Triumph of the Will," and Robinson, "C. L. R. James and the World System." A notable exception is Aldon Nielsen; see both *C. L. R. James: A Critical Introduction* and chapter 2 of *Writing Between the Lines: Race and Intertextuality.*

12. Wright's 1953 existentialist text, *The Outsider,* was also considered inferior to his earlier stateside productions. I find this an interesting coincidence, not for any perceived similarity between it and *Mariners* but because of each author's attempt to critique America within rubrics not previously associated with them: for Wright it was the use of existential philosophy, and for James it was the interweaving of his personal distress with that of "the nation." In addition to the important work of scholars such as Cedric Robinson and Paul Gilroy, which has recently guided readers back to *The Outsider,* Wright's "failed" text, like that of James, demonstrates a line of descent originating in his earlier work on the potential of the black masses in the United States.

Chapter 6

1. Within the pages of *American Civilization* one can discern James's own desire to find creolization in the United States as it exists in the Caribbean, and perhaps even in a more advanced form, a quest that ultimately fails.

2. Chapter 1 offers an extensive discussion of and criteria for my usage of the term "hybridity."

3. For further reading see Beckles and Stoddart, *Liberation Cricket,* and Birbalsingh, *The Rise Of West Indian Cricket.*

4. See especially Sylvia Wynter, "In Quest of Matthew Bondman: Some Cultural Notes on the Jamesian Journey," in Buhle, *C. L. R. James,* 131–45.

5. Nevertheless, when discussing the batting of Rohan Kanhai in the 1966 article "Kanhai: A Study in Confidence" (*At The Rendezvous of Victory,* 1984), James reverts to

an understanding of the cricket personality as representative of a very specific and static national identity.

6. This scene replicates a similar one found in George Lamming's novel *In The Castle of My Skin*, where the shoemaker's shop is the locale for political discussions that lead to political action and resistance.

7. St Louis includes a discussion of James's notions regarding the transmission of genius in *C. L. R. James's Social Theory: A Critique of Race and Modernity*.

WORKS CITED

Alexander, Ziggi. Preface to *The History of Mary Prince: A West Indian Slave, Related by Herself.* 1831. Ed. Moira Ferguson. London: Pandora, 1987.
Anderson, Benedict. *Imagined Communities.* Rev. ed. London: Verso, 1991.
Ashcroft, Bill, Gareth Griffiths, and Helen Tifflin. *Key Concepts in Post-Colonial Studies.* London and New York: Routledge, 1998.
Bakhtin, Mikhail. *The Dialogic Imagination: Four Essays.* Ed. Michael Holquist. Trans. Caryl Emerson and Michael Holquist. Austin: University of Texas Press, 1981.
Balutansky, Kathleen, and Marie-Agnès Sourieau, eds. *Caribbean Creolization: Reflections on the Cultural Dynamics of Language, Literature, and Identity.* Gainesville: University Press of Florida, 1998.
Bambara, Toni Cade. *Deep Sightings and Rescue Missions.* Ed. with a preface by Toni Morrison. New York: Pantheon Books, 1996.
Baraka, Amiri. "Afro-American Literature and Class Struggle." *Black American Literature Forum* 14 (1980): 5–14.
Beckles, Hilary McD, and Brian Stoddart, eds. *Liberation Cricket: West Indies Cricket Culture.* Manchester, Eng., and New York: Manchester University Press, 1995.
Benítez-Rojo, Antonío. *The Repeating Island.* Durham, N.C.: Duke University Press, 1992.
———. "Three Words toward Creolization." In *Caribbean Creolization: Reflections on the Cultural Dynamics of Language, Literature, and Identity,* ed. Kathleen Balutansky and Marie-Agnes Sourieau. Gainesville: University Press of Florida, 1998. 53–61.
Beverly, John. "The Margin at the Center: On Testimonio (Testimonial Narrative)." *Modern Fiction Studies* 35, no. 1 (Spring 1989): 10–32.
Bhabha, Homi. "Signs Taken For Wonders: Questions of Ambivalence and Authority under a Tree Outside Delhi 1817." In *"Race," Writing, and Difference,* ed. Henry Louis Gates Jr. Chicago: University of Chicago Press, 1986. 163–84.

Birbalsingh, Frank. *The Rise of West Indian Cricket: From Colony to Nation.* Antigua: Hansib Publishing, 1996.

Boggs, Grace Lee. *Living For Change: An Autobiography.* Minneapolis: University of Minnesota Press, 1998.

Bogues, Anthony. *Caliban's Freedom: The Early Political Thought of C. L. R. James.* London: Pluto Press, 1997.

Bolland, O. Nigel. "Creolization and Creole Societies: A Culturalnationalist View of Caribbean Social History." In *Intellectuals in the Twentieth-Century Caribbean*, vol. 1: *Spectre of the New Class: The Commonwealth Caribbean*, ed. Alistair Hennessy. Warwick University Caribbean Studies. London and Basingstoke: MacMillan, 1992. 50–79.

Bongie, Chris. *Islands and Exiles: The Creole Identities of Post/Colonial Literature.* Stanford, Calif.: Stanford University Press, 1998.

Brathwaite, Edward Kamau. "Caliban, Ariel, and Unprospero in the Conflict of Creolization: A Study of the Slave Revolt in Jamaica, 1831–32." *Comparative Perspectives on Slavery in New World Plantation Societies*, Annals of the New York Academy of Sciences, 292 (June 27, 1977): 41–62.

———. *Contradictory Omens: Cultural Diversity and Integration in the Caribbean.* Mona, Jamaica: Savacou, 1974.

———. *The Development of Creole Society in Jamaica, 1770–1820.* Oxford: Clarendon, 1971.

———. *History of the Voice: The Development of Nation Language in Anglophone Caribbean Poetry.* London and Port of Spain: New Beacon, 1984.

———. *Roots.* Ann Arbor: University of Michigan Press, 1993.

Brennan, Timothy. *At Home in the World: Cosmopolitanism Now.* Cambridge: Harvard University Press, 1997.

Brody, Jennifer Devere. *Impossible Purities: Blackness, Femininity, and Victorian Culture.* Durham, N.C., and London: Duke University Press, 1998.

Buhle, Paul. *C. L. R. James: The Artist as Revolutionary.* London: Verso, 1988.

———, ed. *C. L. R. James: His Life and Work.* London: Allison and Busby, 1986.

———. "Marxism in America." In *C. L. R. James and Revolutionary Marxism*, ed. Scott McLemee and Paul Le Blanc. New Jersey: Humanities Press, 1994. 55–76.

———. "Rethinking the Rethinking." *C. L. R. James Journal* 1 (1998): 61–71.

Bundy, A. J. M., ed. *Selected Essays of Wilson Harris: The Genesis of An Unfinished Imagination.* London: Routledge, 1999.

Cain, William E. "The Triumph of the Will and the Failure of Resistance: C. L. R. James's Readings of *Moby Dick* and *Othello.*" In *C. L. R. James: His Intellectual Legacies*, ed. Selwyn R. Cudjoe and William E. Cain. Amherst: University of Massachusetts Press, 1995. 260–73.

Cambridge, Alrick. "C. L. R. James: Freedom through History and Dialectics." In *Intellectuals in the Twentieth-Century Caribbean*, vol. 1: *Spectre of the New Class: The Commonwealth Caribbean*, ed. Alistair Hennessy. Warwick University Caribbean Studies. London: MacMillan, 1992. 163–78.

Carby, Hazel V. "Proletarian or Revolutionary Literature? C. L. R. James and the Politics of The Trinidadian Renaissance." *South Atlantic Quarterly* 87 (Winter 1988): 39–52.
———. *Race Men: The W. E. B. Du Bois Lectures*. Cambridge, Mass., and London: Harvard University Press, 1998.
Césaire, Aimé. *Discourse on Colonialism*. Trans. J. Pinkham. New York: Monthly Review Press, 1972.
Cobham, Rhonda. Introduction to *Black Fauns* by A. Mendes. London: New Beacon, 1984.
———. Introduction to *Through a Maze of Colour* by Albert Gomes. N.p., 1974.
———. "Women in Jamaican Literature, 1900–1950." In *Out of The Kumbla: Caribbean Women and Literature*, ed. Carol Boyce Davies and Elaine Savory Fido. Trenton, N.J.: Africa World Press, 1990. 197–218.
Cooper, Carolyn. *Noises in the Blood: Orality, Gender, and the "Vulgar" Body of Jamaican Popular Culture*. Durham, N.C.: Duke University Press, 1993.
Cudjoe, Selwyn, and William E. Cain, eds. *C. L. R. James: His Intellectual Legacies*. Amherst: University of Massachusetts Press, 1995.
Dash, J. Michael. *Edouard Glissant*. Cambridge, Eng.: Cambridge University Press, 1995.
———. Introduction to *Caribbean Discourse* by Edouard Glissant. Charlottesville: University Press of Virginia, 1989.
———. *This Other America: Caribbean Literature in a New World Context*. Charlottesville and London: University Press of Virginia, 1998.
Davies, Carole Boyce. *Black Women, Writing, and Identity: Migrations of the Subject*. London and New York: Routledge, 1994.
Davies, Carole Boyce, and Elaine Savory Fido, eds. *Out of the Kumbla: Caribbean Women and Literature*. Trenton, N.J.: Africa World Press, 1990.
Denning, Michael. *The Cultural Front: The Laboring of American Culture in the Twentieth Century*. London and New York: Verso, 1997.
Diawara, Manthia. "Englishness and Blackness: Cricket as Discourse on Colonialism." *Callaloo* 13, no. 4 (Fall 1990): 835–51.
Edmondson, Belinda, ed. *Caribbean Romances: The Politics of Regional Representation*. Charlottesville: University Press of Virginia, 1999.
———. *Making Men: Gender, Literary Authority, and Women's Writing in Caribbean Narrative*. Durham, N.C.: Duke University Press, 1999.
———. "Race, Tradition, and the Construction of the Caribbean Aesthetic." *New Literary History* 25 (1994): 109–20.
Ellison, Ralph. "Blues People." 1964. *The Collected Essays of Ralph Ellison*. Ed. John F. Callahan. New York: Modern Library, 1995. 278–87.
———. "The Charlie Christian Story." 1958. *The Collected Essays of Ralph Ellison*. Ed. John F. Callahan. New York: Modern Library, 1995. 266–72.
———. *The Collected Essays of Ralph Ellison*. Ed. John F. Callahan. New York: Modern Library, 1995.
———. "The Little Man at Chehaw Station." 1977/78. *The Collected Essays of Ralph Ellison*. Ed. John F. Callahan. New York: Modern Library, 1995. 489–519.

———. "The Novel as a Function of American Democracy." 1967. *The Collected Essays of Ralph Ellison*. Ed. John F. Callahan. New York: Modern Library, 1995. 755–65.

———. "On Bird, Bird-Watching and Jazz." 1962. *The Collected Essays of Ralph Ellison*. Ed. John F. Callahan. New York: Modern Library, 1995. 256–65.

Fanon, Frantz. *The Wretched of the Earth*. New York: Grove Press, 1963.

Farred, Grant, Introduction to *Rethinking C. L. R. James*. Ed. Grant Farred. Oxford, U.K.: Blackwell, 1996.

———. "The Maple Man: How Cricket Made a Postcolonial Intellectual." In *Rethinking C. L. R. James*, ed. Grant Farred. Oxford, U.K.: Blackwell, 1996.

Ferguson, Moira. *Jamaica Kincaid: Where The Land Meets the Body*. Charlottesville: University Press of Virginia, 1994.

Foley, Barbara. *Radical Representations: Politics and Form in U.S. Proletarian Fiction, 1929–1941*. Durham, N.C.: Duke University Press, 1993.

Franklin, Vincent P. "Caribbean Intellectual Influences on Afro-Americans in the United States." In *Intellectuals in the Twentieth-Century Caribbean*, vol. 1: *Spectre of the New Class: the Commonwealth Caribbean*, ed. Alistair Hennessy. Warwick University Caribbean Studies. London: MacMillan, 1992. 179–90.

Gates, Henry Louis, Jr., ed. *"Race," Writing, and Difference*. Chicago: University of Chicago Press, 1986.

Gilroy, Paul. *The Black Atlantic*. Cambridge, Mass.: Harvard University Press, 1993.

———. *Small Acts: Thoughts on the Politics of Black Cultures*. London and New York: Serpents Tail Press, 1993.

———. *There Ain't No Black in the Union Jack*. Chicago: University of Chicago Press, 1989.

Glissant, Edouard. *Caribbean Discourse: Selected Essays*. Trans. J. Michael Dash. Charlottesville: University Press of Virginia, 1989.

Graham, Maryemma. Introduction to *The Outsider* by Richard Wright. New York: Harper Perennial, 1993.

Grimshaw, Anna. "C. L. R. James: A Revolutionary Vision for the Twentieth Century." In *The C. L. R. James Reader*, ed. Anna Grimshaw. Cambridge, Mass. and Oxford: Blackwell, 1992. 1–24.

———, ed. *The C. L. R. James Reader*. Oxford: Blackwell, 1992.

———, ed. *Special Delivery: The Letters of C. L. R. James to Constance Webb, 1939–1948*. Oxford: Blackwell, 1996.

———. "Special Delivery: The Letters of C. L. R. James to Constance Webb, 1939–1948." In *Rethinking C. L. R. James*, ed. Grant Farred. Oxford: Blackwell, 1996. 45–74.

Grimshaw, Anna, and Keith Hart, Introduction to *American Civilization* by C. L. R. James. Oxford: Blackwell, 1992. 1–25.

Hall, Stuart. "C. L. R. James: A Portrait." In *C. L. R. James's Caribbean*, ed. Paget Henry and Paul Buhle. Durham, N.C.: Duke University Press, 1992. 3–16.

———. "A Conversation with C. L. R. James." In *Rethinking C. L. R. James*, ed. Grant Farred. Oxford: Blackwell, 1996. 15–44.

———, ed. *Representation: Cultural Representations and Signifying Practices*. Milton Keynes, Eng.: Open University and Sage Publications, 1997.

———. "What Is This 'Black' in Black Popular Culture?" In *Black Popular Culture*, ed. Gina Dent. Seattle: Bay Press, 1992. 21–33.
Hall, Stuart, David Held, and Tony McGrew, eds. *Modernity and Its Futures*. Oxford: Open University and Polity Press, 1992.
Hamilton, Cynthia. "A Way of Seeing: Culture as Political Expression in the Works of C. L. R. James." *Journal of Black Studies* 22, no. 3 (Mar. 1992): 429–43.
Harding, James. M. "Adorno, Ellison, and the Critique of Jazz." *Cultural Critique*, 31 (Fall 1995): 129–56.
Harlow, Barbara. *Resistance Literature*. New York: Methuen, 1987.
Harney, Stephano. *Nationalism and Identity: Culture and Imagination in a Caribbean Diaspora*. New York: Zed, 1996.
Harris, Wilson. "Creoleness: The Crossroads of a Civilization?" In *Selected Essays of Wilson Harris: The Genesis of An Unfinished Imagination*, ed. A. J. M. Bundy. London: Routledge, 1999. 237–47.
———. "History, Fable, and Myth in the Caribbean and Guianas." In *Anagogic Qualities of Literature*, ed. Joseph P. Strelka. Yearbook of Comparative Criticism 4. University Park: Penn State University Press, 1971. 120–31.
———. *Tradition, the Writer, and Society: Critical Essays*. London: New Beacon, 1967.
Heaney, Seamus. *The Place of Writing*. Atlanta: Scholars, 1989.
Hennessy, Alistair, ed. *Intellectuals in the Twentieth-Century Caribbean*, vol. 1: *Spectre of the New Class: The Commonwealth Caribbean*. Warwick University Caribbean Studies. London: MacMillan, 1992.
Henry, Paget, and Paul Buhle. "Caliban as Deconstructionist." In *C. L. R. James's Caribbean*, ed. Paget Henry and Paul Buhle. Durham: Duke University Press, 1992. 111–42.
———, eds. *C. L. R. James's Caribbean*. Durham, N.C., and London: Duke University Press, 1992.
Hill, Robert A. "In England, 1932–1938" In *C. L. R. James: His Life and Work*, ed. Paul Buhle. London: Allison and Busby, 1986. 61–80.
———. "Literary Executor's Afterword." In *American Civilization*, ed. Anna Grimshaw and Keith Hart. Oxford: Blackwell, 1993. 293–366.
James, C. L. R. "Abyssinia and the Imperialists." 1936. In *The C. L. R. James Reader*, ed. Anna Grimshaw. Oxford: Blackwell, 1992. 63–67.
———. *American Civilization*. Ed. Anna Grimshaw and Keith Hart. Cambridge, Eng.: Blackwell, 1992.
———. *At The Rendezvous of Victory: Selected Writings*. London: Allison and Busby, 1984.
———. "Autobiography: My Early Life and Work in the Caribbean." Untitled transcript of talk at Rutgers University, Sept. 18, 1973. Available at the C. L. R. James Institute, New York, 37 pp.
———. *Beyond a Boundary*. 1963. Durham, N.C.: Duke University Press, 1993.
———. *The Black Jacobins*. 1936. *The C. L. R. James Reader*. Ed. Anna Grimshaw. Oxford: Blackwell, 1992. 67–111.
———. *The Black Jacobins: Toussaint L'Ouverture and the San Domingo Revolution*. 1938. New York: Vintage, 1963.

———. "Black People in the Urban Areas of the United States." 1970. In *The C. L. R. James Reader*, ed. Anna Grimshaw. Oxford: Blackwell, 1992. 375–78.

———. "Black Power." 1967. In *Spheres of Existence*. Westport, Conn.: Lawrence Hill and Co., 1980. 221–36.

———. "Black Studies and the Contemporary Student." 1969. In *The C. L. R. James Reader*, ed. Anna Grimshaw. Oxford: Blackwell, 1992. 390–404.

———. "The Case for West Indian Self-Government." 1933. In *The C. L. R. James Reader*, ed. Anna Grimshaw. Oxford: Blackwell, 1992. 49–62.

———. *Cricket*. Ed. Anna Grimshaw. London: Allison and Busby, 1986.

———. "Cricket and Race." 1975. In *Cricket*, ed. Anna Grimshaw. London: Allison and Busby, 1986. 278–79.

———. "Dialectical Materialism and the Fate of Humanity." 1947. In *The C. L. R. James Reader*, ed. Anna Grimshaw. Oxford: Blackwell, 1992. 153–81.

———. "Discovering Literature in Trinidad: The Nineteen-Thirties." 1969. In *Spheres of Existence*. Westport, Conn.: Lawrence Hill and Co., 1980. 237–44.

———. "Down With Starvation Wages in Missouri." In *The Future in the Present: Selected Writings*. London: Allison and Busby, 1977. 89–94.

———. *Every Cook Can Govern: A Study of Democracy in Ancient Greece and Its Meaning for Today*. 1956. 2nd ed., Detroit: Bewick Editions, 1992.

———. *The Future in the Present: Selected Writings*. London: Allison and Busby, 1977.

———. "The Historical Development of the Negroes in American Society." 1943. In *C. L. R. James on the "Negro Question,"* ed. Scott McLemee. Jackson: University Press of Mississippi, 1996. 63–89.

———. *A History of Pan-African Revolt*. 1938. New York: Charles H. Kerr, 1995. (Originally published as *A History of Negro Revolt*.)

———. "Kanhai: A Study in Confidence." In *At The Rendezvous of Victory: Selected Writings*. London: Allison and Busby, 1984. 166–71.

———. "La Divina Pastora." 1927. In *The C. L. R James Reader*, ed. Anna Grimshaw. Oxford: Blackwell, 1992. 25–28.

———. "Lenin and the Vanguard Party." 1963. In *The C. L. R. James Reader*, ed. Anna Grimshaw. Oxford: Blackwell, 1992. 327–30.

———. "Letters to Constance Webb." 1944, 1945. In *The C. L. R. James Reader*, ed. Anna Grimshaw. Oxford: Blackwell, 1992. 127–52.

———. "The Making of the Caribbean People." 1966. In *Spheres of Existence*. Westport, Conn.: Lawrence Hill and Co., 1980. 173–90.

———. *Mariners, Renegades and Castaways: Herman Melville and The World We Live In*. 1953. London: Allison and Busby, 1985.

———. *Minty Alley*. 1936. London: New Beacon Books, 1971.

———. *Modern Politics*. 1960. Detroit: Bewick, 1973.

———. "A National Purpose for Caribbean Peoples." In *At the Rendezvous of Victory: Selected Writings*. London: Allison and Busby, 1984. 143–58.

———. *Nkrumah and the Ghana Revolution*. London: Allison and Busby, 1977.

———. *Notes on Dialectics: Hegel, Marx and Lenin*. 1948. London: Allison and Busby, 1980.

———. "On *Native Son* by Richard Wright." 1940. In *C. L. R. James on the "Negro Question,"* ed. Scott McLemee. Jackson: University Press of Mississippi, 1996. 55–57.

———. "Preface to Criticism." 1955. In *The C. L. R. James Reader,* ed. Anna Grimshaw. Oxford: Blackwell, 1992. 255–60.

———."The Revolutionary Answer to the Negro Problem in the U.S.A." 1948. In *C. L. R. James and Revolutionary Marxism,* ed. Scott McLemee and Paul Le Blanc. Atlantic Highlands, N.J.: Humanities Press, 1994. 179–87.

———. "The Rise and Fall of Nkrumah." 1966. In *The C. L. R. James Reader,* ed. Anna Grimshaw. Oxford: Blackwell, 1992. 354–61.

———. *Spheres of Existence: Selected Writings.* Conn.: Lawrence Hill and Co., 1980.

———. "Three Black Women Writers: Toni Morison, Alice Walker, and Ntozake Shange." 1981. In *The C. L. R. James Reader,* ed. Anna Grimshaw. Oxford: Blackwell, 1992. 411–17.

———. "Triumph." 1929. In *The C. L. R. James Reader,* ed. Anna Grimshaw. Oxford: Blackwell, 1992. 29–40.

———. "Whitman and Melville." 1950. In *The C. L. R. James Reader,* ed. Anna Grimshaw. Oxford: Blackwell, 1992. 202–19.

———. "With the Sharecroppers." 1941. In *C. L. R. James on the "Negro Question,"* ed. Scott McLemee. Jackson: University Press of Mississippi, 1996. 22–33.

James, C. L. R., Grace Lee Boggs, and P. Chaulieu. *Facing Reality.* 1958. Detroit: Bewick, 1974.

James, C. L. R., et al. *Fighting Racism in World War II.* Ed. Fred Stanton. New York: Pathfinder, 1980.

———. *State Capitalism and World Revolution.* 1956. Chicago: Charles Kerr, 1986.

James, Winston. *Holding Aloft the Banner of Ethiopia: Caribbean Radicalism in Early Twentieth-Century America.* London: Verso, 1998.

Jones, LeRoi (Amiri Baraka). *Blues People.* New York: Morrow Quill Paperbacks, 1963.

Kelley, Robin D. G. Introduction to *A History of Pan-African Revolt* by C. L. R. James. Chicago: Charles H. Kerr, 1995. 1–33.

———. "The World the Diaspora Made: C. L. R. James and the Politics of History." In *Rethinking C. L. R. James,* ed. Grant Farred. Oxford: Blackwell, 1996. 103–30.

Kofsky, Frank. *Black Music, White Business: Illuminating the History and Political Economy of Jazz.* New York: Pathfinder, 1997.

———. *Black Nationalism and the Revolution in Music.* New York: Pathfinder, 1970.

———. *John Coltrane and the Jazz Revolution of the 1960s.* New York: Pathfinder, 1997.

La Guerre, John Gaffer. "The Social and Political Thought of Aimé Cesairé and C. L. R. James." In *Dual Legacies in the Caribbean,* ed. Paul Sutton. London: Cass, 1986. 217–33.

Lamming, George. *The Pleasures of Exile.* 1954. Foreword by Sandra Pouchet Paquet. Ann Arbor: University of Michigan Press, 1992.

———. "Through the People's Eyes: C. L. R. James's Rhetoric of History." *Caribbean Quarterly* 36, nos. 1–2 (June 1990): 85–97.

La Rue Cases Negres (Black Shack Alley). Director, Euzhan Palcy. 1985.

Lima, Maria Helena. "Revolutionary Developments: Michelle Cliff's *No Telephone to Heaven* and Merle Collin's *Angel.*" *Ariel* 24, no. 1 (Jan. 1993): 35–56.

Lowe, Lisa. *Immigrant Acts: On Asian American Cultural Politics*. Durham, N.C.: Duke University Press, 1996.

Mackey, Nathaniel. "Other: From Noun to Verb." *Representations* 39 (Summer 1992): 51–70.

Manley, Michael. *A History of West Indies Cricket*. London: Pan Books, 1988.

Marshall, Paule. *Brown Girl, Brownstones*. Old Westbury, N.Y.: Feminist Press, 1959.

Marx, Karl, and Frederick Engels. *The German Ideology, Part One*. Ed. with an introduction by C. J. Arthur. New York: International Publishers, 1988.

McLemee, Scott, ed. *C. L. R. James on the "Negro Question."* Jackson: University of Mississippi Press, 1996.

———. "Introduction: The Enigma of Arrival." In *C. L. R. James on the "Negro Question,"* ed. Scott McLemee. Jackson: University of Mississippi Press, 1996.

McLemee, Scott, and Paul Le Blanc, eds. *C. L. R. James and Revolutionary Marxism: Selected Writings of C. L. R. James, 1939–1949*. Atlantic Highlands, N.J.: Humanities Press, 1994.

Mitchell, Angelyn, ed. *Within the Circle: An Anthology of African American Literary Criticism from the Harlem Renaissance to the Present*. Durham, N.C.: Duke University Press, 1994.

Murdoch, H. Adlai. "James's Literary Dialectic: Colonialism and Cultural Space in *Minty Alley*." In *C. L. R. James: His Intellectual Legacies*, ed. Selwyn R. Cudjoe and William E. Cain. Amherst: University of Massachusetts Press, 1995. 61–71.

Murray, Jim. "Afterword: The Boy at the Window." In *Rethinking C. L. R. James*, ed. Grant Farred. Oxford: Blackwell, 1996. 205–18.

———. Personal Interview. Mar., Apr., and May 1997; Feb. 1998; May 1999.

Naipaul, V. S. *The Enigma of Arrival*. New York: Knopf, 1987.

———. *A House for Mr. Biswas*. 1961. New York: Vintage, 1984.

———. *The Middle Passage*. 1962. New York: Vintage, 1981.

———. *The Overcrowded Barracoon*. 1972. New York: Vintage, 1984.

Nair, Supriya. *Caliban's Curse: George Lamming and the Revisioning of History*. Ann Arbor: University of Michigan Press, 1996.

Nielsen, Aldon Lynn. *C. L. R. James: A Critical Introduction*. Jackson: University Press of Mississippi, 1997.

———. "Reading James Reading." In *C. L. R. James: His Intellectual Legacies*, ed. Selwyn R. Cudjoe and William E. Cain. Amherst: University of Massachusetts Press, 1995. 348–55.

———. *Writing Between the Lines: Race and Intertextuality*. Athens and London: University of Georgia Press, 1994.

Paquet, Sandra Pouchet. Introduction to *The Pleasures of Exile* by George Lamming. Ann Arbor: University of Michigan Press, 1991.

———. *The Novels of George Lamming*. London: Heinemann, 1982.

———. "West Indian Autobiography." *Black American Literature Forum* 24, no. 2 (Summer 1990): 357–74.

Paule-Emile, Barbara. "Gender Dynamics in James's *Minty Alley*." In *C. L. R. James: His*

Intellectual Legacies, ed. Selwyn R. Cudjoe and William E. Cain. Amherst: University of Massachusetts Press, 1995. 72–78.

Parris, E. Elliot. "Minty Alley." In *C. L. R. James: His Life and Work*, ed. Paul Buhle. London: Allison and Busby, 1986. 200–202.

Puri, Shalani. "Canonized Hybridities, Resistant Hybridities: Chutney Soca, Carnival and the Politics of Nationalism." In *Caribbean Romances: The Politics of Regional Representation*, ed. Belinda Edmondson. Charlottesville and London: University of Virginia Press, 1999. 12–38.

Pyne-Timothy, Helen. "Identity, Society, and Meaning: A Study of the Early Short Stories of C. L. R. James." In *C. L. R. James: His Intellectual Legacies*, ed. Selwyn R. Cudjoe and William E. Cain. Amherst: University of Massachusetts Press, 1995. 51–60.

Rabbitt, Kara M. "C. L. R. James's Figuring of Toussaint-Louverture: *The Black Jacobins* and the Literary Hero." In *C. L. R. James: His Intellectual Legacies*, ed. Selwyn R. Cudjoe and William E. Cain. Amherst: University of Massachusetts Press, 1995. 118–35.

Retamar, Roberto Fernandez. *Caliban and Other Essays*. Trans. Edward Baker. Minneapolis: University of Minnesota Press, 1989.

Richards, Glen. "C. L. R. James on Black Self-Determination in the United States and the Caribbean." In *C. L. R. James: His Intellectual Legacies*, ed. Selwyn R. Cudjoe and William E. Cain. Amherst: University of Massachusetts Press, 1995. 317–27.

Roach, Joseph. *Cities of the Dead*. New York: Columbia University Press, 1996.

Roberts, John. "African-American Folklore in a Discourse of Folkness." *New York Folklore* 18, nos. 1–4 (1995): 61–77.

Robinson, Cedric. *Black Marxism*. New York: Zed, 1983.

———. "C. L. R. James and the World-System." *Race and Class* 34, no. 2 (1992): 49–62.

Rohlehr, Gordon. "The Folk in Caribbean Literature." In *Critical Perspectives on Sam Selvon*, ed. Susheila Nasta. Washington, D.C.: Three Continents, 1988. 29–43.

Roy, Parama. *Indian Traffic: Identities in Question in Colonial and Postcolonial India*. Berkeley: University of California Press, 1998.

Said, Edward W. *Culture and Imperialism*. New York: Vintage, 1993.

———. *Representations of the Intellectual*. New York: Vintage, 1994.

Sander, Reinhard W. "C. L. R. James and the Haitian Revolution." *World Literature Written in English* 26, no. 2 (Autumn 1986): 277–90.

———. *The Trinidad Awakening: West Indian Literature of the 1930s*. Westport, Conn.: Greenwood, 1988.

Schwarz, Bill. "Breaking Bread with History: C. L. R. James and *The Black Jacobins* Stuart Hall Interviewed by Bill Schwarz." *History Workshop Journal* (1998): 17–31.

———. "C. L. R. James in America." *New Formations* 24 (1994): 174–83.

Smith, Faith. "Coming Home to the Real Thing: Gender and Intellectual Life in the Anglophone Caribbean." *South Atlantic Quarterly* 93, no. 4 (Fall 1994): 895–924.

Smith, Valerie. "Alienation and Creativity in the Fiction of Richard Wright." In *Richard Wright: Critical Perspectives Past and Present*, ed. Henry Louis Gates Jr. and K. A. Appiah. New York: Amistad, 1993. 433–47.

———. *Not Just Race, Not Just Gender: Black Feminist Readings*. New York and London: Routledge, 1998.
Spanos, William V. *The Errant Art of Moby Dick: The Canon, the Cold War, and the Struggle for American Studies*. Durham, N.C.: Duke University Press, 1995.
Spivak, Gayatri Chakravorty. *In Other Worlds: Essays in Cultural Politics*. New York: Methuen, 1987.
Stepto, Robert. *From Behind the Veil: A Study of Afro-American Narrative*. Urbana and Chicago: University of Chicago Press, 1979.
———. "I Thought I Knew These People: Richard Wright and the Afro-American Literary Tradition." In *Chant of Saints*, ed. Michael S. Harper and Robert B. Stepto. Urbana: University of Illinois Press, 1976. 195–211.
St Louis, Brett. *C. L. R. James's Social Theory: A Critique of Race and Modernity*. Ph.D. diss., University of Southampton, England, Department of Sociology and Social Policy, 1999.
———. "The Perilous 'Pleasures of Exile': C. L. R. James, Bad Faith, and the Diasporic Life." *Interventions* 1, no. 3 (1999): 345–60.
Surin, Kenneth. "C. L. R. James's Materialist Aesthetic of Cricket." In *Intellectuals in the Twentieth-Century Caribbean*, vol. 1: *Spectre of the New Class: The Commonwealth Caribbean*, ed. Alistair Hennessy. Warwick University Caribbean Studies. London and Basingstoke: MacMillan, 1992. 131–62.
Taylor, Patrick. *The Narrative of Liberation: Perspectives of Afro-Caribbean Literature, Popular Culture, and Politics*. Ithaca, N.Y.: Cornell University Press, 1989.
Thomas, J. J. *Froudacity: West Indian Fables by James Anthony Froude*. With an introduction by C. L. R. James and a biographical note by Donald Wood. London: New Beacon, 1969. (First published by T. Fisher Unwin, London, 1889.)
Tiffin, Helen. "Cricket, Literature, and the Politics of Decolonisation: The Case of C. L. R. James." In *Sport: Money, Morality, and the Media*, ed. Richard Cashman and Michael McKernan. Kensington: New South Wales University Press, 1981. 177–93. (C. L. R. James Institute catalog 1216.)
Torres-Saillant, Silvio. *Caribbean Poetics: Towards an Aesthetic of West Indian Literature*. New York and Cambridge: Cambridge University Press, 1998.
Trotsky, Leon. *Art and Revolution: Writings on Literature, Politics, and Culture*. New York: Pathfinder, 1970. (Originally *Leon Trotsky on Literature and Art*.)
———. *On Black Nationalism and Self-Determination*. Ed. George Breitman. New York: Pathfinder, 1967.
Walcott, Derek. "The Caribbean: Culture or Mimicry?" *Journal of Interamerican Studies and World Affairs* 16 (Feb. 1974): 3–13.
———. "The Muse of History." In *Is Massa Day Dead? Black Moods in the Caribbean*, ed. Orde Coombs. New York: Anchor, 1974. 1–27.
———. *What The Twilight Says: Essays*. New York: Farrar, Straus, Giroux, 1998.
Walmsley, Anne. *The Caribbean Artists Movement, 1966–1972: A Literary and Cultural History*. London: New Beacon, 1992.
Webb, Barbara. *Myth and History in Caribbean Fiction: Alejo Carpentier, Wilson Harris, and Edouard Glissant*. Amherst: University of Massachusetts Press, 1992.

Whitlock, Gillian. "The Bush, the Barrack-Yard, and the Clearing: 'Colonial Realism' in the Sketches and Stories of Susanna Moodie, C. L. R. James, and Henry Lawson." *Journal of Commonwealth Literature* 20, no. 1 (1985): 36–48.

Williams, Eric. *Capitalism and Slavery*. 1944. London: Andre Deutsh, 1964.

———. *From Columbus to Castro: The History of the Caribbean, 1492–1969*. New York: Vintage, 1970.

Wilson-Tagoe, Nana. *Historical Thought and Literary Representation in West Indian Literature*. Oxford: James Curry, and The Press, University of the West Indies, 1998.

Worcester, Kent. *C. L. R. James: A Political Biography*. Albany: New York State University Press, 1996.

———. "A Victorian with the Rebel Seed: C. L. R. James and the Politics of Intellectual Engagement." In *Intellectuals in the Twentieth-Century Caribbean*, vol. 1: *Spectre of the New Class: the Commonwealth Caribbean*, ed. Alistair Hennessy. Warwick University Caribbean Studies. London: MacMillan, 1992. 115–30.

Wright, Richard. *American Hunger*. New York: Harper and Row, 1977.

———. *Black Boy*. New York: Harper Perennial, 1945.

———. "Blueprint for Negro Writing," *New Challenge*, Fall 1937.

———. Introduction to *In the Castle of My Skin* by George Lamming. New York, Toronto, and London: McGraw Hill, 1954.

———. "I Tried to Be a Communist." In *The God That Failed*, ed. Richard Crossman. New York: Harper, 1965.

———. *The Outsider*. 1953. Introduction by Maryemma Graham. New York: Harper Perennial, 1993.

———. *"Native Son" and How "Bigger" Was Born*. 1940. With an introduction by Arnold Rampersad. New York: Harper Perennial, 1993.

———. *Twelve Million Black Voices*. 1941. New York: Thunder's Mouth, 1988.

———. *White Man, Listen!* 1957. Westport, Conn.: Greenwood, 1978.

Young, Robert J. C. *Colonial Desire: Hybridity in Theory, Culture, and Race*. London: Routledge, 1995.

Zobel, Joseph. *La Rue Cases Negres (Black Shack Alley)*. 1950. Trans. Keith Q. Warner. Washington D.C.: Three Continents, 1980.

INDEX

Afrocentrism, 137
Alexander, Ziggy, 63
All-Jamaica Library, 33
Anderson, Benedict, 128
Antiwar Movement (U.S.), 149n 8

Bakhtin, Mikhail, 34
Baldwin, James, 4, 7–8, 21, 90
Balutansky, Kathleen, 13, 14, 15
Baraka, Amiri. See Jones, LeRoi
Baseball, 4, 122
Basketball, 138–39
Beacon, the (group), 5, 33, 55–56, 63, 65, 71–72, 74; (magazine), 33, 72
Benítez-Rojo, Antonio, 10, 128, 137–38
Beverley, John, 64
Bhabha, Homi, 16, 18–19, 21, 121, 146n 9
Bildungsroman, xii, 51, 52–53, 62, 66, 68, 71, 72, 74, 77, 79, 147n 2
Black Power Movement, 18, 99, 119, 130, 133, 149n 3
Black Shack Alley. See *La Rue Cases Negres*
Boggs, Grace Lee, 6, 81, 105, 114, 151n 9
Bogues, Anthony, 103

Bonaparte, Napoleon, 30, 35, 43–44, 46, 146n 5
Bontemps, Arna, 149n 7
Boukman (rebellion leader), 41–42, 47, 49
Boyce Davies, Carole, 148n 1
Brathwaite, Edward Kamau, xi, 10–11, 13–16, 20, 51, 115–16, 120, 124, 138, 147n 7, 148n 8
Brody, Jennifer Devere, 17, 19
Brown, Sterling A., 149n 7
Buhle, Paul, 84, 86
Bunche, Ralph, 148n 2

Cannon, James P., 81
Carby, Hazel V., 53, 55, 57, 127, 148n 1
Caribbean Artists Movement, 18
Carpentier, Alejo, 147n 7
Castro, Fidel, 9, 36, 49–51
Césaire, Aimé, 51, 148n 2
Civil Rights Movement, 95, 107, 111, 133, 149n 8
Civil War (U.S.), 82, 83
Cliff, Michelle, 147n 7
Cobham, Rhonda, 56, 72
Cold War, the, 5, 80, 95, 107, 112, 116
Collins, Merle, 76

Colonial education, 5, 16, 20, 23, 34, 60, 66, 67–69, 70, 123, 148n 9
Columbus, Christopher, 16, 143
Communist Party (U.S.), 79, 80, 82, 88–89, 91, 93–94, 95, 96, 149n 7, 151n 8
Constantine, Sir Learie, 3, 28, 81, 133–34
Cooper, Carolyn, 59
Copeland, Aaron, 138
Creole: language, 14, 15, 145n 5; society, 11, 16, 22, 25, 26, 27, 36, 57, 77, 127, 143
Creolité, 18
Creolization, aesthetics of, x, xiii, 12, 13, 28, 31, 35, 74, 76, 79, 101, 129, 131–32
Cricket, xiii, 22–27, 74, 118–37, 139

Dash, Michael, 14–15, 119, 137–38
de Boissiere, Ralph, 148n 7
De Lisser, Herbert G., 56
Dépestre, René, 40, 147n 7
Dessalines, Jean-Jacques, 38–39, 40–41, 45, 47, 49
Diawara, Manthia, 145n 8
Dickens, Charles, 24–25
Du Bois, W. E. B., 19, 37, 44, 148n 1, 149n 4
Dunayevskaya, Raya, 6, 81, 114–15, 151n 9

Edmondson, Belinda, x, 148n 1
Ellison, Ralph, xiii, 10, 27, 119–20, 129–32, 137–40
Enlightenment aesthetics, 12, 119, 120, 125

Fanon, Frantz, 78, 85, 147n 7, 148n 2
Farred, Grant, 25
Federal Bureau of Investigation (FBI), 150n 3
Foley, Barbara, 53

Folk culture(s), xii, 35, 40, 53, 56, 58, 59, 66, 94, 147n 5, 148n 8
Forest, Freddie. *See* Dunayevskaya, Raya
Franco, General, 34

Garvey, Amy Ashwood, 83
Garvey, Marcus, 72
Gilroy, Paul, 118–19, 140, 148n 1, 151n 12
Glissant, Edouard, xi, 10–11, 13–14, 16, 20, 30, 47, 48, 49, 63, 137–38, 146n 9, 147n 7
Gomes, Albert, 72
Grace, W. G., 28
Gramsci, Antonio, 37
Grimshaw, Anna, 31, 35, 75, 146n 1, 148n 6

Hall, Stuart, 8
Hamilton, Cynthia, 74
Harlem Renaissance, 33, 63, 83, 89, 146n 4
Harlow, Barbara, 102–03
Harris, Wilson, 3, 51, 147n 7
Headley, George, 28
Heaney, Seamus, 102
Hegel, G. W. F., 73
Hitler, Adolf, 34, 108
Hitler-Stalin Pact, 81
Hughes, Langston, 149n 7

International African Friends Service Bureau (IAFSB), 83, 86

James, C. L. R.: *American Civilization*, xiii, 99, 103–07, 113, 116, 150n 2, 150n 3, 151n 8, 151n 10, 151n 1; *Beyond a Boundary*, x, xi, xiii, 19–23, 26, 28, 71, 113, 115–16, 118–29, 131–36, 138–40, 150n 2; *Black Jacobins, The* (history), xi, 5, 11, 18, 28–37, 41, 44, 48–50, 52, 81, 83–84,

103, 112, 133; *Black Jacobins, The* (play), xi, 29–32, 34–38, 41, 49–50, 52, 84, 103; "Black Power: Its Past, Today, and the Way Ahead," 36; *Case For West Indian Self-Government, The*, 34, 61, 75, 112, 134, 148n 6; *History of Negro Revolt, A*, 5, 83, 84, 85, 146n 3; *Invading Socialist Society, The*, 82; "Kanhai: A Study in Confidence," 135; *Life of Captain Cipriani, The*, 33–34, 75, 132; "Making of the Caribbean People, The," 36; *Mariners, Renegades and Castaways*, xiii, 21, 28, 91, 99, 102–05, 107–16, 150n 2, 151n 8, 151n 12; *Minty Alley*, xii, 5, 21, 33, 51–66, 70–77, 94, 103, 115, 148n 7, 148n 11, 150n 2; *Nkrumah and the Ghana Revolution*, 28; "Revolutionary Answer to the Negro Problem in the United States," xiii, 84, 87, 88, 91, 113; *Special Delivery*, 52, 109, 115; *State Capitalism and World Revolution*, 82, 112; "With the Sharecroppers," xiii, 88, 91
Jazz, xiii, 118–19, 122, 128–33, 137–39
Jim Crow, 87, 150n 4, 150n 5
Johnson-Forest Tendency (JFT), 6, 81, 86, 96, 102, 104, 112–15, 150n 5, 151n 9, 151n 10
Jones, LeRoi, 129–31

Kanhai, Rohan, 133, 136, 152n 5
Kelley, Robin D. G., 84, 149n 5
Kincaid, Jamaica, 147n 4

La Guerre, John, 36
Lamming, George, 50, 51, 78, 79, 86, 97–99, 101, 113, 147n 6, 150n 1, 152n 6
La Rue Cases Negres, xii, 53–54, 65–71, 103
Lee, Grace. *See* Boggs, Grace Lee

Lee, Spike, 138–39
Lenin, V. I., 36, 73, 84, 89
Louis, Joe, 88
L'Ouverture, Toussaint, 9, 32, 37–41, 43, 45–47, 50–52, 115, 146n 5
Lowe, Lisa, 20

Mackandal (rebellion leader), 41
Marshall, Paule, 79, 98–101
Marx, Karl, 24, 35, 45, 73, 123
Mays, Willie, 4, 6–8, 21
McCarran Immigration Bill, the, 108
McKay, Claude, 148n 1, 149n 4
McLemee, Scott, 86
Meehan, Kevin, 145n 7, 148n 1
Melville, Herman, 9, 76, 104, 107–11, 114, 116, 151n 7
Mendes, Alfred, 56, 72
Mind/Body split, 57, 58, 64, 75, 76
Murdoch, H. Adlai, 61, 63
Mussolini, Benito, 34

Naipaul, V. S., 20, 51, 135–36
Negritude, 18, 146n 4
"Negro Question," the, xii, 29, 78–83, 98, 100, 101, 105–06, 116, 149n 4
Nielsen, Aldon Lynn, 74, 76, 106, 108, 110, 120
Nkrumah, Kwame, 6, 28

Padmore, George, 83, 148n 1, 148n 2
Paine, Thomas, 45
Palcy, Euzhan, xii, 27, 53–54, 65
Pan-Africanism, 5–6, 26, 33, 80, 83, 95, 149n 3
Paquet, Sandra Pouchet, 36, 46, 136, 150n 1
Parris, D. Elliot, 53
People's National Party (PNP), 6
Pericles, 45
Price-Mars, Jean, 37

Queen's Royal College (QRC), 5

Rabbitt, Kara M., 31, 146n 5
Ramchand, Kenneth, 53
Randolph, A. Philip, 148n 2
Raynal, Abbé, 44–45, 51
Roach, Joseph, 10
Roberts, John, 147,n 5
Robeson, Paul, 31, 99, 148n 2
Robinson, Cedric, 82, 148n 1, 149n 4, 151n 12

Said, Edward W., 78
Sander, Reinhard W., 72–73, 147n 3
Schwarz, Bill, 104–05
Shakespeare, William, 33, 140, 151n 7
Socialist Workers Party (SWP), 5, 28, 79–82, 85, 105, 109, 150n 3
Sourieau, Marie-Agnès, 13, 14, 15
Spivak, Gayatri Chakravorty, 63
St. Louis, Brett, 19, 65, 112, 128, 149n 8, 151n 8, 152n 7
Stalin, Joseph, 34, 108
Surin, Kenneth, 149n 8
Syncretism, cultural, 146n 10

Testimonio, 64
Thackeray, William Makepeace, 24, 25, 73, 123, 151n 7
Torres-Saillant, Silvio, xiii, 9
Toussaint. *See* L'Ouverture, Toussaint
Trinidad (magazine), 33, 55, 72
Trotsky, Leon, 6, 24, 34, 46, 73, 83–84, 86

Universal Negro Improvement Association (UNIA). *See* Garvey, Marcus

Vodun, xi, 30, 32, 35, 37–45, 47–48
Voodoo. *See* Vodun

Walcott, Derek, 17, 47, 140
Walker, Margaret, 149n 7
Webb, Barbara, 48
Webb, Constance, 80, 96, 103–04, 109, 112–15, 150n 5
West Indies Federal Labour Party (WIFLP), 6
West Indies Federation, 6, 50, 109, 112, 140
Whitlock, Gillian, 55
Whitman, Walt, 52, 70, 74, 97
Williams, Eric, 6, 50
Worcester, Kent, 82, 87, 95
Workers Party (WP), 80, 81, 82, 94, 149n 7
World War II, 100
Worrell, Sir Frank, 4–8, 21
Wright, Richard, xii, xiii, 9–10, 19, 27, 76, 79–80, 82, 86–101, 109, 148n 1, 148n 3, 149n 4, 149n 6, 149n 7, 151n 7, 151n 12

Young, Juanita, 150n 5

Zobel, Joseph, 53, 54, 65

www.ingramcontent.com/pod-product-compliance
Lightning Source LLC
Chambersburg PA
CBHW021142230426
43667CB00005B/226